Experience the Living Christ!

Learning to Live in the Presence of God

Norman Mears

Norman Mears
Isa. 55:1 AmP

Copyright © 2015 by Norman Mears

Experience the Living Christ!
Learning to Live in the Presence of God
by Norman Mears

Printed in the United States of America

Edited by Xulon Press

ISBN 9781498415859

All rights reserved solely by the author. The author guarantees all contents are original and do not infringe upon the legal rights of any other person or work. No part of this book may be reproduced in any form without the permission of the author. The views expressed in this book are not necessarily those of the publisher.

Scripture quotations, unless otherwise indicated, are taken from the New King James Version®, Copyright © 1982 by Thomas Nelson, Inc. Used by permission. All rights reserved.

Scripture quotations marked (AMP) are taken from the Amplified Bible, Copyright © 1954, 1958, 1962, 1964, 1965, 1987 by The Lockman Foundation. Used by permission. (www.Lockman.org)

Scripture quotations marked (KJV) are taken from The King James Version—*public domain.*

Scripture quotations marked (NASB) are taken from the New American Standard Bible®, Copyright © 1960, 1962, 1963, 1968, 1971, 1972, 1973, 1975, 1977, 1995 by The Lockman Foundation. Used by permission. (www.Lockman.org)

Scripture quotations marked (NIV) are taken from the Holy Bible, New International Version®, NIV®, Copyright © 1973, 1978, 1984 by the International Bible Society. Used by permission of Zondervan. All rights reserved.

Scripture quotations marked (NRSV) are taken from the New Revised Standard Version Bible, Copyright © 1989 by the Division of Christian Education of the National Council of the Churches of Christ in the United States of America. Used by permission. All rights reserved.

Scripture quotations marked "Phillips" are taken from The New Testament in Modern English, Copyright © 1958, 1959, 1960 by J.B. Phillips and 1947, 1952, 1955, 1957 by The Macmillian Company, New York. Used by permission. All rights reserved.

Scripture quotations marked (RSV) are taken from the Revised Standard Version of the Bible, Copyright © 1946, 1952, 1971 by the Division of Christian Education of the National Council of the Churches of Christ in the United States of America. Used by permission. All rights reserved.

www.xulonpress.com

Dedication

I dedicate this writing to our children and their families. May you increase in faith as you become progressively more intimate with God our Father and our Lord Jesus Christ. May each generation lead the next into greater faith through this deeper intimacy. God bless you, every one.

[That you may really come] to know [practically, through experience for yourselves] the love of Christ, which far surpasses mere knowledge [without experience]; that you may be filled [through all your being] unto all the fullness of God [may have the richest measure of the divine Presence, and become a body wholly filled and flooded with God Himself]!

Ephesians 3:19 AMP

Experience the Living Christ!
Learning to Live in the Presence of God

Contents

Preface xi
Acknowledgments xiii

Part 1: Awakening to God's Spiritual Realities

Chapter 1	Discover God's Unseen Reality	17
Chapter 2	Follow God's Pathway to Ultimate Fulfillment	23
Chapter 3	Come to Know the Living Word	38
Chapter 4	Activate Your Spirit Nature	48
Chapter 5	Be Released from Temporal Limitations	56
Chapter 6	Know Christ as He Really Is	70
Chapter 7	Live in the New Covenant Spiritual Dimension	85
Chapter 8	Activate New Covenant Truth	94

Part 2: Activating Foundational Truths

Chapter 9	Thirst, Come to Jesus, and Drink	109
Chapter 10	Participate in God's Supernatural Commission	125
Chapter 11	Receive Revelation through Grace in Peace	140
Chapter 12	Give Christ Preeminence	151
Chapter 13	Embrace Living Doctrine	162

Chapter 14	Come to Know the Father's Goodness	175
Chapter 15	Live a Lifestyle of Fellowship with Christ	183
Chapter 16	Allow Jesus Christ to Lead	190

Part 3: Yielding to God's Maturing Processes

Chapter 17	Encountering the Living Christ	203
Chapter 18	Increasing Spiritual Strength by Embracing Weakness	213
Chapter 19	Obtaining Ultimate Freedom through Genuine Surrender	221
Chapter 20	Growing into Spiritual Maturity through Intimacy with Christ	236
Chapter 21	Living Eternal Life	247

Endnotes 261

Appendix A: Declarations with Supporting Scriptures 275

Appendix B: Recommended Reading 285

About the Author 287

Preface

God the Father is offering a deeper spiritual life to His people—a closer relationship with Him through greater intimacy with Jesus Christ. I desire to live in this deeper dimension of knowing and experiencing God the Father and the Lord Jesus Christ and to help others do the same. I spend time quietly listening in the presence of the Lord and writing what I "hear" Him saying. I have written this book as a compilation of some of the illumination I received from the Lord in those quiet times.

I have endeavored to write this book, not for rapid reading, but as a work of the Holy Spirit, insightfully helpful, opening awareness of the presence of God to the reader. My intention is not only to communicate knowledge to the mind but also to impart revelation in the heart because the things of God are spiritually discerned. The fullness of Christianity flows out of fellowship with God the Father and the Lord Jesus Christ—intimate sharing of the deepest kind between Christians and their precious Father and Lord. This fellowship is not only possible, it's readily attainable.

In the following pages, I share the way that the Lord speaks to us in our quiet times and then uses what He has revealed to us to bring us into closer fellowship with Him. Each of the following chapters will progressively lead you into the presence of God by unveiling an essential biblical truth, presenting an admonition to enter into that truth, and offering a prayer to enter into the dynamic of that truth. I pray that these truths will bring you into deeper fellowship with God the Father and the Lord Jesus Christ.

Acknowledgments

I would like to express my deep appreciation to my precious wife, Vicki, who has stood by me, encouraged me, and assisted me in the Lord as I proceeded through the writing of this book. You are truly my spiritual completion in Christ.

I also want to express my deep appreciation to others who have been instrumental in this writing through their prayers and encouragement. I am indeed grateful to each one of you whom God has used to pray for me and encourage me as I was writing this book. God revealed to me that every work of the Spirit requires intercessors. Only God knows the magnitude of the contribution you have made in the Spirit through intercession. I could not have completed this work without each and every one of you. Thank you.

Part 1

Awakening to God's Spiritual Realities

Chapter 1

Discover God's Unseen Reality

*The wind blows where it wishes, and you hear the sound of it,
but cannot tell where it comes from and where it goes.
So is everyone who is born of the Spirit.*
John 3:8

God the Father desires to lovingly welcome every one of His children into deep personal fellowship in Him through true personal intimacy with His Son Jesus Christ. Not all Christians, though, are experiencing this wonderful reality.

Reality is not limited to what we observe by natural means. We cannot see the wind, but it is real. We see leaves moving in the trees, hear the rustling of the leaves, and feel the brush of air against our faces. Yet we cannot see this reality called wind—we see only its effects. Unseen reality influences natural reality as the wind invisibly moves the leaves in the trees. It is as genuine as the wind.

Mankind lives in two environments: the natural environment and the supernatural environment. The natural realm is observable with the five senses and is governed by physical laws. The supernatural realm is not observable with the five natural senses and is governed by spiritual laws.

We'll begin our quest to experience the living Christ and live in the presence of God by awakening to eight unseen spiritual realities that are essential to experiencing the living Christ and living in God's presence. Our first spiritual reality is this: living in the presence of God is natural and normal for all believers in Christ.

You Can Perceive God's Presence

From the time of Adam, God has sought to intimately involve Himself in helping people. Adam, unfortunately, decided that he didn't want God's help. He wanted to make his own decisions based on his human reasoning. Adam freely chose to give up his reliance on God, and in so doing, his perception of God became distorted. He became fearful of God and distanced from Him.

As a result of Adam's choice, all mankind's perception became similarly opaque, like trying to see God through a stained-glass window. Even when believers in Christ choose self-reliance over dependence on God, their perception of God becomes distorted, because the things of God are spiritually discerned. We cannot accurately perceive the realm of God's presence while living in this restricted awareness.

God calls this opaque awareness "the flesh." The flesh distracts us from—and persuades us not to believe—the dimension of Christianity that exists beyond our natural awareness.

Faith, on the other hand, perceives the presence of God not discernible by the five senses and natural reasoning. It embraces (recognizes and fully relies upon) the realm of God's presence not observable by natural means.

As we will see in later chapters, perception of God's presence comes by grace through faith. It usually comes as the result of time spent in quietness before the Lord. It comes through our yielding to God's remaking us according to His purpose and through our subordinating our wills to His.

Our enlightenment of the realm of God's presence is progressive. It may take minutes, days, or even years. The Holy Spirit translates supernatural perception into living thoughts and words. As this perception passes through our hearts, souls, and minds, our restricted understanding often taints it with natural comprehension. When we continue in quiet attentiveness to the Holy Spirit, He refines our tainted translation, opening our awareness to the realm of God's presence—unseen reality as real as the wind invisibly moving the leaves in the trees.

Perceiving Unseen Reality Is Practical

Not all believers in Christ perceive unseen reality. Unfortunately, without perceiving the realm of God's presence, they can't receive all His benefits. For example, terrorists flew two commercial airliners into the Twin Towers office buildings in New York City, killing thousands of people on September 11, 2001. Hundreds of people routinely boarded those aircraft, expecting to arrive safely at their destination. Thousands of people reported to work in those towers, expecting to return home at the end of the day. My point is this: a few individuals who were impressed not to go to work that morning escaped.

Here's my question for you: do you hear the voice of the Lord? You can. Hearing the Lord's voice is not fiction. It's part of the supernatural realm of the presence of God. Living in God's presence is open to all who believe in Jesus Christ—not as a character in the Bible, not as a password granting access to God, but as the living, supernatural Son of God.

God Desires to Fellowship with You

God wants to converse with you; He wants to fellowship with you. However, you may not have entered into the dimension of knowing and experiencing God that He is offering. This dimension is a deeper spiritual life, a closer relationship with God the Father through greater intimacy with the Lord Jesus Christ.

The apostle John declared: "This is eternal life, that they may know You, the only true God, and Jesus Christ whom You have sent. You [already] have life, yes, eternal life."[1] Do you personally know God the Father and the Lord Jesus Christ and not just know about them?

Jesus proclaimed, "The sheep that are My own hear and are listening to My voice; and I know them, and they follow Me."[2] Are you listening to Jesus and following what He says?

Jesus informed His disciples, "In that day you will know that I am in My Father, and you in Me, and I in you."[3] Are you aware of your being in Christ and of His being in you?

Knowing the Father and the Lord Jesus Christ, hearing and following Jesus, and being in Christ and His being in us are not theories; neither are they privileges reserved for a chosen few. They are unseen realities. These spiritual realities are available to all who believe in Jesus Christ as Savior and Lord!

Sometimes What Is Abnormal Appears to Be Normal

Sadly, when Christian leaders live their lives outside of the presence of God, believers perceive living outside of God's presence as being the normal Christian life. It's not!

Some Christians don't know the Lord Jesus Christ personally; they only know about Him. They have become complacent in living their lives outside of God's presence; they are not living the normal Christian life. And they don't even realize it.

Living in God's Presence Is Normal for Every Believer

Living in the presence of God is natural and normal for every believer and is the basis for Christ exercising His life and ministry in and through all believers. God makes fellowship with God the Father through intimacy with the Lord Jesus Christ available to every believer. Christian life outside of this intimacy with Christ becomes Spiritless religious activity and loses the supernatural aspect of true Christianity.

Living in God's presence is natural and normal for all Christians for three reasons. First, God is present everywhere. David reasoned: "Where could I go from Your Spirit? Or where could I flee from Your presence? If I ascend up into heaven, You are there; if I make my bed in Sheol (the place of the dead), behold, You are there. If I take the wings of the morning or dwell in the uttermost parts of the sea, even there shall Your hand lead me, and Your right hand shall hold me."[4] He also declared, "The upright shall dwell in Your presence (before Your very face)."[5] Since God is present everywhere, there is nowhere that God is not. Therefore, we simply need to become aware of God's presence in and around us.

Second, we are in Christ and He is in us. Paul prayed for the Ephesians "that Christ may dwell in your hearts through faith . . . that you may be filled with all the fullness of God."[6] The apostle John quotes Jesus: "Dwell in Me, and I will dwell in you. [Live in Me, and I will live in you.]"[7]

Third, living in the presence of God is natural and normal when we are sensitive to His presence. Jesus declared, "The sheep that are My own hear and are listening to My voice; and I know them, and they follow Me."[8] The writer of the book of Hebrews declared, "Today, if you will hear His voice, do not harden your hearts."[9]

Speaking of the Lord Jesus Christ, the apostle Paul declared, "[My determined purpose is] that I may know Him [that I may progressively become more deeply and intimately acquainted with Him."[10] What better example could we follow?

How do we enter into intimacy with Christ? How do we lead others into this personal intimacy? We'll explore answers to these questions in the following chapters.

Admonition to Embrace Unseen Reality

Discover God's unseen reality that affects seen reality as the wind invisibly moves the leaves in the trees. Abandon the opaque awareness of the flesh in favor of clear perception of God's presence. Embrace the realm of God's presence not observable by natural means.

Actually know God the Father and the Lord Jesus Christ. Hear the voice of Jesus and follow Him. Be aware of your being in Christ and His being in you. Enter into deep personal fellowship with God the Father through true personal intimacy with His Son Jesus Christ. Make your determined purpose to become more deeply and intimately acquainted with the Lord Jesus Christ.

Pray to Experience Supernatural Reality

Lord, I desire to know Your truth that transcends natural comprehension. Please open my understanding to unseen supernatural reality. I want to immerse myself in unseen reality, not be restricted to that segment of reality called natural. I desire to become fluent in the perception of unseen supernatural truth. (This is spiritual maturity: being fluent in perception of unseen supernatural truth.)

Thank You, Father, that Your unseen reality influences my natural reality. I want to be as responsive to Your Spirit as the leaves in the trees are to the wind. Please empower me to live in these truths by Your Spirit of grace. All this I ask, not only for my own spiritual growth, but also that our Lord Jesus Christ, in whose name I pray, may be glorified and exalted in and through me. Amen.

Where Do We Go from Here?

In part 1, we are awakening to eight spiritual realities that are essential to experiencing the living Christ and living in the presence of God. In chapter 1, we became aware that we live in the supernatural environment as well as the natural environment. We learned that God the Father desires to fellowship with us through intimacy with His Son. And we found that living in the presence of God is natural and normal for all believers in Christ. In the next chapter, we will continue our journey into the presence of God by tracing Jesus' earthly journey. We'll note three seasons He entered into through three specific events and draw a parallel between His journey on earth and our spiritual journey.

In following chapters, we will first see how God the Father introduces us to His Son and learn how we can actually know the Lord Jesus Christ rather than just know about Him. Then we will trace the spiritual history of mankind from their creation of dust, first to their separation from God, then to their opportunity to be reunited with God, and finally to their restoration into magnificent spirit-beings. We will then learn that mankind lives in two dimensions, the natural and the spiritual, and we'll gain a basic understanding of the spirit nature of mankind. We'll take another step in experiencing the living Christ by gaining a greater perception of Christ as He really is. We'll discover that the way we perceive Christ forms our faith and shapes our earthly and eternal destinies.

We will see how God combines the Spirit nature of Christ and the spirit nature of mankind through the new covenant. This new covenant offers us the opportunity to enter into fellowship with God the Father and His Son Jesus Christ. We'll discover that fellowship with Jesus produces spiritual effectiveness and that all blessing, provision, authority, and power are in Christ.

Let's continue by noting the pattern that Jesus set for us in His life on the earth. We'll find the pathway that leads us to our ultimate fulfillment in the next chapter.

Chapter 2

Follow God's Pathway to Ultimate Fulfillment

*If anyone desires to come after Me, let him deny himself,
and take up his cross, and follow Me.*
Matthew 16:24

We have discovered God's unseen reality that influences seen reality as the wind invisibly moves the leaves in the trees. We learned that living in the presence of God is natural and normal for all believers in Christ. We found that knowing the Father and the Son, hearing and following Jesus, and living in Christ and His living in us are not theories. They are truth.

All this is possible, and it's also readily attainable, but it doesn't happen instantaneously. We progress into experiencing the living Christ and living in the presence of God through our life's spiritual journey, a journey that parallels Jesus' earthly journey. Our second spiritual reality is this: our pathway to ultimate fulfillment follows the spiritual trail that Jesus blazed in His life on earth.

Next, we'll observe the seasons of Jesus' life and ministry on the earth, note the events through which He entered into these seasons, and see how our spiritual journey parallels Jesus' life journey on earth. We are able to follow Jesus' example because He stripped Himself of all the attributes of God and came to earth as a human being (Phil. 2:6–7 AMP).

Our Spiritual Journey Parallels Jesus' Earthly Journey

In Jesus' earthly journey, we can identify three seasons in His life and ministry: (1) preparation, (2) life and ministry in the power of the Spirit, and (3) fulfillment of His ultimate purpose. Jesus entered each of these seasons through a specific event. Our spiritual journey follows Jesus' earthly journey in the same three seasons, which we also enter through similar events. All three are necessary to fully enter into the supernatural lives and ministries that God offers to us in Christ Jesus.

Our use of the term *ministry* is not restricted to the activities of professional clergy. Neither is it restricted to the fivefold ministries of the apostle, prophet, evangelist, pastor, and teacher. It includes everything Christ does through every believer.

Jesus' First Season Was Preparation

Jesus entered the earth through being conceived in a virgin named Mary by the Holy Spirit. He learned the Scriptures as a boy, amazing the people in the temple with His knowledge and wisdom at only twelve years old.

At the appropriate time, Jesus went to John the Baptist to be baptized. The book of Matthew gives this account: "When He had been baptized, Jesus came up immediately from the water; and behold, the heavens were opened to Him, and He saw the Spirit of God descending like a dove and alighting upon Him. And suddenly a voice came from heaven, saying, 'This is My beloved Son, in whom I am well pleased.'"[1]

In baptism, Jesus publicly identified Himself with God, God publicly identified His Son, and Jesus became ready for testing. Following Jesus' baptism, Luke reports, "Jesus, full of the Holy Spirit, returned from the Jordan and was led by the Spirit in the desert, where for forty days he was tempted by the devil."[2]

Our First Season Is Also Preparation

As Jesus' season of preparation brought Him into the fullness of the Holy Spirit, our season of preparation brings us into the fullness of the Holy Spirit as well. This season begins with salvation, continues with baptism, and includes learning the Scriptures. We'll first discuss salvation, then explain baptism, and conclude with briefly discussing studying the Word of God.

Our Preparation Begins with Salvation

We begin our journey by being born again. In this new birth, the Holy Spirit enlightens us that Jesus Christ is the living Son of God. He voluntarily died on the cross to take upon Himself the consequence of death for everyone's sinful disobedience. And He rose again from the dead to provide eternal life for all who believe. We exchange our natural life for Christ's eternal life by relinquishing control of our lives to God, receiving Jesus Christ as Savior and yielding to Him as Lord. Through this supernatural transaction, we enter into eternal life in Christ Jesus. (We will explain mankind's need for salvation and God's provision of salvation in chapter 4.)

The writer to the Hebrews states, "It is appointed for men to die once, but after this the judgment, so Christ was offered once to bear the sins of many."[3] Jesus proclaimed: "For God so loved the world that He gave His only begotten Son, that whoever believes in Him should not perish but have everlasting life. For God did not send His Son into the world to condemn the world, but that the world through Him might be saved."[4] Paul informed Timothy, "God our Savior . . . desires everyone to be saved and to come to the knowledge of the truth."[5]

Salvation doesn't come through knowing the Scriptures, recognizing Jesus as a teacher from God, or conducting our lives according to the requirements of Scripture. Nicodemus believed in God, meticulously ordered his life according to the Scriptures, and was a teacher of the Scriptures. He knew that Jesus was a teacher who came from God. Yet he could not comprehend how a person could be born again (John 3:1-21).

Throughout history, there have been many men named Jesus. Only the Jesus of the Bible is Savior and Lord. When we believe in the Jesus of the Bible, we have biblical faith. In the beginning, Jesus was (and still is) the Word who was with God and was God. He, together with the Father and the Holy Spirit, created the universe. He came to earth to save mankind from eternal destruction. He is the Son of God, born of a virgin. He gave His life as the only payment in full for our sins, was raised from the dead, ascended into heaven, is seated at the right hand of God the Father, and will return to judge the living and the dead.

Paul taught the church at Rome: "If you confess with your mouth the Lord Jesus and believe in your heart that God has raised Him from the dead, you will be saved. For with the heart one believes unto righteousness, and with the mouth confession is made unto salvation."[6] To some, what I'm about to say may seem unduly exclusive, but Jesus did say: "I am the way, the truth, and the life. No one comes to the Father except through Me."[7] This is the only way to enter into eternal life with God, who gives all persons the right of choice. But at physical death, the time to choose salvation in Jesus Christ expires. If you have never done so, please carefully consider and then earnestly pray the following prayer of salvation:

Prayer of Salvation

> Father, I ask you to forgive me for my sins. I believe that Jesus of Nazareth is the Son of God, that He gave His life on the cross for the full payment of my sins. I confess with my mouth that Jesus is Lord, and I believe in my heart that God has raised Him from the dead. I give my temporary life to the Lord Jesus Christ in exchange for His eternal life. I accept Jesus Christ as my Savior and my Lord, and I determine to live for Him and be obedient to Him in all things. All this I pray in Jesus' name. Amen.

If you earnestly prayed this prayer, you are saved and now have eternal life. You are a Christian. You need to join a Bible-believing church and be baptized in water and in the Holy Spirit. You need to read your Bible regularly. A good place to start is the book of John in the New Testament. You need to spend time in prayer every day, both speaking and listening to the Lord.

Our Preparation Continues with Baptism

Baptism follows salvation in God's plan to develop us into the supernatural persons He created us to be. Using Jesus' baptism as our pattern, we will identify two aspects of baptism. The first is John the Baptist immersing Jesus in water: water baptism. The second is the Spirit of God descending upon Jesus: the baptism of the Holy Spirit.

The first aspect is baptism in water. Just as John the Baptist immersed Jesus in the Jordan River, we should be baptized by immersion in water. Water baptism is a symbol of what has taken place in salvation, but it's also much more! Through water baptism, we receive power to live the resurrected life. Properly administered, water baptism (1) releases us from the passions and excesses of the flesh nature, (2) frees us from the power of sin, and (3) relieves us of inner insecurities and fears by giving us inner cleanness and peace with God.

First, Jesus strips us of the "whole corrupt, carnal nature with its passions and lusts" (see quotation below). Through faith in Christ's resurrection, water baptism raises us to a new life in Christ. The apostle Paul taught the Colossian church:

> In Him also you were circumcised with a circumcision not made with hands, but in a [spiritual] circumcision [performed by] Christ by stripping off the body of the flesh (the whole corrupt, carnal nature with its passions and lusts). [Thus you were circumcised when] you were buried with Him in [your] baptism, in which you were also raised with Him [to a new life] through [your] faith in the working of God [as displayed] when He raised Him up from the dead.[8]

Therefore, through baptism in water, we enter into death in Christ, are raised in His resurrection, and are freed from the power of the flesh. Christians who are struggling to overcome the flesh nature with its passions and excesses may not have been taught to expect God's benefits of water baptism.

Second, baptism, according to the apostle Paul, frees us from the power of sin. Paul informed the church at Rome:

> We were buried therefore with Him by the baptism into death, so that just as Christ was raised from the dead by the glorious [power] of the Father, so we too might [habitually] live and behave in newness of life. For if we have

become one with Him by sharing a death like His, we shall also be [one with Him in sharing] His resurrection [by a new life lived for God]. We know that our old (unrenewed) self was nailed to the cross with Him in order that [our] body [which is the instrument] of sin might be made ineffective and inactive for evil, that we might no longer be the slaves of sin.[9]

Third, water baptism saves us from inner questionings and fears by giving us a "good and clear conscience (inward cleanness and peace) before God" (see quotation below). This takes place "[because you are demonstrating what you believe to be yours] through the resurrection of Jesus Christ." The apostle Peter explained to the early church:

Baptism, which is a figure [of their deliverance], does now also save you [from inward questionings and fears], not by the removing of outward body filth [bathing], but by [providing you with] the answer of a good and clear conscience (inward cleanness and peace) before God [because you are demonstrating what you believe to be yours] through the resurrection of Jesus Christ.[10]

The second aspect is the baptism of the Holy Spirit. Please don't let this subject become a divisive issue. Neither Christians baptized in the Holy Spirit nor those who have not experienced this Pentecostal blessing are second-class citizens in the kingdom of God.

We will use the terms *baptism of the Holy Spirit* and *Pentecostal blessing* interchangeably. By both terms, we mean the baptism of the Holy Spirit with the evidence of speaking in tongues.

The baptism of the Holy Spirit does not make one person more spiritually mature than another; neither does it *necessarily* give one person more insight into the things of God than another. Numerous Christians—both those who have and those who have not experienced this Pentecostal blessing—are exemplary in the way they lead their lives, insightful in the Word of God, and productive in the kingdom of God.

The apostle John records Jesus' predicting the coming of the Holy Spirit: "On the last day, that great day of the feast, Jesus stood and cried out, saying, 'If anyone thirsts, let him come to Me and drink. He who believes in Me, as the Scripture has said, out of his heart will flow rivers of living water.' But this He spoke concerning the Spirit, whom those believing in Him would receive; for the Holy Spirit was not yet given, because Jesus was not yet glorified."[11] John the Baptist said that Jesus would baptize believers in the Holy Spirit and fire (Matt. 3:11).

Luke reports Jesus' instructions to His disciples relating to receiving the baptism of the Holy Spirit: "And being assembled together with them, He commanded them not to depart from Jerusalem, but to wait for the Promise of the Father, 'which,' He said, 'you have heard from Me; for John truly baptized with water, but you shall be baptized with the Holy Spirit not many days from now.'"[12] Jesus' prediction took place on the day of Pentecost when the Holy Spirit came to live in believers in Christ.

As the Spirit descended upon Jesus when He was baptized, the Holy Spirit came to live in believers on the day of Pentecost. In Acts 2, after Jesus' ascension, His followers were in an upper room waiting for the promise of the Father. The sound of a rushing wind filled the whole house in which they were assembled. What appeared to be flames of fire came upon the heads of all who were present; they were all filled with the Holy Spirit, and they all began to speak in other tongues. The Holy Spirit came to live in believers as Jesus predicted in John 7:37–39.

The baptism of the Holy Spirit was not only for those who were present in Jerusalem on the day of Pentecost, but is also for all who come to Christ. Peter informed the crowd on this historic day, "The promise [of the Holy Spirit] is to and for you and your children, and to and for all that are far away, [even] to and for as many as the Lord our God invites and bids to come to Himself."[13] If you have received salvation through Jesus Christ, the baptism of the Holy Spirit with the evidence of speaking in tongues is for you!

After Pentecost, believers generally received the baptism of the Holy Spirit with the evidence of speaking in tongues through the preaching of the Word or the laying on of hands. One time Paul came upon some disciples in Ephesus who believed in Jesus but had not heard about the Holy Spirit. Luke records that "as Paul laid his hands upon them, the Holy Spirit came on them; and they spoke in [foreign, unknown] tongues (languages) and prophesied."[14] Another time, as Peter preached to Cornelius's household, the Holy Spirit came on all who heard the message, and they began speaking in tongues and praising God (Acts 10:44–46).

Although some believers receive this Pentecostal blessing by waiting on the Lord, most people today receive the baptism of the Holy Spirit by the preaching of the Word and the laying on of hands in church services, private homes, and other locations.

Through the baptism of the Holy Spirit with the evidence of speaking in tongues, we who are diligent in the faith become more sensitive to the Spirit of God, acquire greater insight into God's Word, receive greater understanding of the kingdom of God, and receive God's power to *be* witnesses—not only *tell* others *about* Jesus, but live our lives in the power and demonstration of the Holy Spirit.

Our Preparation Includes Learning the Word of God

Learning the Word of God is an essential part of our preparation. The apostle Paul taught Timothy, "All Scripture is given by inspiration of God, and is profitable for doctrine, for reproof, for correction, for instruction in righteousness, that the man of God may be complete, thoroughly equipped for every good work."[15] Paul encouraged him, "Study and be eager and do your utmost to present yourself to God approved (tested by trial), a workman who has no cause to be ashamed, correctly analyzing and accurately dividing [rightly handling and skillfully teaching] the Word of Truth."[16]

Through the baptism of the Holy Spirit, we are equipped to learn the Scriptures, because the things of God are spiritually discerned. The apostle Paul taught the Corinthian church, "The natural man does not receive the things of the Spirit of God, for they are foolishness to him; nor can he know them, because they are spiritually discerned."[17] By spiritually discerning the Scriptures, we become knowledgeable of the doctrines of the faith, among which are those we will discuss in chapter 13.

The baptism of the Holy Spirit transforms our perception of the Word of God from being intellectual to being alive and personal. Paul explained: "What man knows the things of a man except the spirit of the man which is in him? Even so no one knows the things of God except the Spirit of God. Now we have received, not the spirit of the world, but the Spirit who is from God, that we might know the things that have been freely given to us by God."[18]

Jesus' Second Season Was Life and Ministry in the Power of the Spirit

Jesus entered into His season of life and ministry in the power of the Spirit through His wilderness experience. Baptism prepared Jesus for temptation. Immediately following Jesus' being recognized in baptism, the Holy Spirit led Him into the wilderness, where He fasted for forty days. There Satan challenged Jesus to prove His identity, even though God had publicly identified Him in baptism. Matthew described this experience in these words:

> Jesus was led up by the Spirit into the wilderness to be tempted by the devil. And when He had fasted forty days and forty nights, afterward He was hungry. Now when the tempter came to Him, he said, "If You are the Son of God, command that these stones become bread."
>
> But He answered and said, "It is written, 'Man shall not live by bread alone, but by every word that proceeds from the mouth of God.'"
>
> Then the devil took Him up into the holy city, set Him on the pinnacle of the temple, and said to Him, "If You are the Son of God, throw Yourself down. For it is written: 'He shall give His angels charge over you,' and, 'In their hands they shall bear you up, lest you dash your foot against a stone.'"
>
> Jesus said to him, "It is written again, 'You shall not tempt the Lord your God.'"
>
> Again, the devil took Him up on an exceedingly high mountain, and showed Him all the kingdoms of the world and their glory. And he said to Him, "All these things I will give You if You will fall down and worship me."
>
> Then Jesus said to him, "Away with you, Satan! For it is written, 'You shall worship the Lord your God, and Him only you shall serve.'"

> Then the devil left Him, and behold, angels came and ministered to Him.[19]

Satan tempted Jesus by appealing to His natural reasoning three times. Twice he tempted Jesus to prove His spiritual identity. The third time, he tempted Jesus to take the easy way of the world rather than the difficult way that God had planned. First, Satan appealed to Jesus' physical needs. Second, he tempted Jesus to presumptively "step out in faith." Third, Satan tempted Jesus to rule in the way of the world rather than through the kingdom of God. All three times, Satan tempted Jesus with subtle misinterpretation of Scripture.

Jesus overcame the devil in confidence and boldness with the Word of God. He did not ask His Father for help. Notice that angels came and ministered to Jesus after He successfully resisted temptation in all three confrontations. After having fasted forty days and nights and successfully resisting these temptations, Jesus entered His earthly ministry in power. According to the gospel of Luke, "Jesus returned in the power of the Spirit to Galilee, and news of Him went out through all the surrounding region."[20] Jesus entered the wilderness after His baptism *full* of the Spirit and exited the wilderness after successfully resisting the devil's temptations in the *power* of the Spirit.

In this season, Jesus called His disciples, preached the kingdom of God, and worked miracles. Indeed, Jesus worked His first miracle at the wedding in Cana after returning from the wilderness in the power of the Spirit.

Our Second Season Is Also Life and Ministry in the Power of the Spirit

We also enter our season of life and ministry in the power of the Spirit through our wilderness experiences. Just as Satan tempted Jesus in the wilderness, he also tempts believers today in three ways. He appeals to our physical needs, as he tempted Jesus to turn stones into bread. He tempts us to enter into presumption, as he tempted Jesus to presume that God would protect Him if He of His own volition threw Himself down from the temple pinnacle. And he tempts us to do things in the way of the world rather than in the way of the kingdom of God, as the devil tempted Jesus to rule the world by worshiping him.

Many believers today succumb to these temptations, compromising their lives and ministry callings in pursuits not initiated or sustained by their new nature in Christ. In other words, they live their lives and conduct their ministries within the limitations of the natural realm instead of waiting for the prompting and empowering of the Holy Spirit.

We confront the devil in our wilderness experiences by refusing to use our natural reasoning and abilities to engage in deceptively attractive opportunities. In other words, we must be mindful of entering into attractive opportunities without the leading of the Holy Spirit, regardless of how attractive those opportunities may seem. We enter into life and ministry in the power of the Holy Spirit when we (1) resist avoiding the hardships that God has brought our way, (2) refuse to prove our spirituality by presumptively stepping out in faith without the leading of the Holy Spirit, and (3) reject pursuing spiritual accomplishments by worldly means.

As the devil confronted Jesus when He was physically weak, he approaches us in our times of weakness. Even though we feel weak, we should always confront the devil as Jesus did—with confidence and boldness. We should confront him with the Word of God. Going through a wilderness experience is unfortunately not a one-time occurrence. The devil presents us with numerous opportunities to rely on ourselves rather than God.

Jesus' Third Season Was Fulfilling His Ultimate Purpose

Jesus prepared Himself to fulfill His ultimate purpose in the Garden of Gethsemane. Even though Jesus successfully resisted the devil's temptations, He had yet to meet His greatest challenge in this garden. Through His Garden-of-Gethsemane experience, Jesus overcame His self-nature, enabling Him to accomplish His ultimate purpose: taking on Himself the consequences for the sins of all mankind. By *self-nature*, we mean the self-protective drive that God builds into every human being, the human motivation to resist physical, mental, or emotional harm. In the garden, Jesus prepared Himself to accept being tortured, executed by crucifixion, forsaken by God the Father, and to suffer the consequences for the sins of all mankind in Hades.

According to the book of Matthew, Jesus went to the Garden of Gethsemane with His disciples immediately preceding His betrayal by Judas Iscariot. He became extremely sorrowful and greatly distressed, knowing that He would endure extreme physical and spiritual suffering. Three times Jesus prayed that the Father's will be done instead of His own.

Luke gave this account of Jesus' Garden-of-Gethsemane experience in the twenty-second chapter of his gospel: "He knelt down and prayed, saying, 'Father, if it is Your will, take this cup away from Me; nevertheless not My will, but Yours, be done.' Then an angel appeared to Him from heaven, strengthening Him. And being in agony, He prayed more earnestly. Then His sweat became like great drops of blood falling down to the ground."[21]

While confronting His self-nature in the garden, Jesus was emotionally distressed, in agony, and grieved in His soul. He prayed so earnestly that His sweat became like drops of blood. Note that an angel ministered to Him during the confrontation.

Jesus surrendered His self-will through prayer, overcoming His self-nature through His relationship with the Father. Through His Garden-of-Gethsemane experience, Jesus fulfilled the ultimate purpose for which He came into this world: He offered Himself as the sin offering for all mankind.

Our Third Season Is Fulfilling Our Ultimate Purpose

As Jesus fulfilled His ultimate purpose on earth through His garden experience, we fulfill the purpose for which God brought us into this world through our Garden-of-Gethsemane experiences. In our garden experiences, God gives us the opportunity to deny our will and accept His. Confronted with these opportunities, we choose between our will and God's will, which is in direct opposition to our own.

When we surrender our self-will in our garden experiences, we yield all that we are, all that we have, and all that we desire to God. By surrendering our self-will to God, we achieve a self-sacrificing ability to accomplish our God-given purpose—our ultimate fulfillment.

As Jesus' Garden-of-Gethsemane experience was extremely stressful, our garden experiences are agonizingly stressful. Confronting our self-nature is excruciating. We become terribly distressed at releasing our self-preservation into God's hands.

Comparing Jesus' confrontation with the devil in the wilderness with His confrontation with self-nature in the Garden of Gethsemane, we find that His time in the garden was much more stressful than His time in the wilderness. In the wilderness, Jesus was hungry and physically tired. He confronted the devil with confidence and boldness. Angels ministered to Jesus *after* His third temptation.

In the garden, Jesus was emotionally distressed, in agony, and grieved in His soul. His sweat became as drops of blood as He wrestled to choose the Father's will over His own. An angel strengthened Him *during* His confrontation. Based on this comparison, we conclude that our confrontations with our self-will in our garden experiences are more stressful than our confrontations with the devil in our wilderness experiences.

Paul instructed the Philippian church, "As you have always obeyed, not as in my presence only, but now much more in my absence, work out your own salvation with fear and trembling."[22] We shouldn't fear the devil in our wilderness experiences, but we certainly encounter fear and tremble in our Garden-of-Gethsemane experiences. We don't fear the devil, but we do work out our own salvation in fear and trembling.

The writer of the book of Hebrews exhorts us: "Consider Him who endured such hostility from sinners against Himself, lest you become weary and discouraged in your souls. You have not yet resisted to bloodshed, striving against sin."[23] Jesus did not resist when He shed His blood on the cross. He resisted to bloodshed in the Garden of Gethsemane. Our garden confrontation with our self-will is excruciating, but we are unlikely to shed blood as Jesus did.

Our Garden-of-Gethsemane experience, however, is not a one-time event—it's a lifestyle. We surrender our self-will in prayer, overcoming our self-nature through our relationship with our Father in the strength of His Son.

Admonition to Follow God's Pathway to Ultimate Fulfillment

Be born of the Spirit. Be baptized in water for (1) release from passions and excesses of the flesh, (2) freedom from the power of sin, and (3) relief from inner insecurities and fears by attaining inner cleanness and peace with God. Receive the baptism of the Holy Spirit with the evidence of speaking in tongues to become more sensitive to the Spirit of God, acquire greater insight into God's Word, receive greater understanding of the kingdom of God, and receive God's power to be a witness—telling others about Jesus and living in the power and demonstration of the Holy Spirit. Learn the Scriptures with the enlightenment of the Holy Spirit.

If you are still not sure that the baptism of the Holy Spirit is a blessing that God is offering to you, please at least tell God that if He is offering it to you, you are open to receiving it in His way and in His time.

Boldly confront the devil with the Word of God in your wilderness experiences. Enter into the power of the Holy Spirit by resisting temptations to avoid the hardships that God brings your way, refusing to prove your spirituality by presumptively stepping out in faith, and rejecting pursuit of spiritual accomplishments by worldly means.

Surrender your self-will to God in your Garden-of-Gethsemane experiences. Know that the Lord Jesus Christ is with you. He who has already overcome all obstacles is strengthening and guiding you. Be encouraged that the fulfilling of your life purpose—your ultimate fulfillment—awaits you on the other side of your garden experiences.

Pray to Follow God's Pathway to Ultimate Fulfillment

Father, I desire to grow into spiritual maturity. I want to be born of the Spirit. I want to enter into death and resurrection with Christ in water baptism, releasing me from the passions and excesses of the flesh, freeing me from the power of sin, relieving me of inner insecurities and fears by giving me an inner cleanness and peace with God. I want to be more sensitive to the Spirit of God, acquire greater insight into Your Word, receive greater understanding of the kingdom of God, and receive Your power to be a witness through the baptism of the Holy Spirit with the evidence of speaking in tongues.

Father, I want to yield all that I am, all that I have, and all that I desire to You. Please strengthen me by Your Spirit so that I can withstand the devil's temptations to avoid hardships You bring my way, to prove my spiritual identity or accept deceptively attractive opportunities by presumptively stepping out in faith, and to conduct spiritual ministry through worldly methods. Please also strengthen me as I confront my self-will in my Garden-of-Gethsemane experiences. I strongly desire to fulfill my

God-given purpose in Your strength. All this I ask, not only for my own spiritual growth, but also that our Lord Jesus Christ, in whose name I pray, may be glorified and exalted in and through me. Amen.

Where Do We Go from Here?

Since we are dependent on Jesus to successfully progress through our life's spiritual journey, we need to know Him. Next, we will discover how the Bible brings us into a closer relationship with Jesus Christ. We'll learn that our approach to the Bible defines our relationship with God, forms the boundaries of our faith, and determines our earthly and eternal destinies. Finally, we will come to know Jesus as the living Word.

Chapter 3

Come to Know the Living Word

> In the past God spoke to our forefathers through the prophets
> at many times and in various ways, but in these last days
> he has spoken to us by his Son.
> Hebrews 1:1 NIV

In our quest to experience the living Christ and live in the presence of God, we observed Jesus' earthly journey and noted that our spiritual journey progresses through the same three seasons: preparation, life and ministry in the power of the Spirit, and fulfilling our ultimate purpose. In our wilderness and Garden-of-Gethsemane experiences, we look to Jesus for guidance, strength, and encouragement. Being dependent on Jesus, we need to know Him, not just know about Him. This is our third spiritual reality: we can personally meet, become acquainted with, and become intimate with the Lord Jesus Christ through the Bible.

The Father Introduces Us to Jesus in the Bible

Experiencing the living Christ begins with the Father's invitation to meet His Son in the Holy Bible. Through it we come to personally know the Lord Jesus Christ, and through Christ, we come to know God the Father and the Holy Spirit. When we read the Bible by enlightenment of the Holy Spirit, we receive the Father's invitation. When we study the Bible without the Spirit's enlightenment, we only know about Him.

Having learned about Christ, we presume to know Him when we don't even hear His voice.

By introducing us to Jesus, the Father gives us the opportunity to enter into fellowship with Him. *Fellowship*, as we will use the term, is more than the social gathering of church members that produces the pleasures of friendship. It is the spirit realm coming together of a believer in Christ with God the Father, with the Lord Jesus Christ, or with other believers that supernaturally edifies the people involved. Two factors determine the depth of our fellowship with God the Father and the Lord Jesus Christ: (1) our willingness to enter into the realm of God's presence and (2) our taking time to wait quietly before them.

When we've been introduced to people, we may later say that we know them. The truth is, however, we don't really *know* them; we've only been introduced to them. By meeting them, we have the *opportunity* to know them. Through casual conversation, we may become acquainted with them, learning their interests and opinions. Even then, we don't really know them. As we progress from casual conversation to sharing from our hearts, we come to *know* them. Similarly, having learned about Jesus, some believers think that they know Him. But they've only been introduced.

Having been introduced to Jesus, we may enter into conversation with Him in prayer. If we listen as well as talk to Him, we learn His interests and opinions. When we progress from casual prayer to listening to Christ as He shares His heart, we come to know Him in fellowship.

Whether or not we accept the Father's invitation and how well we become acquainted with His Son are influenced by three things: (1) our perception of the Bible, (2) our application of the Bible, and (3) our interpretation of the Bible.

Our Perception of the Bible Defines
Our Relationship with Christ

The Holy Spirit wrote the Bible through holy men with living words, because ordinary words are incapable of expressing the full dimensions of its truth. Therefore, the Bible cannot be understood through the meaning of its words alone. One must discern the supernatural life hidden within the words to perceive what God is offering to the reader. As Paul advised the Corinthian church, "The natural man does not receive the things of the Spirit of God, for they are foolishness to him; nor can he know them, because they are spiritually discerned."[1] What is written by the Spirit must be read through the Spirit to receive the life, power, and wisdom of the Spirit. In other words, the illumination of the Holy Spirit opens spirit-realm truth to the discerning reader.

Not everyone, however, discerns the Bible in this dimension. We can identify four ways that people perceive the Bible. They view the Bible (1) as an ordinary book, (2) as a spiritual book naturally written, (3) as the Word of God, or (4) as the written record of God's Spirit-empowered Word.

First, some people view the Bible as an ordinary book. If they read the Bible at all, they do so out of curiosity and probably with a critical eye. Without a sovereign act of God, they receive no spiritual benefit. They are unlikely to perceive the Father's invitation to know His Son.

The Bible is a book, words formed by ink printed on paper pages or letters appearing on an electronic screen. Neither the ink nor the paper and neither the letters nor the screen has any significance. Without the illumination of the Holy Spirit, these are merely ordinary words. People can spend a lifetime diligently studying the Bible without the enlightenment of the Holy Spirit and never receive the life, power, and wisdom hidden in its words.

Even when viewed as a normal book, the Bible is extraordinary. Written by a number of people over hundreds of years, its teachings are remarkably consistent. The fact that minor variations exist without negating the truth of its message attests to its authenticity. The Bible is painfully truthful, even exposing the weaknesses of Christ's disciples. Yet they willingly martyred themselves to bring its message to mankind.

Prophecies in the Bible have come true, and biblical facts that at one time were thought to be erroneous have been archaeologically proven accurate. Not understanding the Bible does not invalidate its spiritual truth any more than not understanding Einstein's theory of relativity invalidates its natural truth.

In spite of the efforts of unenlightened people to destroy the Bible, it has endured throughout time. It continues to be one of the most, if not the most, commonly owned and frequently read books in the world.

The second way people view the Bible is as a naturally written spiritual book. They are selective in accepting its truth, discrediting portions they find contrary to their natural reasoning or personal experiences. They rarely receive the life of God hidden in the Bible's Spirit-empowered words.

A third group of people perceive the Bible as the Word of God written by the Holy Spirit through mankind. They believe that the Bible is without error and that it teaches them principles by which they govern their conduct. Some may govern their inner thoughts and motivations by the Bible's principles as well. They believe, as Paul taught Timothy, "All Scripture is given by inspiration of God, and is profitable for doctrine, for reproof, for correction, for instruction in righteousness, that the man of God may be complete, thoroughly equipped for every good work."[2] They may not, however, know the Lord Jesus Christ well enough to converse with Him.

The fourth way people perceive the Bible is as the written record of God's Spirit-empowered Word. They believe it was written by the Holy Spirit through mankind. They receive the life, power, and wisdom hidden in the Bible's Spirit-empowered words and share these living benefits with other people.

These people converse with God. By the Spirit, they receive answers to questions not answered in the Bible, such as, Where should I live? Whom should I marry? What occupation should I choose?

The Holy Spirit opens the understanding of these discerning readers to perceive the Father's introduction to His Son, who came that mankind "may have life, and have it abundantly,"[3] and who is "the Power of God and the Wisdom of God."[4]

Our Application of the Bible Determines Its Effectiveness in Our Lives

People generally apply the principles of the Bible in one of four ways: (1) they make no application, (2) they make religious application, (3) they make unenlightened personal application, or (4) they give themselves to God for His application. Let's take a closer look at each group.

First, the people who make no application of the Bible cannot see its relevance to their daily lives. They consider the Bible outdated. For them, the Bible is too restrictive, forbidding pleasurable behaviors and contradicting their societal values and view of world affairs.

Second, some see the relevance of biblical principles, but they make religious application. They may belong to a church or denomination that neglects fellowship with the Lord Jesus Christ; they have no interactive relationship with Him. Some are unaware of salvation. Others are unaware that God's Spirit can work effectively in their lives. They don't benefit from the life, power, and wisdom of the Word of God.

Third are those who make unenlightened application of the Word of God. They desire advantages offered through the application of biblical principles such as prosperity, healing, and protection. They don't fellowship with the Lord Jesus Christ. They don't hear His voice. They outwardly appear surrendered to Him but in truth are not.

Then fourth, people give themselves entirely to God to work His will and good pleasure in their lives. These people come to know Jesus intimately.

Our Interpretation of the Bible Determines Our Destiny

The way we interpret the Bible shapes our earthly and eternal destinies. We can identify three ways in which mankind interprets the Bible: (1) intellectually, (2) conceptually, and (3) spiritually.

Some Interpret the Bible Intellectually

Those who interpret the Bible intellectually limit themselves to the mental understanding of its words. They become knowledgeable of biblical facts, and they may obtain salvation, but they don't perceive the living power and wisdom of God's Word.

Some contemporary Christians unknowingly limit themselves to an intellectual gospel. They study to understand the written Word. They know about the Lord Jesus Christ, but they don't know Him personally. They don't have fellowship with Jesus.

In Jesus' time, a group called the Pharisees limited themselves to an intellectual understanding of the Word of God. They were an elite religious group, highly educated in the Scriptures, diligent in meticulously adhering to the Scripture's requirements, zealous in enforcing the requirements of Scripture on others, and committed to silencing those who threatened their beliefs. Even though they were knowledgeable, diligent, zealous, and committed to their intellectual interpretation of Scripture, they did not recognize the Son of God as He stood in their presence. In fact, Jesus rebuked them, saying, "You diligently study the Scriptures because you think that by them you possess eternal life. These are the Scriptures that testify about me, yet you refuse to come to me to have life."[5]

Not only did the Pharisees not recognize the Son of God, but they also aggressively opposed Him, condemning Him to death on the cross. By intellectually interpreting the Scriptures, they made them an idol. Serving that idol, they crucified the Son of God—the God they thought they were vehemently serving!

Some Christians today study the Bible, but they don't know the Son of God. Their lives outwardly conform to the Scriptures, yet they are void of the life, power, and wisdom offered through fellowship with God's Son. Like the Pharisees, they make the Scriptures an idol.

Seminaries and Bible schools teach their students biblical knowledge. Some neglect, however, to lead them into fellowship with the Lord Jesus Christ. As a result, when these students enter the ministry, their preaching and teaching convey information without imparting the illumination of the Holy Spirit. They preach intellectual instruction, not the Spirit-empowered Word of God. Some even preach sermon content produced by unsaved persons, substituting the principles of the world for the anointing of God. Their sermons and lessons may be biblically accurate, but they are void of the life, power, and wisdom of God. Signs and wonders rarely occur; the Lord is not working with them (Mark 16:20).

Paul challenged the Colossian church, "If you died with Christ from the basic principles of the world, why, as though living in the world, do you subject yourselves to regulations?"[6] We might similarly ask ourselves, If Christ has delivered us from the principles of the world, why are they so prominent in the church? Could the reason be that some of the leadership in the church today lacks fellowship with the Lord Jesus Christ?

According to the gospel of Matthew, Jesus warned the multitudes in one of the more sobering passages in the Bible:

> Not everyone who says to Me, Lord, Lord, will enter the kingdom of heaven, but he who does the will of My Father Who is in heaven. Many will say to Me on that day, Lord, Lord, have we not prophesied in Your name and driven out demons in Your name and done many mighty works in Your name? And then I will say to them openly

(publicly), I never knew you; depart from Me, you who act wickedly [disregarding My commands].[7]

These people appeared to be spiritually successful, prophesying and casting out demons. However, they lacked one thing: they disregarded Jesus' commands. How can we obey Christ's commands if we don't listen to His voice? How can we hear His voice if we don't know Him as a living being? (We will address living a lifestyle that is attentive to the Lord in chapter 15.)

Others Interpret the Bible Conceptually

Those who view the Bible conceptually apply its principles to their lives to achieve favorable results. This interpretation is widely publicized from pulpits and by Christian television and radio ministries today. One popular form of teaching is to *intellectually* formulate the steps to accomplish a desired spiritual result. Another popular form of teaching motivates believers to claim—or even demand—that God activate *intellectually selected* (as opposed to Spirit-led) portions of Scripture on their behalf.

These people put their faith in principles instead of a person—the Lord Jesus Christ. Their works-centered approach tries to manipulate God to make desired provisions. Unfortunately, many well-intentioned Christians attempt to lead people into the benefits of God's Word through this pursuit. They don't lead them into fellowship with the Lord Jesus Christ, in whom is all provision.

Still Others Interpret the Bible Spiritually

Those who interpret the Bible spiritually recognize it is the writing of the Holy Spirit. These people discern the written words of the Bible as they are quickened, or made alive, by the Holy Spirit. They don't use the Bible as a medium to communicate with the spirit world, but they are sensitive to the Holy Spirit as He brings the words on the printed page to life. These enlightened words produce spiritual growth by God working through them and reveal Jesus as the living Word.

Spiritual Growth Is the Work of God

It's good to conform our conduct to the requirements of Scripture, but we must guard against attempting to apply God's Word without the inner working of God. Paul disclosed to the Corinthian church: "I planted, Apollos watered, but God gave the increase. So then neither he who plants is anything, nor he who waters, but God who gives the increase."[8] He encouraged the Philippian church, saying he was "confident of this very thing, that He who has begun a good work in you will complete it until the day of Jesus Christ."[9] He told them, "It is God who works in you both to will and to do for His good pleasure."[10]

Spiritual growth is therefore not the work of man; it's the work of God. The written Word is the objective measure, the holy standard, which is achieved, not by natural discipline alone, but through faith in our Lord Jesus Christ.

Jesus Is the Living Word

The Bible is commonly known as the Word of God. But there is another Word of God. Jesus Christ is the Word. The apostle John opened his gospel with these words: "In the beginning was the Word, and the Word was with God, and the Word was God. He was in the beginning with God. All things were made through Him, and without Him nothing was made that was made. And the Word became flesh and dwelt among us, and we beheld His glory, the glory as of the only begotten of the Father, full of grace and truth."[11]

Paul informed the Corinthian church that Christ is "the power of God and the wisdom of God"[12] to those who believe. Paul labored to form Christ in believers. He addressed the Galatians, "My little children, for whom I am again suffering birth pangs until Christ is completely and permanently formed (molded) within you."[13] Indeed, Jesus Christ is "the author and finisher of our faith."[14]

Anointed lives and ministries flow out of fellowship with the Lord Jesus Christ. Mark described the ministry of the early church in this way: "They went out and preached everywhere, the Lord working with them and confirming the word through the accompanying signs."[15] Usually, when miracles take place, someone has entered into fellowship with Christ to attain them.

Fellowship with the Lord Jesus Christ avails us of all that God has provided for us in Christ. As we become increasingly intimate with the Lord, we experience His love, compassion, and faithfulness. We trust Him with greater control of our lives. As we surrender to Him, He takes over a greater portion of our lives, and the spirit of the world is forced to relinquish control. Our personal relationship with Jesus (the living Word), not a mere intellectual understanding of the Bible (the written Word), establishes the kingdom of God within us. God's kingdom is the environment in which sin, sickness, and the world cannot endure.

Elevating the written Word over the living Word impersonalizes our relationship with Jesus Christ. Paul did not say he knew *what* he believed; he said he knew *whom* he believed. He testified to Timothy, "I know whom I have believed and am persuaded that He is able to keep what I have committed to Him until that Day."[16] Reading about Jesus in the Bible is not the same as knowing Him!

The written Word can never substitute for the living Word, in whom all things exist. Paul emphasized this point to the believers in Colossae: "By Him all things were created that are in heaven and that are on earth, visible and invisible, whether thrones or dominions or principalities or powers. All things were created through Him and for Him. And He is before all things, and in Him all things consist."[17] The living Word is a person— Jesus Christ, the Son of God.

The Bible, or written Word, is similar to a biography of the Lord Jesus Christ, the living Word. We learn about a person by reading his or her biography, but we cannot really know the person without actually meeting and interacting with him or her. Let's come to know our Lord Jesus Christ beyond just reading His biography and live with Him in intimate fellowship. Let's do more than put our faith and trust in the written Word; let's put our faith and trust in the living Word—the Lord Jesus Christ.

Admonition to Know the Living Word

Allow the Father to introduce you to His Son through His written Word. Receive the Bible as God's written record of His Spirit-empowered Word. Allow the Lord to bring your thoughts, attitudes, emotions, and conduct up to His holy standard. Study the Bible with the enlightenment of the Holy Spirit. Come to personally know the Lord Jesus Christ. Listen for His voice, and be attentive when He speaks.

Pray to Know the Living Word

Father, I joyously receive Your invitation to know Your Son. Please forgive me for emphasizing Your written Word above Your living Word. Lord Jesus, I want to know You and not just know about You. I want to hear Your voice every time You speak to me. All this I ask, not only for my own spiritual growth, but also that our Lord Jesus Christ, in whose name I pray, may be glorified and exalted in and through me. Amen.

Where Do We Go from Here?

Now that we have received the Father's invitation to know His Son, we can enter into fellowship with God the Father and the Lord Jesus Christ. Adam brought death on all mankind, separating us from God. Jesus makes alive all who believe in Him, bringing us into fellowship with God. Next, we'll activate our spirit nature by choosing obedience to God over independence from God and by choosing spiritual discernment over intellectual opinion.

Chapter 4

Activate Your Spirit Nature

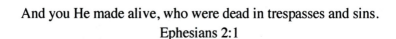

And you He made alive, who were dead in trespasses and sins.
Ephesians 2:1

Now that we know Jesus as the living Word, we will continue our journey into the presence of God by learning that Jesus brings our human spirits to life. Our fourth spiritual reality is this: we can live in the realm of God's presence beyond the limitations of the natural mind and five senses.

We'll note that people are spirit-beings in physical bodies. Adam chose independence from God rather than dependence on God, eternally separating mankind from God. Jesus Christ chose dependence on God over independence from God, bringing those who believe back to Him. Finally, we will activate our spirit nature by choosing dependence on God over independence from God, and spiritual discernment over intellectual opinion.

Adam Separated Mankind from God, but Jesus Brings Us Back

Mankind is created in the image of God. Genesis tells us: "God said, 'Let Us make man in Our image, according to Our likeness. . . .' So God created man in His own image; in the image of God He created him; male and female He created them."[1] God refers to Himself in the plural. He is a triune, or three-part, being—Father, Son, and Holy Spirit. And He created man as a triune being—spirit, soul, and body. God created mankind in two events. He first created Adam and later created Eve.

God Created Adam of the Dust of the Ground

Genesis describes God's creation of Adam: "The Lord God formed man of the dust of the ground, and breathed into his nostrils the breath of life; and man became a living soul."[2] God first formed *man* of the dust of the ground. He then breathed the *breath of life* into his nostrils, and man became a *living soul*. The lifeless body of dust was man before God breathed His life into it. When God breathed His life into man, he became a living soul.

Thus we see that mankind is composed of spirit, soul, and body. The spirit is a portion of God's breath of life. The soul is the living being created when God's breath contacted the body. And the body is the formation of dust into which God breathed His life breath. Paul referred to this three-part composition when he prayed for the church in Thessalonica: "Now may the God of peace Himself sanctify you completely; and may your whole spirit, soul, and body be preserved blameless at the coming of our Lord Jesus Christ."[3]

God Formed Eve out of Adam's Side

God created woman in this manner: "The Lord God caused a deep sleep to fall upon Adam; and while he slept, He took one of his ribs or a part of his side and closed up the [place with] flesh. And the rib or part of his side which the Lord God had taken from the man He built up and made into a woman, and He brought her to the man."[4]

The material that God took from Adam to form Eve was more than the lifeless dust out of which He had formed man. The substance God took from Adam was a living portion of the being God created when He breathed His breath into the body of dust to create a living soul. Since Adam was living, the material that God took from Adam was living. There must have been elements of the breath of God, the living soul, and the body of dust in the part of Adam from which God made Eve. Accordingly, Adam and Eve shared more than the dust out of which man was originally made.

They Shall Become One Flesh

Immediately following this account, Genesis continues, "Therefore a man shall leave his father and his mother and shall become united and cleave to his wife, and they shall become one flesh."[5] When a man leaves his father and mother, he is to become united and cleave to his wife and to become one flesh with her. Two separate people, who were not one flesh, are to become one flesh.

Mark records Jesus quoting this scripture to the Pharisees: "From the beginning of the creation, God 'made them male and female. For this reason a man shall leave his father and mother and be joined to his wife, and the two shall become one flesh'; so then they are no longer two, but one flesh."[6] A man and his wife were to no longer be two, but to become one flesh, because God made them male and female.

A man and a woman with two separate bodies become one flesh. God brings them together as one flesh in marriage. But becoming one flesh involves more than becoming religiously related in matrimony. The husband and wife are the spiritual completion of one another.

Christ and the Church Are One

A man and his wife becoming one flesh describes the relationship between Christ and the church. Paul taught the Ephesian believers: "For this reason a man shall leave his father and mother and be joined to his wife, and the two shall become one flesh. This is a great mystery, but I speak concerning Christ and the church."[7] A husband and wife are one, as Christ and the church are one. This spiritual phenomenon, although not observable with the natural senses, is nevertheless true.

Paul called becoming one flesh a mystery. A mystery is an occurrence that cannot be verified by the five natural senses or explained through natural reasoning. Therefore, one flesh is not a theological concept; it's a spiritual reality. If a husband and wife being one flesh were a theological concept, the relationship between Christ and the church would be a theological concept. If the relationship between Christ and the church were a theological concept, Christianity would be mere religion; our faith in Christ would be in vain.

All believers together (the church) are one with Christ. Since each believer is a part of the church, each believer is a portion of this oneness with Christ. Each believer is a separate person, yet all believers together are one with Christ. Paul wrote to the church at Rome, "We, being many, are one body in Christ, and individually members of one another."[8]

Therefore, the body of Christ is more than an assembly of physical beings who believe in Jesus as Lord. The body of Christ is a spiritual entity that encompasses the spirits, souls, and bodies of all believers.

The body of Christ is one body, and each member of the body affects the others. Paul informed the Corinthian church: "God has combined the members of the body and has given greater honor to the parts that lacked it, so that there should be no division in the body, but that its parts should have equal concern for each other. If one part suffers, every part suffers with it; if one part is honored, every part rejoices with it."[9] This interrelatedness of the body of Christ is spiritual reality.

Early in human history, though, Adam and Eve nullified their interrelatedness with God when they chose to be independent of Him. They ate the forbidden fruit of the tree of the knowledge of good and evil.

Adam and Eve Chose Independence from God over Dependence on God

God told Adam that he might eat the fruit of every tree in the garden, except one. He warned Adam that if he ate the fruit of the tree of the knowledge of good and evil, he would die. Satan enticed Eve, asserting that if she ate the forbidden fruit, she would not die but would become wise and would be like God.

When Adam and Eve ate the fruit of the tree of the knowledge of good and evil, they forfeited the right to eat the fruit of the tree of life, not only for themselves but for all their descendants. God drove Adam and Eve out of the Garden of Eden and placed a guard around the tree of life so that they could not eat its fruit. We call this course of events "the fall of man."

Adam and Eve declared their independence from God in willful rebellion. From that time, mankind began to function independently from God, having to depend upon their natural abilities rather than God's empowerment. They began to make distinctions between right and wrong based on their limited natural judgment instead of the all-knowing insight of God.

No longer did God's breath of life continually empower them with His strength, ability, and wisdom. No longer did Adam and Eve enjoy fellowship with God.

Eating the fruit of the tree of the knowledge of good and evil opened an awareness of the natural realm in Adam and Eve. Before they ate the forbidden fruit, Adam and Eve were innocent, childlike, dependent on God, and without sin consciousness. After they ate it, they became aware of their physical nakedness; they experienced shame and became fearful of God. They changed from being God-centered to being self-centered.

As the result of their independence, Adam and Eve experienced death—separation from God. Before Adam and Eve ate the forbidden fruit, their souls and bodies continuously received the replenishing flow of God's life through their human spirits. But upon eating this fruit, their human spirits ceased to function. Their only source of life was the stagnant life already deposited in their souls. Their bodies began irreversible deterioration leading to physical death because they were no longer sustained by God's continuous, replenishing life source through the human spirit.

Adam and Eve ceased to function in the image of God. They no longer lived as three-part beings but functioned in only two parts: soul and body. While their human spirits were functioning, they enjoyed the pure, continuously flowing wisdom of God. When they chose to live independently from God, they limited their wisdom to the understanding of the soul. They exchanged the unlimited life source of their spirits for the limited life source of their souls. Because of their independence from God, they had to toil to survive without God's empowerment.

This fallen state of mankind binds people in spiritual darkness. They cannot make fully informed choices, the chief of which is to be reconciled to God and know Him as He really is.

Fallen men and women are captive to the power of sin. Their spirits are deadened, their hearts are hardened, and their souls are darkened. Their spirits are deadened because all human spirits ceased to function after the fall of man. Their hearts are hardened because they no longer receive the softening life of God's Spirit through their human spirits. Their souls are darkened because the light of God no longer shines through their deadened human spirits and hardened hearts. Only the sacrifice of God's Son can rescue mankind from this dire state of being.

Jesus Christ Chose Dependence on God over Independence from God

The first Adam separated all mankind from God by choosing independence from God. Jesus Christ, the last Adam, came to bring all mankind back to God through His dependence on God. Jesus Christ, God's Son, gave Himself as the only perfect, sinless sacrifice to redeem mankind from the consequences of Adam and Eve's rebellion. We call this redemption of mankind "salvation."

Salvation brings the human spirit to life. Saved people no longer function as two-part beings (soul and body). No longer handicapped by a nonfunctioning human spirit, they are restored to the full function of their entire being—spirit, soul, and body—as God originally designed mankind.

God gives every person the right to choose to live eternally in His presence by accepting His gift of salvation in Christ. Everyone is free to accept God's gift to live eternally in His presence or to reject it and exist eternally outside of His presence. If you have not yet prayed the prayer of salvation, please return to the prayer in chapter 2.

The Enlivened Human Spirit Enables Spiritual Discernment

Physical life came first, then spiritual life. The apostle Paul informed the Corinthian church, "It is not the spiritual life which came first, but the physical and then the spiritual."[10] In the creation of Adam, God made the physical body first and then breathed into it the breath of life. As the physical body came before the spiritual life in the formation of Adam, our physical existence comes before our spiritual life today. We initially find ourselves with our bodies and souls functioning and our human spirits deadened because of the fall of man.

Through salvation, God brings our human spirit to life. After salvation, we can choose to no longer eat from the tree of the knowledge of good and evil. But this choice is more than a one-time decision; it's a lifetime of decisions that determine the course and pace of our spiritual journey.

Eating the fruit of the tree of the knowledge of good and evil is judging right and wrong by our human intellect rather than deferring judgment to God. Each time we judge for ourselves through our five senses and natural mind, rather than looking to God for His evaluation, we eat the fruit of the tree of the knowledge of good and evil. We cannot judge with our human intellect and defer judgment to God at the same time. Doing the first forfeits the second and increases our tendency to continue making the same choice.

All Christians choose repeatedly between forming their own opinions and exercising spiritual discernment. Some believers stunt their spiritual growth by routinely relying on their intellects. They seldom venture beyond the limitations of their natural understanding.

Even so, the opportunity of entering into the realm of God's presence beyond the limitations of the human mind and the five natural senses remains open to all believers. We who have accepted Jesus Christ as Savior and Lord have freedom of choice. We can freely choose between forming intellectual opinions and exercising spiritual discernment.

Admonition to Activate Your Spirit Nature

Enter the realm of God's presence beyond the natural mind and five senses. Enter into fellowship with God through Jesus Christ. Enjoy the continuous life source of His Spirit. Choose to be like the last Adam (Jesus), not the first Adam. Be reliant on God, not reliant on self. Choose dependence on God over independence from God. Look continually to God for His all-knowing wisdom rather than forming your own opinions.

Pray to Activate Your Spirit Nature

Father, I know that Adam separated himself and his descendants from You by relying on his limited judgment rather than Your unlimited knowledge and wisdom. Please forgive me for doing the same. Help me to rely on You instead of on myself. I want to be obedient to You rather than independent from You. I want to defer all judgment to You rather than judging by my human intellect, to exercise spiritual discernment rather than forming personal opinions. I want to live in Your continuously replenishing life breath. All this I ask, not only for my own spiritual growth, but also that our Lord Jesus Christ, in whose name I pray, may be glorified and exalted in and through me. Amen.

Where Do We Go from Here?

People—being spirit, soul, and body—live in two dimensions: (1) the spiritual realm and (2) the physical realm. Next, we will see that we relate to the realm of God's presence with the heart and relate to the physical world with the mind. We'll conform our minds to the dimension of God's Spirit. We will perceive the things of the Spirit by the Spirit.

Chapter 5

Be Released from Temporal Limitations

God raised us up with Christ and seated us with him
in the heavenly realms in Christ Jesus.
Ephesians 2:6 NIV

We know that God created mankind as a three-part being: spirit, soul, and body. Adam separated mankind from God by choosing independence from God; Jesus Christ brings those who believe back into fellowship with God through His dependence on God, making God's continuous life breath, strength, ability, and wisdom available to them. Next, we'll advance toward experiencing the living Christ and living in the presence of God by finding freedom from our temporal limitations.

Our fifth spiritual reality is this: Jesus Christ releases us from temporal-realm limitations. We'll recognize that mankind lives in two dimensions: (1) the body functions in the physical dimension, and (2) the human spirit and soul live in the spiritual dimension. We'll find that people discern the realm of God's presence through the heart. The mind either helps or hinders this perception. Jesus Christ opens the awareness of those who believe in Him to God's presence. Finally, we will receive freedom from our temporal-realm limitations.

Mankind Lives in Two Dimensions

In chapter 4, we noted that a man and his wife becoming one flesh describes the relationship between Christ and the church. As Christ and the church are one, so are a husband and wife. This leads us to a radical conclusion: there is a dimension of mankind that transcends the physical body.

There are two dimensions of human existence: one is physical, and the other is spiritual. The Bible refers to these two dimensions as *temporal* and *eternal*. Everything in the temporal realm has a limited lifespan. These things have physical characteristics that people can understand with the natural mind and observe with the five natural senses: seeing, hearing, smelling, touching, and tasting. Everything in the eternal realm will live forever. Since eternal things have no physical form or function, human beings can neither observe them with the five natural senses nor understand them with the natural mind. The body is temporal; the human spirit and soul are eternal.

The Body Is Temporal

As we have discussed, God formed man's body from the dust of the earth. The body, being made from physical material, has a tangible form readily observable with the five natural senses.

The body is subject to the limitations of time and space and has physical vulnerabilities such as physical injury, disease, aging, and death. Temporal things wear out. Homes, automobiles, other possessions, and even our physical bodies deteriorate to dust over time. Those who believe in Christ, however, have this hope that the apostle Paul expressed to the Corinthian church:

> We do not lose heart. Though outwardly we are wasting away, yet inwardly we are being renewed day by day. For our light and momentary troubles are achieving for us an eternal glory that far outweighs them all. So we fix our eyes not on what is seen, but on what is unseen. For what is seen is temporary, but what is unseen is eternal.[1]

The body is not the person; it's the housing in which the person lives while on the earth. For believers in Christ, though, the body is much more than just an earthly dwelling place; it's the temple of the Holy Spirit. In fact, our bodies don't belong to us; they belong to God, and we are to keep them holy. The apostle Paul confronted believers in Corinth: "Do you not know that your body is the temple of the Holy Spirit who is in you, whom you have from God, and you are not your own? For you were bought at a price; therefore glorify God in your body and in your spirit, which are God's."[2] Keeping our bodies holy enhances our sensitivity to the presence of God.

People are not just living bodies; they are spirit, soul, and body. The body, being made of dust, has a limited lifespan, but the spirit and soul live after the physical body ceases to function. From the viewpoint of the world, the human spirit and soul appear to pass away. In truth, however, the invisible human spirit and soul continue to live; only the visible body passes away.

Even though the body is the part of mankind that is naturally observable, the human spirit and soul make up the greater being. As stated in our opening scripture, we who have received salvation live in more than the body—we live also in Christ. The physical body, with its temporary and natural nature, is therefore not to dominate but to serve the human spirit and soul. Fasting weakens the influence of the body and opens awareness to the realm of God's presence.

The Spirit and Soul Are Eternal

The human spirit and soul live forever. The human spirit, being a portion of the breath of God, has no tangible form; neither does the soul, which was created by the breath of God contacting the earthen body. The human spirit and soul, although invisible, are finite entities. They are defined, not by physical form, but by dimensions not observable with the five natural senses. The human spirit and soul are practically indistinguishable with our natural understanding; they are so similar that we can hardly tell them apart.

The soul gives the human spirit individual expression. People reason, decide, and feel emotions in the soul. The soul interrelates with the realm of God's presence through the heart and human spirit, and with the natural world through the mind and body. The heart is the door to the realm of God's presence, and the mind is the gate to the natural world.

Human spirits of believers in Christ are one with the Lord, because Scripture tells us that "he who is joined to the Lord is one spirit with Him."[3] Solomon wrote, "The spirit of man is the lamp of the Lord, searching all the innermost parts of his being."[4] God primarily relates to mankind through the human spirit.

As believers progress in spiritual maturity, they become increasingly sensitive to God's presence through their hearts and human spirits. Paul explained to believers in Corinth that only the spirit of a person knows the inner thoughts, motivations, and values within that person. Likewise, only the Spirit of God knows the thoughts, motivations, and values hidden deep in God. And only the Holy Spirit can reveal them (1 Cor. 2:11 AMP).

Even though our spirit is one with the Lord, our soul hinders our spiritual awareness. Our soul, tainted by the world through the five senses and the natural mind, dulls our sensitivity to the presence of God. We have difficulty discerning God's presence until He separates our soul and spirit.

According to the writer of Hebrews, "The Word that God speaks is alive and full of power [making it active, operative, energizing, and effective]; it is sharper than any two-edged sword, penetrating to the dividing line of the breath of life (soul) and [the immortal] spirit, and of joints and marrow [of the deepest parts of our nature], exposing and sifting and analyzing and judging the very thoughts and purposes of the heart."[5] Notice that it is *the Word that God speaks* that frees the human spirit from the limitations imposed by the soul. God may speak by quickening, making alive and personal, the words of the Bible to the discerning reader. He may speak by giving the believer an inner prompting. God also actually speaks words that the believer "hears" in his or her inner being. Remember, Jesus said that His sheep hear His voice and follow Him.

God separates our soul and spirit by exposing a portion of the sinful thoughts and purposes of our heart. He reveals our heart's condition to us inwardly or by allowing circumstances to which we react carnally. These thoughts and purposes may include previously unnoticed qualities such as pride, rebellion, unforgiveness, bitterness, resentment, "righteous" indignation, envy, strife, covetousness, self-centeredness, lust, and many other aspects of the flesh such as those listed in Galatians 5:19–21.

We receive this separation by making ourselves available to God in times of quietness, accepting God's judgment of our inner sinfulness, asking His forgiveness, and obeying His instructions. God may, among other things, have us release our sinful thoughts or motivations to Him, command a spirit to leave us, forgive someone who has hurt us, or go to someone and ask for forgiveness.

Over time, God continues to expose the condition of our heart to us. As God gradually erodes this hardness of heart through our repentant obedience, our human spirit becomes less limited by the soul. Division of our soul and spirit accordingly releases our human spirit from domination of our worldly-influenced soul, giving us greater sensitivity to the presence of God. Dividing the soul and spirit thereby enhances our fellowship with God the Father and the Lord Jesus Christ.

Similarly, separation of the joints and marrow enhances our fellowship with other believers. Since joints connect the parts of the body, they represent the members of the body of Christ relating to one another (Eph. 4:16). Since marrow is the deepest life-giving matter of the natural body, it corresponds to God's presence in our inner being. By the dividing of joints and marrow, our relationships with others become more governed by God's Spirit within us and less influenced by the conduct of other people.

The Heart Interacts with the Realm of God's Presence

Mankind accesses the realm of God's presence with the heart. With the heart, mankind (1) believes, (2) receives life, (3) hears the voice of God, (4) receives the indwelling Christ, and (5) prefers supernatural reality over natural reality. Let's look at each one of these.

First of all, people believe with the heart. Paul taught the church at Rome, "If you confess with your mouth the Lord Jesus and believe in your heart that God has raised Him from the dead, you will be saved."[6] People don't believe because of the hardness of their hearts. Mark records Jesus' rebuking of His disciples for hardness of heart: "He rebuked their unbelief and hardness of heart, because they did not believe those who had seen him after he had risen."[7]

Second, the heart receives life from the realm of God's presence. Jesus proclaimed in the temple, "He who believes in Me, as the Scripture has said, out of his heart will flow rivers of living water."[8] Solomon advised his sons, "Above all else, guard your heart, for it is the wellspring of life."[9] This supernatural life force of God cannot be received through the mind. It cannot be received through the five natural senses. The life of God is received with the heart, the wellspring of life.

Ironically, we cannot guard our heart by hardening or closing it to other people. Instead, we guard our heart by keeping it softened and open to God through holiness. This is the importance of true holiness, not mere outward conduct, but purity of heart: to keep the heart soft and keep the life-giving flow of the Spirit of God undefiled as it passes through our heart, soul, and mind.

Third, the condition of our heart is crucial in hearing the voice of God. The book of Hebrews quotes David, "Today, if you will hear His voice, do not harden your hearts."[10]

Fourth, hardness of the heart must be broken and removed to experience Christ beyond the limitations of religious intellect. Paul prayed for the Ephesian church "that Christ may dwell in your hearts through faith."[11] Jesus taught in the Sermon on the Mount, "Blessed are the pure in heart, for they shall see God."[12] Therefore, we fellowship with God the Father and the Lord Jesus Christ through a pure heart.

We keep our heart pure by being quick to repent and by being selective in what we see, hear, think, say, and do. We don't judge the purity of the heart in ourselves or in others, because the heart is deceptive and not readily observable. The prophet Jeremiah proclaimed, "The heart is deceitful above all things, and desperately wicked; who can know it?"[13] We therefore look to God to reveal the condition of the heart.

And fifth, softening our heart enables us to prefer the greater supernatural reality over the lesser natural reality. The children of Israel failed to achieve this preference because of the hardness of their hearts. God spoke through the psalmist: "They are a people whose hearts go astray, and they have not known my ways. So I declared on oath in my anger, 'They shall never enter my rest.'"[14] Blinded by their hardness of heart, they were not thankful for God's supernatural provision of manna in the wilderness. Instead, they longed to return to the natural provision of Egypt.

The writer of the book of Hebrews warns, "Do not harden your hearts as in the rebellion, in the day of trial in the wilderness, where your fathers tested Me, tried Me, and saw My works forty years."[15] He continues, "Beware, brethren, lest there be in any of you an evil heart of unbelief in departing from the living God; but exhort one another daily, while it is called 'Today,' lest any of you be hardened through the deceitfulness of sin."[16]

Let's not harden our hearts as the children of Israel did in the wilderness. Let's not prefer with our minds the natural reality that is so comfortable to our self-nature. Instead, let's prefer with pure hearts the supernatural reality that God is so graciously offering to us.

The Mind Either Helps or Hinders Perception of God's Presence

The mind works well in learning a profession or a trade, learning to eat healthful foods, or learning the benefits of exercising regularly. With the mind, people learn not to touch a hot stove, to look for traffic before crossing the street, and to wear a coat in cold weather. The mind in its natural state functions well in the natural world. But it cannot discern Spirit-realm reality. In fact, the mind that is not illuminated by God's Spirit hinders true spiritual discernment.

The Bible calls the mind that is not illuminated by God's Spirit "carnal," "natural," or "not renewed." Paul explained to the Roman church, "The carnal mind is enmity against God; for it is not subject to the law of God, nor indeed can be."[17] In other words, the mind in its natural state actively opposes God. And it *cannot* do otherwise!

The renewed Christian mind sees God as a loving, invisible Father who is passionately calling His beloved children to come to Him through His Son and be blessed. In contrast, the mind that is not renewed tends to gravitate to two opposite extremes. At one extreme, the natural mind tends to be acutely sensitive to evil spirits, focusing on protection from these spirits or pacifying easily agitated, angry gods. Some of these people worship man-made idols, various aspects of nature, or different kinds of animals. Others follow ancient philosophies.

At the other extreme, the carnal mind thinks in the dimensions of time, physical form, and geographic location. These people, being insensitive to the spirit world, think in these terms because of their earthly limitations. God, however, is not subject to these limitations. The realm of God's presence extends beyond physical dimensions. People with this mind-set cannot accept these spiritual realities.

This thinking, which is limited to time and space, restricts a person's understanding to the temporal realm. It generally ignores or denies the spirit nature of mankind. The mind that is not renewed frequently denies the existence of anything it cannot verify with its five senses—most emphatically, God. These intellectual people believe that what can be validated through science is real and what cannot be so validated is not real.

The mind should not so limit believers in Christ, because what is seen is made of that which is not seen. What is unseen is actually more real than what is seen. The writer to the Hebrews taught believers that "by faith we understand that the worlds were framed by the word of God, so that the things which are seen were not made of things which are visible."[18] To understand the realm of God's presence, believers must be freed from such natural limitations.

Our mind relates to the world through our five senses, but it should not be controlled by the world through the five senses. God wants us to have dominion over the world, not be dominated by its natural perception. We can decide what we think. Paul instructed Philippian believers to "think about these things."[19] He taught the Corinthians to bring "every thought into captivity to the obedience of Christ."[20] We therefore should control our thoughts by choosing what we think and by choosing what we don't think. Disciplining the mind, however, is different from renewing the mind.

The apostle Paul admonished the Ephesian church, "Be renewed in the spirit of your mind."[21] Paul also urged the Roman believers, "Be transformed by the renewing of your mind."[22] Notice that these phrases are both stated in the passive voice. Mind renewal is therefore not something we do for ourselves. In fact, J. B. Phillips expresses Romans 12:2 in this way: "Let God re-make you so that your whole attitude of mind is changed."[23] Renewal of the mind is something that God does for us when we give ourselves unreservedly to Him by offering our bodies to Him as a living sacrifice as we will discuss in chapter 19. It enables us to prove the "good and acceptable and the perfect will of God."[24]

Mind renewal gives believers in Christ an additional flow of consciousness. The original, natural train of thought operates through the mind and natural senses. It works well when relating to the world, but it hinders spiritual discernment. We can illustrate this natural flow of consciousness in this way: world → natural senses → mind.

When God renews our mind, He gives us an additional flow of consciousness that enables us to exercise spiritual discernment and allows the flow of His Spirit. In this way, God communicates to us through the human spirit and heart. We can illustrate this spiritual flow of consciousness in this way: God → human spirit → heart. This new flow of consciousness also enables us to communicate with God by reversing this order: heart → human spirit → God.

The original flow of consciousness is being carnally minded; this new flow of consciousness is being spiritually minded. Paul informed the Roman church, "To be carnally minded is death, but to be spiritually minded is life and peace."[25]

In carnal people, the mind that is not renewed takes a primary role in spiritual matters, initiating thoughts and actions. In the spiritual person, the renewed mind takes a secondary role in such matters. Rather than originating thought or action, it validates by the Word of God all communications received through the human spirit and heart. The spiritual person receives God's communications through the heart, and the heart receives those communications through the human spirit, the part of the saved person that is one with the Lord.

The Heart and Mind Are Not Interchangeable

The heart and mind are similar in many ways, but they are also very different. They perform many of the same functions, but in two distinctly different realms. We run into problems when we use our mind to do the things that God designed our heart to do. Using our mind instead of our heart is similar to trying to do something with our foot that we would normally do with our hand. Some things we can't do as well with our foot, and others, we can't do at all. Using our mind when we should use our heart degrades Christianity to mere Spiritless religion.

Our mind is obviously necessary to understand the meanings of the words printed in the Bible. But it is not equipped to discern the hidden Spirit of the passage that we read, because the things of God are spiritually discerned. For instance, we can read with our mind that God loves us, but until we receive God's love through our heart, we cannot experience it.

The heart has to do with the deep, inner spirit-being of a person, the part of the person that is closest to God and is most like Him. It is best suited to relate to the supernatural Spirit nature of God. The mind functions on a more natural, superficial level. Whether we use our mind or our heart determines the spiritual depth of our prayers and our ability to enter into God's presence.

We Communicate with God on Three Levels

We communicate with God (1) with the mind, (2) with the heart, and (3) with the spirit. The first way we can pray is with the mind. When we pray with the mind we determine what we pray for and how we pray. We don't have to exercise any degree of spiritual sensitivity. We communicate with God intellectually, contacting Him on a mental level. Praying with our mind is therefore our most natural and superficial level of communicating with God.

The second way we can pray is with the heart. By praying with the heart we communicate with God on a deeper, more spiritually sensitive level than praying with the mind. We attain this sensitivity by quieting the mind and the soul. When we pray in this way God can direct our praying through the new flow of consciousness. Therefore, praying with the heart is the purest, most spiritually effective form of comprehensible prayer. By comprehensible prayer, we mean praying with our understanding.

Third, we can pray with the spirit. When we pray with the spirit, also known as praying in tongues, God prays through us. He bypasses our mind so that we don't understand what we're praying. The apostle Paul taught the Corinthian church: "If I pray in a tongue, my spirit prays, but my mind is unfruitful. So what shall I do? I will pray with my spirit, but I will also pray with my mind."[26] An additional way we pray without our understanding is by praying with groans according to Romans 8:26. Since these two forms of prayer are not tainted with our natural understanding they can be more spiritually effective than praying with the mind or with the heart.

We Enter God's Presence Through the Heart

We can pray with the mind, but we enter into God's presence through the heart. There is a time to communicate with God with the mind, and there is a time to enter into God's presence through the heart. The heart opens Spirit-realm fellowship with God by being sensitive to His presence.

The Lord spoke through the prophet Jeremiah, "You will seek Me and find Me, when you search for Me with all your heart."[27] Surely, we enter God's presence, not with the mind, but through the heart.

Entering the realm of God's presence is accordingly beyond the capability of the mind. God has chosen the foolish things of this world to confound the wise. Therefore, not many people considered wise by the world are sensitive to God's presence. Worldly people have difficulty believing spiritual truth because they rely on their minds rather than their hearts. Focusing attention on the mind retards reliance on the heart and dulls its sensitivity to God's presence.

We focus on our heart by paying attention to our inner being while quieting the clamor within us, because living water flows out of our "innermost being."[28] I generally sense a knowing or prompting, or I "hear" the Lord's voice within my inner being. At other times, I "see" a picture before my closed eyes or superimposed over my natural vision.

If I rely on my natural mind at these times, I generally lose my sense of the Lord's presence. For instance, when writing this book, I wrote with assurance from my heart. But when my mind interfered, I experienced difficulty expressing what the Lord had shown me. My mind was necessary to form the words but was incapable of expressing the spiritual truth that the Lord had revealed to me.

Believers Live in Both the Temporal and Eternal Realms

Before salvation, people function in the temporal realm. After being born again, believers also live in the eternal realm. As the apostle Paul expressed in our opening scripture, "God raised us up with Christ and seated us with him in the heavenly realms in Christ Jesus." Therefore, when we speak of being in the presence of God, we are speaking of being in God's presence in Christ.

Paul distinctly stated in the past tense, "God raised us up and seated us with him." We who believe are therefore now seated with God in the heavenly realms in Christ Jesus. Our human spirits live in Christ in heavenly places as well as in our bodies.

The natural person's inability to comprehend this Spirit-realm reality does not invalidate it. Paul taught the Corinthian church, "The natural man does not receive the things of the Spirit of God, for they are foolishness to him; nor can he know them, because they are spiritually discerned."[29] The natural man is not only the unsaved man, but also the saved person who is not open to the supernatural realm of God's presence. Yes, Christians can be carnally minded.

Jesus Sets Us Free from Temporal Limitations

In salvation, Jesus extends our *presence* beyond the natural confines of the physical body so that we live not only in the body, but also in Christ. By this presence, we can receive inspired thought, insight supernaturally opened to our natural mind. Jesus then opens our *awareness* to this presence by the baptism of the Holy Spirit with the evidence of speaking in tongues. Through this awareness, we can receive revelation—supernatural opening of our perception beyond the limitations of the natural mind—extending our understanding into the realities of His presence and revealing truth not naturally perceived.

Revelation is accompanied with power when unrestrained by carnal thought. This power is the anointing, or supernatural working, of the Holy Spirit. It ranges from receiving the spiritual ability to understand and communicate the supernatural things of God to the working of miracles.

For instance, the revelation of salvation, as opposed to the knowledge of salvation, comes with the ability to minister salvation in the power of the Holy Spirit. After His resurrection, Jesus commanded His followers to wait for the promise of the Father, saying, "You shall receive power when the Holy Spirit has come upon you."[30] Peter, empowered by the revelation of the prophet Joel's prophecy, preached a message of salvation on the day of Pentecost. And God added three thousand people to the church!

God activates and directs this power. The person receiving the revelation doesn't act or speak on his own initiative. God prompts the person who receives the revelation to act on it in His way and at His time.

Believers in Christ accordingly have spiritual influence beyond the outer dimensions of the physical body. God uses members of the body of Christ to produce positive change in other people's lives by prayer through the spiritual flow of consciousness. Prayer influences people through the realm of God's presence, producing supernatural results observed in the physical realm. Prayer—in its purest form—originates with God, comes to an individual by the prompting of the Holy Spirit, is returned to God as prayer, and then returns again to mankind as God's answer to that prayer.

For instance, the Holy Spirit may prompt me to pray for someone for a specific need. In obedience to God's prompting, I allow the Lord to pray through me for that person, as the branch bears the fruit of the true vine, the Lord Jesus Christ (John 15:1–8). God then answers the prayer that He impressed me to pray. In this way, God initiates the prayer by prompting me to pray. I return that prayer to Him by allowing the Lord to pray through me. And God then answers His prayer that He prompted me to pray.

Admonition to Be Released from Temporal Limitations

Exceed the limitations of your natural mind by opening your awareness to God's presence through your heart, the wellspring of life. Receive God's separation of your soul and spirit by spending time in quietness before Him, accepting God's judgment of your inner sinfulness, asking His forgiveness, and obeying His inner promptings. Enter the realm of God's presence by the spiritual flow of consciousness. Receive spiritual insight. Receive revelation accompanied with power through the baptism of the Holy Spirit with the evidence of speaking in tongues. Allow God to use you to produce positive change in other people's lives by praying in the spiritual flow of consciousness.

Here's a gentle word of caution. There is a spirit realm that is not of God. This is the realm of Satan, principalities, powers, rulers of darkness of this world, spiritual wickedness in high places, and demon spirits (Eph. 6:12). The apostle Paul cautioned the believers in Corinth that "even Satan disguises himself as an angel of light."[31] There is no need to fear this realm or to avoid the supernatural realm of God's presence because of it. Believers have authority over this realm in Christ. We just don't want to yield ourselves to it.

An easy, definitive way to determine whether or not a spirit is of God is to notice the character of the spirit. One helpful passage is Galatians 5:22–23. Although the context of this scripture is human conduct, any spirit that does not meet this description is not of God. Paul wrote, "The fruit of the Spirit is love, joy, peace, longsuffering, kindness, goodness, faithfulness, gentleness, self-control." The Holy Spirit may convict a person of sin, but any spirit that condemns or forcibly tries to take control is definitely *not* of God.

It is wise to be specific concerning the spirit-being to which we yield. At times, the Holy Spirit may impress us to add one or more qualifying phrases as we yield ourselves to God. For instance, when surrendering to God the Father, we might identify Him as "the creator of the heavens and the earth," "the God of Abraham, Isaac, and Jacob," or "the Father of our Lord and Savior Jesus Christ." When surrendering to Jesus, we might add "my Lord and Savior," "Son of God," or "the Word of God." When yielding to the Holy Spirit, we might include such phrases as "who hovered over the waters when the earth was without form and void," "who came upon Jesus of Nazareth when He was baptized," or "who came to earth to dwell in believers in Christ on the day of Pentecost."

Pray to be Released from Temporal Limitations

Heavenly Father, please release me from the limitations of my natural reasoning and open my awareness to Your presence. I desire to receive both inspired thought and revelation accompanied with power. Please renew my mind, giving me Your spiritual flow of consciousness. Father God, I want to experience Your presence in Christ Jesus. Please use me to produce positive change in other people's lives through prayer in the spiritual flow of consciousness. Please empower me to yield my entire being to You. All this I ask, not only for my own spiritual growth, but also that our Lord Jesus Christ, in whose name I pray, may be glorified and exalted in and through me. Amen.

Where Do We Go from Here?

God gives us, as Christians, a new flow of consciousness through which He gives us access to Him through our hearts and human spirits. Next, through this flow, we will learn to perceive Jesus Christ by the Spirit, thereby increasing the magnitude of our faith. We will perceive Jesus Christ as the magnificent supernatural being that He really is.

Chapter 6

Know Christ as He Really Is

[Now] He is the exact likeness of the unseen God [the visible representation of the invisible]; He is the Firstborn of all creation. For it was in Him that all things were created, in heaven and on earth, things seen and things unseen, whether thrones, dominions, rulers, or authorities; all things were created and exist through Him [by His service, intervention] and in and for Him. And He Himself existed before all things, and in Him all things consist (cohere, are held together).
Colossians 1:15–17 AMP

We have seen that mankind lives in two dimensions. Through the heart, people relate to the eternal realm, and with the mind, they relate primarily to the temporal realm. Although people can communicate with God with their minds, they understand and experience the supernatural realm of God's presence, not with their minds, but through their hearts. Having established that believers enter into God's presence with the heart, we are prepared to perceive Jesus Christ as the supernatural being that He really is.

Here is our sixth spiritual reality: we can know the Lord Jesus Christ as He really is—in His supernatural dimension. We will review the three dimensions of Christ, see how our perception of Christ determines the magnitude of our faith, ponder the descriptions of Christ given by prominent persons in the Bible, identify seven common perceptions of Christ, see Jesus as God and man, and pray to know Christ as He really is.

We will call the supernatural being that Christ really is *the glorified Lord*. Let's start with His glorification—His supernatural being endued with all power and authority.

At the Feast of Tabernacles, Jesus spoke in the temple, foretelling His postincarnate ministry—His ministry after His death and resurrection. The apostle John records His announcement:

> On the last and greatest day of the Feast, Jesus stood and said in a loud voice, "If anyone is thirsty, let him come to me and drink. Whoever believes in me, as the Scripture has said, streams of living water will flow from within him." By this he meant the Spirit, whom those who believed in him were later to receive. *Up to that time the Spirit had not been given, since Jesus had not yet been glorified.*[1]

The glorification of Christ ushered in the postincarnate ministry of Christ. Only through the glorification of Christ can we actually be in Him and He be in us. As we discuss different dimensions of Christ, we will, of course, not be discussing different Christs, but different aspects of the Lord Jesus Christ.

The Bible Reveals Christ in Three Dimensions

The Bible describes Christ in three dimensions: (1) preincarnate (before His coming to earth), (2) incarnate (while He was on the earth), and (3) postincarnate (after His leaving the earth). Knowing the preincarnate Christ reveals Christ as deity. Knowing the incarnate Jesus Christ reveals His humanity. Knowing the postincarnate Christ reveals Him in His glory.

The Preincarnate Dimension of Christ Reveals His Deity

In His preincarnate dimension, Jesus is God. He participated in the creation of all things. John describes the preincarnate Christ in the first chapter of his gospel: "In the beginning was the Word, and the Word was with God, and the Word was God. He was in the beginning with God. All things were made through Him, and without Him nothing was made that was made."[2]

The Incarnate Dimension of Christ Reveals His Humanity

Jesus of Nazareth walked this earth as a human being. He is someone we can visualize, a real person with whom we can relate. John continues in the first chapter of his gospel: "The Word became flesh and dwelt among us, and we beheld His glory, the glory as of the only begotten of the Father, full of grace and truth."[3] Luke described Him this way: "God anointed Jesus of Nazareth with the Holy Spirit and with power, who went about doing good and healing all who were oppressed by the devil, for God was with Him."[4]

Jesus demonstrated a measure of the power of God by performing healings and miracles in His earthly ministry, but He did not use the infinite power of God that He now possesses. The thrust of His ministry was revealing God as Father and showing mankind the way back to Him. According to the apostle John, God sent His Son to the earth so that "the world might find salvation and be made safe and sound through Him."[5] Jesus demonstrated the Father's boundless love for mankind by performing miracles, but He did not exert His preincarnate or postincarnate authority and power in His incarnate ministry.

The Postincarnate Dimension of Christ Reveals His Glory

In our opening scripture, Paul describes the present, postincarnate dimension of Christ: "[Now] He is the exact likeness of the unseen God [the visible representation of the invisible]; He is the Firstborn of all creation. For it was in Him that all things were created, in heaven and on earth, things seen and things unseen, whether thrones, dominions, rulers, or authorities; all things were created and exist through Him [by His service, intervention] and in and for Him."

In His postincarnate dimension, Christ possesses all authority and power. God "raised Him from the dead and seated Him at His right hand in the heavenly places, far above all principality and power and might and dominion, and every name that is named, not only in this age but also in that which is to come. And He put all things under His feet, and gave him to be head over all things to the church, which is His body, the fullness of Him who fills all in all."[6] This is the glorification of Christ.

Our Perception of Christ Determines the Magnitude of Our Faith

The postincarnate Christ also encompasses His preincarnate and incarnate dimensions. God gave the glorified Christ as the head of the church; He is the one in whom we believe. Many Christians know about Christ as Jesus of Nazareth but, unfortunately, have never experienced Christ glorified.

Christ is the central life and order of all things; in Him all things consist. Our being in Christ is therefore more than being located in Christ; it is being sustained in Him and by Him. He is our life; without Him, we cannot take our next breath. He is our knowledge and wisdom; apart from Him, we cannot know or understand truth. He is our empowerment; without Him, we can do nothing. Being in Christ, we recognize our dependence on Him in every aspect of our lives.

In response to His great love for us, we should seek Christ for who He is, not only for what He can do for us. Jesus rebuked the people who sought Him only for their natural needs: "I tell you the truth, you are looking for me, not because you saw miraculous signs but because you ate the loaves and had your fill. Do not work for food that spoils, but for food that endures to eternal life, which the Son of Man will give you. On him God the Father has placed his seal of approval."[7] These people observed the incarnate Christ. They did not, however, perceive His supernatural nature.

Jesus proclaimed: "I am the bread of life. Your fathers ate the manna in the wilderness, and are dead. . . . I am the living bread which came down from heaven. If anyone eats of this bread, he will live forever; and the bread that I shall give is My flesh, which I shall give for the life of the world."[8] This passage speaks of Christ giving us eternal life, but it also speaks of His growing us spiritually. Jesus informed the Pharisees who challenged Him, "I have come that they may have life, and that they may have it more abundantly."[9]

Only through Christ are we spiritually nourished; only in Him can we grow into the supernatural beings that God created us to be. All that God does for us He does in and through the Lord Jesus Christ. Our perception of Christ therefore determines the magnitude of our faith.

Today, however, we still tend to look to God for "food that spoils." We look to God to help us, but we are too fearful or too impatient to venture beyond our natural understanding and abilities. We limit our faith by perceiving Christ as Jesus of Nazareth without also perceiving Him as the postincarnate Christ.

We must do more than picture Christ in our minds; we must perceive Christ in our hearts. We are not trying to *visualize* Christ; we are seeking to *know* Him. We must not only know Christ as our Good Shepherd, but also know Him in His full authority, power, and glory. If we envision Jesus as a man but don't also know Christ the postincarnate Word of God, we radically reduce our faith. I am convinced of this: if we had the briefest glimpse of the true being of the Lord Jesus Christ, there would be nothing we would not do for Him, and nothing He could not do through us.

Let's know Christ beyond His human form. Let's experience Him as the Word in and through whom all things were created, the one in and through whom all things consist. In so doing, we're not taking away from Christ's humanity; we are perceiving His supernatural being.

Perceiving Christ Supernaturally

There are two dimensions of perceiving Christ: natural and supernatural. We can visualize Christ *with* our natural understanding, or we can perceive Christ *beyond* our natural understanding. Scripture records examples of these two perceptions.

One example depicts Philip's natural perception of Christ. At one time, Philip perceived Jesus with his mind rather than with his heart. Before His crucifixion, Jesus told His disciples that He was going away to make a place for them. He disclosed that no one comes to the Father except through Him. The apostle John records the following exchange between Jesus and Philip:

> Philip said to Him, "Lord, show us the Father, and it is sufficient for us."
>
> Jesus said to him, "Have I been with you so long, and yet you have not known Me, Philip? He who has seen Me has seen the Father; so how can you say, 'Show us the Father'?"[10]

At this time, Philip perceived Jesus only as the incarnate Christ. He lacked spiritual discernment.

The second example is when Peter knew Christ by revelation:

> He [Jesus] said to them [His disciples], "But who do you say that I am?"
>
> Simon Peter answered and said, "You are the Christ, the Son of the living God."
>
> Jesus answered and said to him, "Blessed are you, Simon Bar-Jonah, for flesh and blood has not revealed this to you, but My Father who is in heaven."[11]

At that moment, Peter perceived Christ supernaturally. He perceived Him with his heart rather than just observing Him through his mind.

The true perception of Christ is the supernatural perception of the heart. Paul prayed for those in the church at Ephesus that they would know spiritual truths "according to the working of His [God's] mighty power."[12] By this power, the eyes of our understanding are enlightened, and we spiritually see Christ as more than the incarnate Jesus who lived on earth in human form.

Natural perception limits faith in Christ to intellectual belief. An intellectual concept of Christ may be biblically accurate yet omit His living presence. Salvation, deliverance, healing, atonement for sins, and victory over the power of sin are all in the person of Christ. In fact, all blessing and provision are in Christ—the person of Christ, not a concept of Christ. Let's leave our intellectual concepts behind and accurately perceive our supernatural Lord.

Accurately Perceiving the Supernatural Christ

Our perception of Christ—not a concept in the mind, but a perception of the heart—forms our faith. How we perceive Christ determines the strength of our faith, His presence in our lives, and His empowering activity in our lives and ministries. Perceiving Jesus as the supernatural Christ catapults our faith to a higher, supernatural dimension.

To accurately perceive the supernatural dimension of Christ, we'll examine descriptions given by three prominent people in the Bible:

(1) the writer of the book of Hebrews, (2) the apostle John, and (3) the Lord Jesus Christ. We'll first examine Christ's authority and power. We'll then observe His supernatural appearance. Finally, we'll note His holy character. Our purpose is not to *imagine* Christ so described, but to *perceive* Christ in His infinite authority and power, His supernatural appearance, and His holy character.

Ordinary language is inadequate to describe the Lord Jesus Christ. He is greater than natural words can express. The Bible, written by the Holy Spirit in living words, reveals the supernatural dimension of Christ to the discerning reader.

As you read the following passages, take time to allow the Holy Spirit to reveal Christ in your heart. Remember, we perceive spiritual truths with the heart, not with the mind. Quiet yourself in the Spirit, and ask the Lord Jesus Christ to reveal Himself to you as you reverently read the following Scripture passages. These Scripture references are purposely lengthy. The cursory reader who skips over these passages may not receive deeper spiritual insight or revelation into the glorified Lord.

The Author of Hebrews Portrays Christ

In the first chapter of the book of Hebrews, the writer describes the postincarnate Christ in this way:

> [The Son], whom He [God the Father] has appointed heir of all things, through whom also He made the worlds; who being the brightness of His glory and the express image of His person, and upholding all things by the word of His power, when He had by Himself purged our sins, sat down at the right hand of the Majesty on high, having become so much better than the angels, as He has by inheritance obtained a more excellent name than they. . . .
>
> But to the Son He [God the Father] says: "Your throne, O God, is forever and ever; a scepter of righteousness is the scepter of Your kingdom. You have loved righteousness and hated lawlessness; therefore God, Your God, has anointed You with the oil of gladness more than Your companions." And: "You, Lord, in the beginning laid the

foundation of the earth, and the heavens are the work of Your hands. They will perish, but You remain; and they will all grow old like a garment; like a cloak You will fold them up, and they will be changed. But You are the same, and Your years will not fail."[13]

The Apostle John Described Christ as He Appeared to Him

The apostle John gives a detailed description of the Lord Jesus Christ as He appeared to him on the island of Patmos:

> His head and His hair were white like white wool, [as white] as snow, and His eyes [flashed] like a flame of fire. His feet glowed like burnished (bright) bronze as it is refined in a furnace, and His voice was like the sound of many waters. In His right hand He held seven stars, and from His mouth there came forth a sharp two-edged sword, and His face was like the sun shining in full power at midday. When I saw Him, I fell at His feet as if dead. But He laid His right hand on me and said, Do not be afraid! I am the First and the Last, and the Ever-living One [I am living in the eternity of the eternities]. I died, but see, I am alive forevermore; and I possess the keys of death and Hades (the realm of the dead).[14]

Christ Described Himself to John for the Seven Churches

The Lord Jesus Christ gives this description of Himself to the apostle John for the seven churches in the book of Revelation:

> The First and the Last, Who died and came to life again . . . Him Who has and wields the sharp two-edged sword . . . the Son of God, Who has eyes that flash like a flame of fire, and Whose feet glow like bright and burnished and white-hot bronze . . . Him Who has the seven Spirits of God [the sevenfold Holy Spirit] and the seven stars . . . the Holy One, the True One, He Who has the key of David, Who

opens and no one shall shut, Who shuts and no one shall open . . . the Amen, the trusty and faithful and true Witness, the Origin and Beginning and Author of God's creation.[15]

Take a few minutes to meditate on these scriptures. Ask God to reveal the postincarnate Christ to you. First, note Christ's extraordinary authority and power: (1) He is "the Origin and Beginning and Author of God's creation." (2) He upholds all things by the word of His power. (3) He laid the foundation of the earth. (4) The heavens are the work of His hands. (5) He will fold up the earth and the heavens like a cloak. (6) He shuts and no one can open, and He opens and no one can shut. (7) A sharp sword comes from His mouth "with which to strike down the nations."[16] (8) The apostle John knew Jesus of Nazareth intimately, yet upon seeing Him as the glorified Lord, John fell at His feet as though dead. These statements describe the authority and power of the glorified Lord.

Next, consider Christ's supernatural appearance: (1) He is the brightness of God's glory. (2) He is the express image of God's person. (3) His head and hair are white like white wool, as white as snow. (4) His eyes are like a flame of fire. (5) His feet glow like bright, white-hot bronze being refined in a furnace. (6) His voice thunders like the roar of gigantic waterfalls. (7) A sharp, two-edged sword comes from His mouth. (8) His face shines like the sun shining in full power at midday. This is the supernatural being who is Christ our Lord.

Then, look at the description of Christ's character: (1) He is the Holy One. (2) He is the True One. (3) He is "the trusty and faithful and true Witness." (4) He passes judgment and wages war in righteousness. This is our holy, true, faithful, and righteous Lord.

Now that we have seen how the writer of Hebrews, the apostle John, and Jesus described the supernatural Christ, let's look at seven ways that people commonly perceive Him. These common perceptions pale in contrast to those of the people who actually experienced Him firsthand.

Seven Common Perceptions of Christ

People have many perceptions of Christ. We can identify seven common perceptions. Each of the seven bears a genuine truth, but only one embraces the totality of truth. Each perception recognizes at least one essential element of faith in Christ.

Please keep in mind that these are perceptions, not hard-and-fast categories of persons. An individual's perception of Christ will typically be a combination of these perceptions. In fact, a mature believer's perception should have elements of all seven.

The Historical Christ

The first perception is the historical Christ. Those who hold this perception believe that Jesus was a teacher or prophet, but they don't know Him as deity or Savior. They do, however, recognize that there actually was a man named Jesus of Nazareth, whose teaching has had a great impact on mankind. This perception is important, because if Jesus were not a historical person, our faith would be only a myth.

The Christ Child

Second, people perceive Christ as the baby in the manger in the Christmas tradition. They identify with Christianity, but their faith is limited to belief in a powerless baby Jesus. They do, however, generally recognize that Jesus is the Son of God and was born of a virgin.

The Crucified Christ

Third, others perceive Christ crucified. This perception is characterized by the period between Christ's crucifixion and His resurrection. During this time, the disciples huddled together in fear, dismay, and powerlessness. They had not yet experienced Christ resurrected.

Those with this perception celebrate the suffering of Christ but are void of the power of His resurrection. They emphasize confession of sins but have not received victory over the power of sin. Their faith is limited to belief in a preresurrected Christ.

They do recognize two essential elements of the faith: the confession of sins and the selfless characteristics of the crucified Christ. These are essential characteristics for spiritual growth in all Christians.

The Resurrected Christ

The fourth perception people hold is Christ resurrected. This perception is derived from the period after Christ's resurrection and before His ascension. Christ generally revealed Himself in fleeting encounters during this period. The focus was on the fact that Jesus was alive, not on establishing a relationship with Him. This perception lacks the abiding presence essential for active, abiding faith.

One example is when Jesus joined two of His followers who were walking on the road to Emmaus. As He walked and talked with them, they did not recognize Him. Later, when Jesus joined them for their evening meal, their eyes were opened and they knew who He was. He then vanished (Luke 24:13-31). They interacted with Him briefly, but they did not have a relationship with Him.

Many with this perception believe in Christ's resurrection, but like the men who encountered Christ on the road to Emmaus, they are not aware of His being present with them. They do, however, believe the essential element of Christ's victory over the grave.

The Ascended Christ

The fifth perception of Christ is Christ ascended. The Bible describes this perception in the period between Christ's ascension and the day of Pentecost. This period lacked spiritual activity other than waiting and prayer. Christ had instructed His disciples to wait for the promise of the Father. There was no leading of the Holy Spirit; the disciples actually drew lots to select the disciple to replace Judas Iscariot.

Those with this perception view Christ as being at the right hand of the Father and believe in eternal life. They embrace Him as their mediator making intercession for them with the Father, but He may not be routinely active in their lives. They recognize that He has risen from the dead, and they worship Him and glory in His resurrection, but they are void of His power.

They embrace the Great Commission: "All authority has been given to Me in heaven and on earth. Go therefore and make disciples of all nations, baptizing them in the name of the Father and of the Son and of the Holy Spirit, teaching them to observe all things that I have commanded you; and lo, I am with you always, even to the end of the age."[17] They do not, however, embrace Christ's accompanying command to wait to receive power: "Being assembled together with them, He commanded them not to depart from Jerusalem, but to wait for the Promise of the Father, 'which,' He said, 'you have heard from Me; for John truly baptized with water, but you shall be baptized with the Holy Spirit not many days from now.'"[18]

Those with this perception have received and minister salvation. But they have not received the baptism of the Holy Spirit with the evidence of speaking in tongues and are void of its power. People with this perception recognize Christ the Savior and effectively exercise the ministry of salvation by grace through faith. Those with this perception may be responsible for leading more people to Christ than those with any other perception.

The Glorified Christ

The sixth perception that people hold of Christ is Christ glorified. They embrace both the Great Commission and the historical command to wait to receive power. They have received the baptism of the Holy Spirit with the evidence of speaking in tongues, but they generally conduct their lives and ministries within the limitations of their natural knowledge and abilities. They are working for God rather than God working through them. They rarely venture beyond their own abilities into the realm of God's presence in total dependence on Him.

Those with this perception recognize the essential element of the supernatural empowerment of the Holy Spirit. But they usually rely on their own strength instead of venturing beyond their natural abilities. Therefore, Christ cannot routinely express Himself through them.

The Glorified Lord

In the seventh perception, people honor Jesus Christ as the Lord. They continually listen to His voice, and then say what they hear Him say and do what they see Him do. Those with this perception embrace the truths of the first six perceptions. They believe (1) that there actually was a man named Jesus of Nazareth, (2) that Jesus is the Son of God and was born of a virgin, (3) in the confession of sins and the selfless character of the crucified Christ, (4) in Christ's victory over the grave, (5) in the ministry of salvation through Christ, and (6) in the supernatural empowerment of the Holy Spirit.

These people have personally encountered the Son of God in a significant way, as we will discuss in chapter 17. They abide in Christ, and He abides in them. They relate to Him in genuine, holy reverence. Being dependent on Him, these believers are attentive to His slightest desire to express Himself in or through them. They receive both spiritual insight and revelation accompanied with power.

Those with this perception are branches grafted into the true vine (Christ). Their life is that which flows into them from the vine. The fruit they bear is the fruit produced by the life of Christ flowing through them. They bear the fruit that Christ is producing rather than producing fruit for Him. They spend time waiting quietly before the Lord, listening for what He might say. They also continuously wait upon the Lord concurrently with their ongoing activities. They are attentively mindful of the voice of the Lord at all times. Christ lives within them and ministers through them.

Like Paul, they do not rely on their own abilities. Paul expressed his utter dependence on Jesus Christ: "And I, brethren, when I came to you, did not come with excellence of speech or of wisdom declaring to you the testimony of God. For I determined not to know anything among you except Jesus Christ and Him crucified. I was with you in weakness, in fear, and in much trembling. And my speech and my preaching were not with persuasive words of human wisdom, but in demonstration of the Spirit and of power, that your faith should not be in the wisdom of men but in the power of God."[19]

Jesus Christ Is Fully God and Fully Man

What a wondrous being our Savior is! What a fantastic being of reconciliation! He is wholly God and wholly man. He is holy God and holy man. In one being, we relate to man and we relate to God. As Jesus of Nazareth, He is a man with whom we can identify; He is compassionate and understanding of our human frailties. As Christ Jesus, He is the creator and sustainer of all things, who has all power and authority in this age and in the age to come.

As Jesus of Nazareth, He was a man whom we can visualize today. He walked this earth healing the sick, casting out demons, miraculously feeding thousands, stilling the storm, raising the dead, having compassion on the weak and downtrodden, and revealing God as Father to mankind. As the Lamb of God, He bore our penalty for sin, redeemed us to God the Father, and broke the power of sin. He is the express image of the Father, the visible image of the invisible.

As the Word, He created all things and upholds all things by the word of His power. And He will return as the King of Kings and the Lord of Lords.

As the glorified Lord, He sits at the right hand of God the Father and has all authority and power in this age and in the age to come. His throne will be forever and ever. Through His glorification, God sent the Holy Spirit to dwell within us. The glorified Lord lives in our hearts by faith. He is the Bread of Life, and He is the true vine into whom the Father has grafted us. We are His branches, through whom He produces His fruit to the glory of God the Father. In Christ, all things are possible to those who believe!

Admonition to Know Christ as He Really Is

Know Christ with your heart, beyond the limitations of your natural understanding. Know Christ as the creator and sustainer of all things. Know Him as the one who was raised from the dead, is seated at the right hand of the Father, and is far above all principalities and powers. Know Him as the head of the church, with all things under His feet. Increase the strength of your faith, Christ's presence in your life, and His empowering activity in your life and ministry by perceiving Him beyond your natural intellect. Enter into Christ in total dependency—as a branch grafted into the true vine, bearing the fruit that He produces. Live in fellowship with Him—in genuine, personal, holy reverence.

Pray to Know Christ as He Really Is

Father, I desire to know my Lord Jesus Christ with my whole heart. I want to know Him as the creator and sustainer of all things. I must know Him as the one who was raised from the dead, is seated at the right hand of the Father, and is far above all principalities and powers. I want to know Him as the head of the church, with all things under His feet. I want to be a branch grafted into the true vine, bearing the fruit that He produces. I want to live in fellowship with Him—in genuine, personal, holy reverence. I want to be attentive to His slightest inclination to express Himself in or through me. All this I ask, not only for my own spiritual growth, but also that our Lord Jesus Christ, in whose name I pray, may be glorified and exalted in and through me. Amen.

Where Do We Go from Here?

Now that we know we are spirit-beings and know Christ as He really is, we are prepared to enter into the new covenant life that God has provided for us in Christ. We will throw off the religious limitations of old covenant living and enter into new covenant life. We'll learn that God has opened a new spiritual dimension to those of us who believe in Christ—a dimension that brings our spirit-being together with the Spirit-being of Christ, sets us free from the limitations of the flesh, and empowers us with the Holy Spirit.

Chapter 7

Live in the New Covenant Spiritual Dimension

> But now He [Jesus] has obtained a more excellent ministry, inasmuch as He is also Mediator of a better covenant, which was established on better promises. For if that first covenant had been faultless, then no place would have been sought for a second.
>
> Hebrews 8:6–7

We have established that mankind has a supernatural dimension with influence beyond the physical body and that the Lord Jesus Christ has a supernatural dimension beyond the natural observance of mankind. Our seventh spiritual reality is this: God brings the supernatural nature of believers and the supernatural nature of Christ together in the new covenant.

God has made the way for us to experience the living Christ and live in the presence of God by joining our spirit-being with Christ's Spirit-being through the new covenant. God joins the believer's spirit to Christ's Spirit, because "he who is joined to the Lord is one spirit with Him."[1]

This new covenant life is available to all believers, but it cannot be attained in an old covenant lifestyle. We enter into this greater spiritual dimension by abandoning our old covenant ways; we release our reliance on our natural abilities and become reliant on the Spirit of God.

Jesus Commanded His Disciples to Wait

From the time of Abraham, God has related to mankind by covenant. The old covenant and the new covenant define two ways that people approach and interact with God. After the fall, mankind could no longer interact with God without an intermediary. During the old covenant, people approached God through the blood sacrifice of animals. Today, in the new covenant, people approach God through the blood sacrifice of His Son.

Just before Jesus' ascension, He told His disciples to go into the entire world and preach the gospel. He also commanded them not to begin witnessing until they received the promise of the Holy Spirit.

First, Jesus told His disciples, "Go therefore and make disciples of all the nations, baptizing them in the name of the Father and of the Son and of the Holy Spirit, teaching them to observe all things that I have commanded you; and lo, I am with you always, even to the end of the age."[2] He then "*commanded* them not to depart from Jerusalem, but to wait for the Promise of the Father, 'which,' He said, 'you have heard from Me; for John truly baptized with water, but you shall be baptized with the Holy Spirit not many days from now.'"[3] Jesus exhorted His disciples, "You shall receive power when the Holy Spirit has come upon you; and you shall be witnesses to Me in Jerusalem, and in all Judea and Samaria, and to the end of the earth."[4]

Jesus commanded His disciples to wait for "the promise of the Father." To understand why Jesus commanded His disciples to wait, we'll compare the old and new covenants.

Comparing the Covenants and the Testaments

The old covenant and the new covenant are roughly equivalent to the Old Testament and the New Testament. The Old Testament ends with Malachi 4, and the New Testament begins with Matthew 1. However, the old covenant ends with Acts 1, and the new covenant begins with Acts 2. The old covenant and the New Testament overlap in the period between Matthew 1:1 and Acts 1:26. The following table compares the Old and New Testaments with the old and new covenants:

Comparison of Covenants and Testaments		
Genesis 1:1–Malachi 4:6	Matthew 1:1–Acts 1:26	Acts 2:1–Revelation 22:21
Old Testament	New Testament	
Old Covenant		New Covenant

Identifying the Transitional Period

A transitional period begins at Jesus' crucifixion and ends on the day of Pentecost. In the Bible, this period begins at John 19:31 and ends at Acts 1:26. During this time, the old covenant was still in effect. The new covenant had not been activated because Jesus had not been glorified as disclosed in John 7:39. This period is illustrated in the following table:

Transitional Period		
Old Covenant	Transitional Period	New Covenant
Genesis 1:1–John 19:30	John 19:31–Acts 1:26	Acts 2:1– Revelation 22:21

Theologians may differ on whether this transitional period is part of the old covenant or the new covenant. But the ministry of the Holy Spirit through believers in Christ unquestionably began at Pentecost. Indeed, Jesus Christ birthed His church on the day of Pentecost.

This transitional period was a time of waiting rather than ministry. Even though the disciples had seen Christ resurrected, and some had even witnessed His ascension, Jesus instructed them not to begin witnessing until Pentecost. He commanded His disciples to wait for the promise of the Father, by which they would receive power through the baptism of the Holy Spirit. One reason Jesus did this is because the effectiveness of the old covenant was limited by the weakness of the flesh, but the operation of the new covenant is empowered by the Spirit.

Comparing the Old and New Covenants

Jesus' disciples *could not* begin witnessing until the new covenant began for this reason: the message of Christ the Savior is a spiritual message. The salvation message is foolishness to those whom the Holy Spirit does not enlighten. Only by the quickening of the Holy Spirit does an unsaved person become a believer in Christ.

The Old Covenant Was Weakened by the Flesh

The old covenant depended on the flesh. It could only minister the letter of the law. People in the time of the old covenant generally relied on prophets, priests, or kings to hear the voice of God. God's people brought specified sacrifices to human priests, who then enacted rituals pursuant to the law on their behalf. Only the high priest could enter the presence of God beyond the temple veil, and only once a year.

The New Covenant Is Empowered by the Holy Spirit

The new covenant depends on the Holy Spirit. In the new covenant, all believers can freely receive the Holy Spirit and not only enter into the presence of God, but also live continually in His presence. Revelation is available to all. The Holy Spirit births new covenant faith by bringing the spoken or written Word of God to life in the hearts of those who believe.

On the day of Pentecost, people in a crowd from many nations were perplexed to hear those who had received the baptism of the Holy Spirit speaking in the crowd's native languages. Peter addressed the crowd, informing them that God was pouring out His Spirit as the prophet Joel had prophesied: "It shall come to pass in the last days, says God, that I will pour out of My Spirit on all flesh; your sons and your daughters shall prophesy, your young men shall see visions, your old men shall dream dreams. And on My menservants and on My maidservants I will pour out My Spirit in those days; and they shall prophesy."[5]

Contrasting Two Spiritual Dimensions

The coming of the Holy Spirit on the day of Pentecost opened not only a new covenant to mankind, but also a completely new spiritual dimension. The writer of the book of Hebrews makes this distinction between the old and new covenants: "In the past God spoke to our forefathers through the prophets at many times and in various ways, but in these last days he has spoken to us by his Son, whom he appointed heir of all things, and through whom he made the universe."[6]

People under the old covenant understood their covenant intellectually because they did not have the Holy Spirit to illuminate it. Now people under the new covenant have the Holy Spirit to enlighten them. New covenant truths are spiritually discerned, not merely intellectually understood. Paul taught the Corinthian church that natural people don't receive the things of God because they are foolishness to them, and they cannot know them because they are spiritually discerned. Remember, the natural man is not only the unsaved person, but also the saved person not enlightened by the Holy Spirit.

Accordingly, the old and the new covenants are two different *spiritual dimensions*. The apostle Paul explained how the new covenant is superior to the old covenant in his letter to the Romans:

> God has done what the Law could not do, [its power] being weakened by the flesh [the entire nature of man without the Holy Spirit]. Sending His own Son in the guise of sinful flesh and as an offering for sin, [God] condemned sin in the flesh [subdued, overcame, deprived it of its power over all who accept that sacrifice], so that the righteous and just requirement of the Law might be fully met in us who live and move not in the ways of the flesh but in the ways of the Spirit [our lives governed not by the standards and according to the dictates of the flesh, but controlled by the Holy Spirit].[7]

The Difference between the Two Spiritual Dimensions Illustrated

We can illustrate the difference between the old and new covenant dimensions by comparing it to the difference between two-dimensional and three-dimensional drawings. Two-dimensional drawings have only height and width. Three-dimensional drawings also have the appearance of depth. As a two-dimensional drawing does not fully reflect the reality of the three-dimensional world, the old covenant spiritual dimension does not fully reflect the realm of God's presence.

Further, a drawing can appear to have three dimensions yet have only two. It can appear to have three-dimensional depth yet is drawn on a two-dimensional surface. This distinction relates to the old and new covenant spiritual dimensions in the following way.

In the transitional period between Jesus' crucifixion and His ascension, Jesus ministered salvation to His disciples. Romans 10:9 tells us, "If you confess with your mouth the Lord Jesus and believe in your heart that God has raised Him from the dead, you will be saved." After Jesus' resurrection and before His ascension, He entered the room where the disciples were assembled. On that occasion, they confessed with their mouths that Jesus is Lord and believed in their hearts that God raised Him from the dead.

According to the gospel of John, the disciples were gathered in a house where they had locked the doors because they were afraid of the Jews. Jesus appeared, stood with them, and showed them His hands and His side. The disciples were delighted to see the Lord. He told them that as the Father had sent Him, He was also sending them. He breathed on them and told them to receive the Holy Spirit. Thomas was not present, so when he returned, "the other disciples . . . said to him, 'We have seen the Lord.'"[8]

When the disciples told Thomas, "We have seen the Lord," they confessed with their mouths the Lord Jesus and expressed their belief that God had raised Him from the dead. Therefore, according to Romans 10:9, the disciples received salvation before Pentecost—directly from Jesus, not through others. The disciples received salvation, even though the time of the new covenant spiritual dimension had not yet come.

Likewise, many believers today have received salvation but have not entered into the new covenant spiritual dimension. Like a three-dimensional drawing, they appear to have depth. They have the appearance of living in the new covenant dimension, but in truth, they have restricted themselves to old covenant lifestyles.

The Illustration Applied

The weakness of the flesh rendered the old covenant ineffective. People had to try to meet its requirements with their natural knowledge and abilities. Some present-day believers still live in the old covenant spiritual dimension. They are not willing to leave their reliance on their natural understanding and abilities and enter into the supernatural realm of God's presence. Their reliance on the flesh confines them in the old covenant spiritual dimension.

The new covenant spiritual dimension frees believers from the limitations of the flesh, as long as they freely leave the limitations of the natural realm and move into the dimension of God's Spirit. To live in the new covenant spiritual dimension is to "live and move not in the ways of the flesh but in the ways of the Spirit [our lives governed not by the standards and according to the dictates of the flesh, but controlled by the Holy Spirit]." However, some ministers restrict their ministries and some believers confine their lives to the old covenant spiritual dimension by relying on their intellects to understand new covenant truths rather than depending on the Holy Spirit to reveal them.

What Has Happened to Some Denominations?

Some denominations, even those founded and once firmly established in the validity of Scripture, are now straying from new covenant truth. They deny the divinity of Christ, reject the virgin birth, disclaim the inerrancy of Scripture, refute the present-day ministry of the Holy Spirit, and ordain persons not prepared to minister in the realm of God's presence. How is this happening? Paul explained to the Roman church, "They exchanged the truth of God for a lie, and worshipped and served created things rather than the Creator—who is forever praised."[9]

Today's idols are not only statues formed by craftsmen, but also doctrines formed with human reasoning—mere human opinions defiantly opposing the Word and Spirit of God. Stubbornly elevating their opinions over the Word of God, they worship themselves rather than their creator. Denying the revelation of the Holy Spirit, they blind themselves in self-imposed unbelief.

Live in the Timing of God

Christians today are living in the spiritual season of the new covenant. The spiritual season of the old covenant has passed. To live in the old covenant spiritual dimension is to live out of the timing of God.

When we are living out of the timing of God, we cannot be living in the fullness of God's natural or spiritual provision. Living in the old covenant spiritual dimension is no longer pleasing to God. He wants us to experience the living Christ and to live in His presence beyond the limitations of our natural intellects. In the book of Hebrews, the writer admonished believers, "Without faith it is impossible to please Him, for he who comes to God must believe that He is, and that he is a rewarder of those who diligently seek *Him*."[10]

God the Father has made the way for us to experience the living Christ and to live in His presence by joining our spirit nature with Christ's Spirit nature through the new covenant. We must, however, throw off the religious limitations of old covenant living to experience the living Christ and to live in the presence of God. He is reaching out to you now. Will you seek Him in the new covenant spiritual dimension? Or will you revert to old covenant ways, rendering His new covenant benefits for you inoperative?

Admonition to Live in the New Covenant Spiritual Dimension

Become aware of God's joining your spirit nature with the Spirit nature of Christ in the new covenant spiritual dimension. Be enlightened by the Holy Spirit beyond natural comprehension. Understand the Word of God, not just intellectually, but through enlightenment of the Holy Spirit. Be free from the limitations of the flesh; freely leave the limitations of the natural realm and move into the dimension of God's Spirit. Receive freedom from self-imposed unbelief by conforming your opinions to God's Word. Live in the timing of God—in the new covenant spiritual dimension.

Experience the living Christ and live in God's presence by entering fully into the new covenant spiritual dimension.

Pray to Live in the New Covenant Spiritual Dimension

Father, thank You for joining my spirit-being with the Spirit-being of Christ in the new covenant spiritual dimension. Please forgive me for relying on my own limited understanding and abilities and not entering fully and unreservedly into the realm of Your presence. I want to understand the things of God, not just intellectually, but through enlightenment of the Holy Spirit.

Please set me free from the limitations of the flesh as I freely leave the limitations of the natural realm behind and move into the dimension of Your presence. Please expose my self-imposed unbelief to me so that I may repent and conform my opinions to Your Word. I want to live in Your timing—in the new covenant spiritual dimension. I want to experience the living Christ and live in Your presence by entering fully into the new covenant spiritual dimension. All this I ask, not only for my own spiritual growth, but also that our Lord Jesus Christ, in whose name I pray, may be glorified and exalted in and through me. Amen.

Where Do We Go from Here?

God desires all His children to live in His presence through the new covenant. Next, we'll find that all believers are ministers of new covenant truth. Fellowship with Jesus produces spiritual effectiveness. Ministry is Jesus Christ working through us. We'll recognize that God's anointing is His active presence. And we'll activate new covenant truth in our lives.

Chapter 8

Activate New Covenant Truth

When they saw the boldness and unfettered eloquence of Peter and John and perceived that they were unlearned and untrained in the schools [common men with no educational advantages], they marveled; and they recognized that they had been with Jesus.
Acts 4:13 AMP

We have seen that God has brought the spirit-being of believers together with the Spirit-being of Christ in the new covenant spiritual dimension. God frees us from the limitations of our flesh to experience the living Christ and live in His presence in the spiritual dimension of the new covenant.

This is the eighth and last spiritual reality that we will discuss: old covenant ministry ministers the letter of the Word; new covenant ministry ministers the Spirit of the Word. We will now progress toward experiencing the living Christ and living in the presence of God by discovering that believers who are intimate with Jesus are needed for a mighty move of God to occur in the world today. We'll find that fellowship with Jesus produces spiritual effectiveness, that God's anointing is His active presence, and that all blessing, provision, authority, and power are in Christ. Finally, we will activate new covenant truth in our lives.

Contrasting Old and New Covenant Ministry

Some Christians conduct their lives and ministries in the old covenant way: they rely on mental comprehension instead of revelation. Solomon, however, advised, "Trust in the Lord with all your heart, and lean not on your own understanding; in all your ways acknowledge Him, and He shall direct your paths."[1] Jesus warned, "Whoever does not receive the kingdom of God as a little child will by no means enter it."[2] Children typically believe in things beyond their understanding. (One very important note of caution, though: All revelation should be confirmed by the written Word. Any revelation inconsistent with the Holy Bible is definitely *not* of God.)

Old covenant leaders minister the letter of the Word by only teaching biblical facts. They strip God's Word of its life and power by not also imparting the Spirit of the Word. The apostle Paul informed the Corinthian church that God "has made us competent as ministers of a new covenant—not of the letter but of the Spirit; for the letter kills, but the Spirit gives life."[3]

New covenant ministry is not the physical act of ministry itself, but the impartation of the Spirit of that ministry. It imparts the Spirit of the Word. For instance, when teaching or preaching divine healing, we not only present biblical facts about divine healing, but also impart the Holy Spirit who heals. The same principle is valid for every topic. When teaching or preaching divine comfort, we impart the Holy Spirit who comforts.

Old covenant leaders neglect leading people into fellowship with God the Father and the Lord Jesus Christ. New covenant pastors, teachers, and other ministers lead people into fellowship with God the Father and the Lord Jesus Christ. The apostle John defined the Christian life, saying, "That which we have seen and heard we declare to you, that you also may have fellowship with us; and truly our fellowship is with the Father and with His Son Jesus Christ."[4] Leading people into fellowship with the Father and the Lord Jesus Christ is new covenant ministry.

They Had Been with Jesus

Peter and John are examples of people who lived the new covenant lifestyle. Peter and John, ordinary men, produced great fruit for God because they lived in consistent, intimate fellowship with the Lord Jesus Christ. On one occasion, Peter and John were on their way to the temple to attend Sabbath prayer. At the Beautiful Gate, a lame man asked them for alms. Peter responded, "Silver and gold I do not have, but what I do have I give you: In the name of Jesus Christ of Nazareth, rise up and walk."[5]

The lame man immediately rose, walked, and leaping and praising God, he accompanied Peter and John into the temple.

The religious leaders arrested Peter and John for healing the man on the Sabbath because it violated their intellectual interpretation of the law of Moses. They brought them before the Sanhedrin—the same religious rulers who were responsible for Jesus' crucifixion. The Sanhedrin demanded to know by what power and authority Peter and John had healed the lame man. Peter replied, "In the name and through the power and authority of Jesus Christ of Nazareth, Whom you crucified, [but] Whom God raised from the dead, in Him and by means of Him this man is standing here before you well and sound in body."[6]

Peter addressed the rulers boldly, respectfully, and eloquently. He was not disrespectful or arrogant. The rulers first marveled and then realized that Peter and John had been with Jesus. According to our opening scripture, "when they saw the boldness and unfettered eloquence of Peter and John and perceived that they were unlearned and untrained in the schools [common men with no educational advantages], they marveled; and they recognized that they had been with Jesus." Believers who are intimate with Jesus, not educated believers without this intimacy, are needed for a mighty move of God to occur throughout the world today.

Peter addressed the Sanhedrin boldly "[because he was] filled with [and controlled by] the Holy Spirit."[7] The Holy Spirit exercised the power and authority of the Lord Jesus Christ through Peter and John to first heal the lame man and then to stand boldly before the men who had crucified Christ—because they had been with Jesus. If we want to be filled with the Holy Spirit as Peter and John were filled with the Holy Spirit, we must spend time with Jesus.

Fellowship with Jesus Produces Spiritual Effectiveness

The ministry of the Spirit comes out of a life lived in the Spirit. Note that Peter and John healed the lame man as they were going to the temple to pray, not when they were coming from the temple after having prayed. They were filled with the Holy Spirit because of the life they were living in Christ.

To be effective for the Lord, we must live our lives sufficiently free of distractions to allow God to fill us with and control us by His Holy Spirit.

We must maintain sufficient inner quietness to routinely hear the voice of our Good Shepherd, Jesus Christ. We cannot live a life filled with busyness and distractions, much less a sinful life, and expect the Lord to use us supernaturally.

The anointing of God, short of the supernatural gift, comes out of intimacy with the glorified Lord Jesus Christ. Just as only the high priest could enter into the Holy of Holies in the old covenant, we can enter the presence of God only through our High Priest, the glorified Lord Jesus Christ.

Therefore, our intimacy with the Lord Jesus Christ is foremost. It is the foundation of our personal life, and our personal life is the foundation of the Lord's ministry through us. Our intimacy with the Lord Jesus Christ defines our ministry. The measure of our intimacy with Christ determines our spiritual effectiveness: our depth of spiritual sensitivity and the strength of our spiritual authority and power. The spiritual quality of the way we live determines the spiritual quality of the ministry we give.

We cannot enter more deeply into ministry to others than the depth of our intimacy with the Lord Jesus Christ. Ministry flows from the presence of God within us. The indwelling of Christ and the work of the Holy Spirit produce the measure of the life of Christ within us. This life is the measure of our spiritual sensitivity and the spiritual authority and power that the Lord Jesus Christ ministers through us by the Holy Spirit. The apostle John disclosed, "In him [Jesus Christ] was life, and that life was the light of men. The light shines in the darkness, but the darkness has not understood it."[8] Ministry is the light of the Lord Jesus Christ shining through us. Our intimacy with Christ determines the brightness of that light.

Ministry Is Jesus Christ Working through Us

People generally think of ministry as the formal functions of the fivefold ministry gifts—apostle, prophet, evangelist, pastor, and teacher. Ministry, however, is everything that the Spirit of God does through any believer. It encompasses roles commonly considered secular, such as conducting business, teaching, and practicing law or medicine. It also includes participation in church meetings, family activities, or practically any activity not in violation of Scripture.

Ministry is dispensing the life of the Lord Jesus Christ to others. Whether it's by a reassuring smile, an encouraging word, or a formal sermon, the Holy Spirit dispenses the life of Christ through the individual who has prepared himself or herself before the Lord. This person has received Christ's life and Spirit and is full to overflowing.

The Ministry *of Christ* Differs from Ministering *for Christ*

Not everything we do for God in a religious setting is ministry, but everything God does through us—within or without a religious setting—is ministry. As we will discuss it, the ministry *of Christ* differs from ministering *for Christ*. The ministry *of Christ* is what the Spirit of God does *through* us. Ministering *for Christ* is what we do *for* God.

The ministry of Christ has spiritual influence, authority, and power that ministering for Christ does not have. Unfortunately, some of the church (the body of Christ at large) has lost this influence, authority, and power by substituting ministering for Christ for the ministry of Christ.

God does His greatest works through believers who are in fellowship with the Lord Jesus Christ. Normally, where there is no fellowship with the Lord Jesus Christ, there is no real ministry of the Holy Spirit. Where there is minimal fellowship with the Lord Jesus Christ, there is minimal ministry of the Spirit. Where there is much fellowship with the Lord Jesus Christ, there is much ministry of the Spirit. And where there is rich fellowship with the Lord Jesus Christ, there is rich ministry of the Holy Spirit.

One reason that God has taken His ministry outside of the local church through parachurch organizations such as radio and television ministries is that church leaders are ministering for Christ instead of imparting the ministry of Christ. He wants to return the ministry of Christ into His local assembly. Some of the church, however, is too preoccupied with ministering for Christ to enter into the ministry of Christ. The current move of the Spirit of God is to bring the ministry of the Lord Jesus Christ back into the local assembly of His church.

When the Lord ministers through us, we surpass ministering for Christ by imparting the life of Christ through the ministry of the Holy Spirit. We reach this worthy objective by intimate fellowship with the Lord Jesus Christ.

God's Anointing Is His Active Presence

The anointing of God is not separate from God but is the active presence of God. It is the evidence of a life lived with God in Christ. We cannot separate Christ from His blessings, His atonement, His promises, His anointing, or His authority.

All blessing, provision, authority, and power are in Christ and attained only in Christ. If we don't take time for Jesus to pour His life into us, there is nothing of Him in us that the Holy Spirit can later pour out to others. Therefore, prayers of others alone cannot secure the anointing of God for us. Their prayers may help to temporarily prop us up, but they cannot maintain God's anointing over time.

The message received from Christ is superior to the message prepared for Christ. Paul informed the church at Rome, "Faith comes by hearing [what is told], and what is heard comes by the preaching [of the message that came from the lips] of Christ (the Messiah Himself)."[9] The effective, anointed message comes from Christ. The Spirit of God is saying to the church, "The hour is coming and now is when the sermons of man will no longer suffice; only the sermons of God through man will suffice."

Jesus admonishes us: "I am the vine, you are the branches. He who abides in Me, and I in him, bears much fruit; for without Me you can do nothing. If you abide in Me, and My words abide in you, you will ask what you desire, and it shall be done for you."[10] In these verses, Jesus underscores the supreme importance of our abiding in Him and His abiding in us. Take a few moments to reflect on this: let's not presume we're abiding in Christ if in truth we are not!

All Believers Are Ministers of New Covenant Truth

God makes living and ministering in the new covenant spiritual dimension available to all believers. He empowers all believers to lead people into fellowship with God the Father and the Lord Jesus Christ through imparting the Spirit of the Word.

Just as Jesus commanded His disciples to wait to receive spiritual power by the promise of the Father at Pentecost, so each believer waits to individually receive spiritual power by his or her personal promise of the Father. To live in and effectively minister new covenant truth, we first progress through our personal transition period, an actual period of waiting. After this, we continue in times of waiting, but we also wait continuously—concurrently proceeding in our lives and ministries.

This waiting for our personal promise of the Father is the lifestyle of waiting to receive power. Hearing and obeying the voice of the Lord brings spiritual power. To receive it, we spend time in isolated quietness and in continuous and concurrent waiting on Him. When we wait on Christ, He enacts His ministry in and through us in His timing and in His way. New covenant ministry is hearing the word of the Lord and obeying Him. The apostle James instructed the early church, "Faith, if it does not have works (deeds and actions of obedience to back it up), by itself is destitute of power (inoperative, dead)."[11] Without hearing and obedience, new covenant ministry cannot take place.

Enacting the Ministry of Christ

The Lord Jesus Christ, whom we hear and obey, must be the same one of whom the Old and New Testaments bear record. Christ's ministry on the earth has not changed. The writer of the book of Hebrews clearly stated, "Jesus Christ is the same yesterday, today, and forever."[12] Jesus stressed to His disciples, "Most assuredly, I say to you, he who believes in Me, the works that I do he will do also; and greater works than these he will do, because I go to My Father."[13]

Jesus Christ is no longer working through one physical body; He is working the same and greater works through *one spiritual body—the church*. His body, the church, is now composed of many physical bodies. As Paul taught the Colossian church, "You are complete in Him [Christ], who is the head of all principality and power."[14] Christ is the head of the church, the body of Christ. The church is the embodiment of the glorified Lord.

By the glorification of Christ, the Holy Spirit came to live in believers. Through the lordship of the glorified Christ, the Holy Spirit invokes the authority and power of Christ through believers. Glorification brought His presence to us. Lordship (our attentive obedience) releases His authority and power through us. By glorifying Jesus as Lord, we become dependent on Him; we come to know Christ as He really is—the Son of God.

Receiving the Empowering Revelation That Jesus Is the Son of God

Revelation that Jesus is the Son of the living God—not Spiritless knowledge—empowers new covenant ministry. One time Jesus asked His disciples who they said that He was. Peter replied that Jesus was the Christ, the Son of the living God. Jesus then revealed that Peter did not know this by natural means but had received it from the Father.

Jesus then told Peter in the presence of His disciples, "I will give you the keys of the kingdom of heaven; and whatever you bind (declare to be improper and unlawful) on earth *must be what is already bound in heaven*; and whatever you loose (declare lawful) on earth *must be what is already loosed in heaven*."[15] Illumination of Christ as the Son of the living God qualifies us to receive from Him the keys of the kingdom of heaven.

When the eyes of our heart are opened to know Jesus as the Son of the living God, He gives us the keys to the kingdom of heaven—discernment of what is already bound or loosed in heaven. Illumination of what is already bound or loosed in heaven is the foundation of new covenant authority.

Exercising New Covenant Authority

Under the new covenant, Jesus exercises His authority through His body, the church. New covenant believers are not people who possess power; they are vessels for the Lord's use. They have no spiritual power in themselves. They are filled and poured out by the Lord Jesus Christ. Under the old covenant, Jesus gave His followers delegated authority; now the church is the body through which Jesus Christ Himself, as the head of the church, exercises His authority.

One time before Pentecost, Jesus sent seventy people out to heal the sick. They healed the sick and cast out devils, but the kingdom of God was not in them. He enabled them to heal the sick and cast out devils under old covenant authority. They did not have Christ in them because He had not yet been glorified; the spiritual dimension of the Holy Spirit living in believers had not yet come.

New covenant authority exceeds the authority that Jesus granted to the seventy in Luke 10:19. Jesus is no longer restricted to *delegating* us authority in the new covenant dimension. He now *enacts* His authority in and through us. The Lord Jesus Christ Himself ministers in and through us by the Holy Spirit. This is the way to minister new covenant authority: discern what Christ has already loosed or bound in heaven, and allow Him to enforce it through you by the leading, authority, and power of the Holy Spirit.

Speaking of this period, Jesus advised His disciples, "At that day you will know that I am in My Father, and you in Me, and I in you."[16] The pastor of a local church has long been viewed as the shepherd or undershepherd of the flock. In the new covenant spiritual dimension, however, the pastor is the embodiment (vessel) of the Good Shepherd, the Lord Jesus Christ. Likewise, the teacher is the embodiment of the Teacher, and the evangelist is the embodiment of the Evangelist. Indeed, Christ lives in and can minister through every believer.

Progressing from Ritual to Revelation

We know that God replaced the old covenant because it was weakened by the flesh. Under the old covenant, priests ministered by strictly adhering to prescribed rituals. Under the new covenant, however, all believers minister by the leading, authority, and power of the Holy Spirit.

When teaching and preaching new covenant truth, we lead people into reliance on the Lord Jesus Christ, rather than presenting them with formulas. For our purposes, we will define a formula as a humanly reasoned process by which one expects to reach a predetermined spiritual result. Formulas remove the simplicity of the gospel and negate dependence on God. They introduce human reasoning and carnal effort into the divine equation, producing a tainted result—ministry that is void of the authority and power of the Lord Jesus Christ, the Son of the living God.

Whenever there is revelation, the carnal mind tends to reduce it to a formula. Whenever there is spiritual success, the flesh seeks to repeat the process that produced it. By reducing spiritual success to a formula, the unsuspecting believer removes the supernatural dimension from spiritual success, rendering it powerless. Spiritual success is not accomplished through repetitious, carnal methodology.

The flesh is always looking for a formula, but the only valid new covenant formula is following the Spirit of God. The ministry of Jesus defied carnal methodology. This is the way that Jesus ministered: He heard what the Father said, saw what the Father did, and said and did likewise. This is the methodology of new covenant ministry.

The new covenant method is following the leading of the Holy Spirit—being filled with and controlled by the Holy Spirit. By the leading and empowerment of the Holy Spirit, believers minister in Jesus' name.

Praying and Ministering in Jesus' Name

This is the meaning of praying or ministering in Jesus' name: "presenting all that I AM." Immediately after Jesus told His disciples that anyone who believes would do greater things than He did, He promised: "I will do [I Myself will grant] whatever you ask in My Name [as presenting all that I AM], so that the Father may be glorified and extolled in (through) the Son. [Yes] I will grant [I myself will do for you] whatever you shall ask in My Name [as presenting all that I AM]."[17]

"I AM" indicates Jesus' deity. Jesus tells us He will do all that we ask, "presenting all that I AM." We must know Jesus as the Son of God to "present all that I AM."

Ministering in Jesus' name is the Holy Spirit supernaturally enlightening and empowering us to speak His words of divine power into an individual or situation. Note that "I AM" is present tense. Ministering in Jesus' name is not asking Him to come and do something in the future; it is presenting Him as all that He is now.

Being with Jesus Speaks for Itself

When we have been with Jesus, the evidence—even physical evidence of a life changed or a miracle done—will speak undeniably for itself. At the conclusion of Luke's account of Peter and John standing before the Sanhedrin, he triumphantly stated, "Seeing the man who had been healed standing with them, they [the Sanhedrin] could say nothing against it."[18]

Admonition to Activate New Covenant Truth

Become intimate with Jesus. Live in the Spirit. Allow Christ to minister through you, rather than ministering for Christ. Lead people into fellowship with God the Father and the Lord Jesus Christ by imparting the Spirit of the Word.

Receive the keys of the kingdom of heaven through the illumination that Jesus Christ is the Son of the living God. Discern what is already loosed or bound in heaven and enforce it in the earth. Allow Jesus Christ to exercise His authority through you. Live and minister the power of the divinity of Christ.

Live in God's presence. Recognize that God's anointing is His active presence. Remember, all blessing, provision, authority, and power are in Christ and attained only in Christ. Spend time alone with Jesus. Listen to Him when you pray. Fellowship with Jesus and attain spiritual effectiveness—spiritual sensitivity, authority, and power. There will be evidence that you have been with Jesus!

Pray to Activate New Covenant Truth

Father God, I want to be prepared for life and ministry as Peter and John were when the Lord healed the lame man through them and enabled them to stand boldly before the Jewish rulers. I want to be filled with and controlled by the Holy Spirit. I want to impart the Spirit of Your Word. I want to impart Your Spirit-empowered salvation message to other people and lead people into fellowship with God the Father and the Lord Jesus Christ. I want to be intimate with Jesus and live my life in the Spirit so that the ministry of the Spirit will flow out of me. I desire to allow Christ to minister through me, rather than my ministering for Him.

Please enlighten me by Your Spirit so that I may come into fellowship with Your Son. I want to truly exalt Him as the Word and the Son of God. I desire to live and minister in Your new covenant authority, discerning what is already bound or loosed in heaven and enforcing it in the earth. I want to minister by presenting Jesus as "all that I AM." All this I ask, not only for my own spiritual growth, but also that our Lord Jesus Christ, in whose name I pray, may be glorified and exalted in and through me. Amen.

Part 1 Summary

In this first part, we have discovered, accepted, and embraced spiritual realities that are essential to experiencing the living Christ and living in the presence of God. We began by recognizing that God the Father desires to have a close, personal relationship with all of His children and is reaching out to mankind through His Son Jesus Christ. We discovered that every believer can enter into actual, intimate fellowship with God the Father and the Lord Jesus Christ. We then lovingly embraced God's desire for us to enter into deep personal fellowship with Him through intimacy with His Son Jesus Christ.

We followed Jesus' earthly journey, noting key events and drawing a parallel between His journey on earth and our spiritual journey. We then noted how God the Father introduces us to His Son and learned that we can actually know the Lord Jesus Christ rather than just know about Him. Next, we traced the spiritual history of mankind from their creation, to their separation from God, to their opportunity to be reunited to God, and finally to their restoration into magnificent spiritual beings.

We then learned that mankind lives in two dimensions, the natural and the spiritual, and we gained a basic understanding of the spirit nature of mankind. Stressing the importance of knowing Christ as He really is, we discovered that the way we perceive Christ forms our faith and shapes our earthly and eternal destinies. We saw how God joins the spirit-being of believers with the Spirit-being of Christ through the new covenant, and we entered into spirit-dimension fellowship with God the Father and the Lord Jesus Christ. Finally, we began living and ministering new covenant truth by the active presence of God.

Where Do We Go from Here?

In part 1, we began by embracing spiritual realities that are essential to experiencing the living Christ and living our lives in the presence of God. In part 2, we will activate foundational truths that are also essential for experiencing the living Christ, living our lives in the presence of God, and leading others to experience Christ and live in God's presence as well. We will begin in the next chapter by identifying thirst as a prerequisite to entering the new covenant spiritual dimension. We will see that when we come to Jesus and drink, believe, and glorify the Lord Jesus Christ, streams of living water will flow from within us. We will see that we should thirst for the living Christ to be revealed in us.

Part 2

Activating Foundational Truths

Chapter 9

Thirst, Come to Jesus, and Drink

> On the last and greatest day of the Feast, Jesus stood and said in a loud voice, "If anyone is thirsty, let him come to me and drink. Whoever believes in me, as the Scripture has said, streams of living water will flow from within him." By this he meant the Spirit, whom those who believed in him were later to receive. Up to that time the Spirit had not been given, since Jesus had not yet been glorified.
> John 7:37–39 NIV

In the previous chapter, we observed how the Lord used Peter and John to heal a lame man at the Beautiful Gate because they lived in intimate fellowship Him. These two ordinary, uneducated men then astonished the sophisticated Jewish leaders who had arrested them by boldly and eloquently responding to their interrogation—because they had been with Jesus.

Likewise, the depth of our relationship with Jesus determines the depth of our spiritual sensitivity and the strength of our spiritual authority and power. The Bible characterizes our desire to deepen our relationship with Christ and to be more effective for Him as thirst. We will now advance toward experiencing the living Christ and living in the presence of God by activating eight foundational truths.

Our first foundational truth is this: the ministry of the Holy Spirit flows from within us when we thirst and come to Jesus and drink according to the Scriptures. Next, we will see that the glorification of Christ makes the new covenant spiritual dimension available to all Christians. Thirsting for more of Christ opens this dimension to individual believers. Properly responding to the thirst within us activates the ministry of the Holy Spirit in and through us. It brings us closer to experiencing the living Christ and living in the presence of God.

Streams of Living Water Will Flow from Within You

The apostle John explained the meaning of our opening scripture with these words: "By this he meant the Spirit, whom those who believed in him were later to receive." The streams of living water flowing from within us are the ministry of the Holy Spirit. This passage sets out the requirements for the Holy Spirit to become active and effective in our lives and ministries.

We cannot live or minister in the Holy Spirit by expecting Him to mysteriously descend upon us. The Holy Spirit comes from within believers in Christ. He comes through a prepared heart. How do we prepare for the Holy Spirit to live and minister in and through us? According to this passage, streams of living water will flow from within us when we meet the following four conditions: (1) thirst, (2) come to Jesus and drink, (3) believe, and (4) glorify the Lord Jesus Christ. Let's begin with the first one: thirst.

What Is Thirst?

Natural thirst is a primal drive, an intense desire for something we cannot live without. It is an intense desire to live, to survive. Spiritual thirst is the supernatural drive for spiritual life. The Holy Spirit is as necessary to our spiritual life as water is to our natural life. We cannot live without Him. We are spiritually dead without the Holy Spirit—spiritually inactive, inoperative, and lifeless.

In this passage, Jesus announced, "If anyone is thirsty . . ." This is the first and most important requirement for life and ministry in the Holy Spirit: thirst. Thirst is the recognition of the need for water. Water is a symbol of the Holy Spirit. Spiritual thirst is recognizing and experiencing our life-sustaining need for the Holy Spirit. When we thirst, we are dry—spiritually dry. We recognize our spiritual depravity. We seek from the Lord the refreshing life of the Holy Spirit—the Spirit who gives life.

We thirst, not with our minds, but with our hearts. Spiritual thirst powerfully motivates us to come to Jesus and drink. The writer to the Hebrews urged them, "We must give the more earnest heed to the things we have heard, lest we drift away."[1] The words "give the more earnest heed" express the urgency and intensity of thirsting for more of the Holy Spirit.

The apostle John expressed the desperation of thirst in his gospel when he quoted Jesus as saying, "Without Me you can do nothing."[2] Our thirst goes beyond our saying, "I can't do this without You, Lord." It says, "I can't live without You! You are my very life! You must do everything in and through me! I must live in Your presence!"

The enlightenment that we can do nothing without Christ is the realization that awakens thirst. When we become aware of our spiritual depravity, we are prepared to come to Jesus and drink.

Come and Drink

To thirst is not all that is required for streams of living water to flow from within us. After Jesus proclaimed, "If anyone is thirsty," He continued with "come to Me and drink." Jesus is our source of life. The apostle John quoted Jesus as saying, "I have come that they may have life, and that they may have it more abundantly."[3] Speaking of Jesus, John wrote, "In Him was life, and the life was the light of men."[4]

Jesus called those who thirst to come to Him. He did not say to go to knowledge and drink, nor did He say to go to a church service and drink. He said, "Come to Me and drink." So how do we drink? We drink purposefully and spiritually.

Drinking Is Purposeful

Drinking is purposeful, something we do: (1) We come to Jesus Christ, and (2) we drink. If we come to Him without drinking, we do not receive living water. This living water cannot flow out unless it has first been taken in. Living water is taken in by drinking. What is the living water that we drink? The living water we drink is the Holy Spirit.

How do we come and drink? The heart is the reservoir, and the mind is the filter. The heart must be open, and the mind must be surrendered to God and renewed. It's much like entering into the revelatory flow. We enter reverently—in quietness and peacefulness, in full reliance, submission, and humility. The prophet Isaiah proclaimed, "Wait and listen, everyone who is thirsty! Come to the waters; and he who has no money, come, buy and eat! Yes, come, buy [priceless, spiritual] wine and milk without money and without price [simply for the self-surrender that accepts the blessing]."[5]

Under the old covenant, people had to rely on the chief priest to enter into the presence of God for them. Under the new covenant, believers can actually wait in the presence of God. When we are in Christ, we are in the presence of the Father because Christ is one with the Father and is seated at the right hand of God. We wait in the Father's presence reverently, attentively, and expectantly. Isaiah wisely advises us, "Seek, inquire for, and require the Lord while He may be found [claiming Him by necessity and by right]; call upon Him while He is near."[6] The words "while He may be found" imply that He may not be found at a later time. Therefore, we should not take our spiritual thirst lightly but make the most of it by promptly coming to Jesus to drink. We must not put off coming to Jesus to quench our spiritual thirst.

Drinking Is a Spiritual Act

Drinking is a spiritual act. To quench our physical thirst, we go to a water source and drink. To quench our spiritual thirst, we come to Jesus, our spiritual source, and drink. To come to Jesus to drink, we first enter into His presence. He then saturates us with His Spirit.

In this sense, we don't drink physically or mentally, but we spiritually receive what Christ is releasing within our heart. This drinking takes place as we become aware of the life of Christ that He progressively reveals in our heart. And it continues as we actively allow Him to expand that life throughout our entire being. We drink actively, yet responsively. We surrender and yield to the life of Christ stirring within us. A baby instinctively knows how to suck, but a young child must learn how to drink. Likewise, we learn to drink spiritually.

Believe

The third condition for streams of living water to flow from within us is to believe. Returning to our opening scripture, Jesus proclaimed,

"Whoever believes in me, as the Scripture has said, streams of living water will flow from within him." It is not enough to thirst and to come to Jesus and drink to experience the Holy Spirit flowing out of us. It is also not enough to believe in His promises.

We must believe in Him. We need to believe that God will consistently and faithfully reward us when we diligently seek Him. The writer to the Hebrews informed believers, "Without faith it is impossible to please Him, for he who comes to God must believe that He is, and that He is a rewarder of those who diligently seek Him."[7] Jesus taught His disciples, "Whatever things you ask when you pray, believe that you receive them, and you will have them."[8]

Obedience is the evidence of believing. James warned his readers, "Faith, if it does not have works (deeds and actions of obedience to back it up), by itself is destitute of power (inoperative, dead)."[9] How do we believe?

We believe with our heart. Paul prayed for the church at Ephesus, "having the eyes of your heart flooded with light, so that you can know and understand . . . the immeasurable and unlimited and surpassing greatness of His power in and for us who believe, as demonstrated in the working of His mighty strength."[10] Jesus works in and through us by this power.

Jesus never said His works or ministry would decrease after His crucifixion. He specifically said His works would increase. He declared, "Most assuredly, I say to you, he who believes in Me, the works that I do he will do also; and greater works than these he will do, because I go to My Father."[11]

Glorify the Lord Jesus Christ

The fourth requirement to experience the Holy Spirit filling us and flowing out of us is to glorify the Lord Jesus Christ. Jesus told Philip in the presence of His other disciples, "Whatever you ask in My name, that I will do, that the Father may be glorified in the Son."[12]

According to the apostle John, this ministry of the Holy Spirit by which streams of living water would flow from within could not take place at the time of Jesus' announcement because He had not yet been glorified. For the Holy Spirit to actively dwell within us and effectively minister through us, we glorify Jesus in two ways: historically and personally.

Glorify Christ Historically

The Holy Spirit actively dwells in us and effectively ministers through us when we recognize Jesus' historical glorification. The evidence of His historical glorification was the arrival of the Holy Spirit on the day of Pentecost. Just before Jesus' ascension, He commanded His disciples "not to leave Jerusalem but to wait for what the Father had promised, of which [He said] you have heard Me speak. For John baptized with water, but not many days from now you shall be baptized with (placed in, introduced into) the Holy Spirit."[13] Later He continued, "You shall receive power (ability, efficiency, and might) when the Holy Spirit has come upon you, and you shall be My witnesses in Jerusalem and all Judea and Samaria and to the ends (the very bounds) of the earth."[14]

Jesus Christ baptizes believers in the Holy Spirit. John the Baptist testified, "I did not know Him nor recognize Him, but He Who sent me to baptize in (with) water said to me, Upon Him Whom you shall see the Spirit descend and remain, that One is He Who baptizes with the Holy Spirit."[15]

Pentecost, when the Holy Spirit came to live in believers, was a one-time historical occurrence. But experiencing the baptism of the Holy Spirit was not only for those who were present in Jerusalem on that historic day! Peter informed the crowd on the day of Pentecost, "The promise [of the Holy Spirit] is to and for you and your children, and to and for all that are far away, [even] to and for as many as the Lord our God invites and bids to come to Himself."[16] The baptism of the Holy Spirit is for all who come to Christ. If Jesus has invited you to come to Him, this promise is for you!

Glorify Christ Personally

For streams of living water to flow from within us, we also personally glorify Jesus by recognizing, knowing, and reverencing Him as the glorified Lord as we described in chapter 6. We glorify Christ when we (1) obey Him, (2) cooperate with the Holy Spirit, (3) honor Christ's headship, and (4) keep our hearts pure.

   1. *Personally glorify Christ by obedience.* Jesus taught His disciples that He would reveal Himself to those who love and obey Him:

"He who has My commandments and keeps them, it is he who loves Me. And he who loves Me will be loved by My Father, and I will love him and manifest Myself to him."[17] Referring to Jesus, Luke quoted Peter and the apostles in the book of Acts: "Him God has exalted to His right hand to be Prince and Savior, to give repentance to Israel and forgiveness of sins. And we are His witnesses to these things, and so also is the Holy Spirit whom God has given to those who obey Him."[18] Obedience is therefore indispensable to coming to Jesus, and coming to Jesus is indispensable for spiritual life to flow out of us.

Old covenant obedience was by the flesh. New covenant obedience is by the Spirit. Old covenant obedience was to the *written Word* or to the words of the prophets. New covenant obedience is to the *living Word*—the Lord Jesus Christ. It encompasses obedience to the written Word but also includes obedience to the Holy Spirit. Proper motivation of new covenant obedience is love for God the Father and the Lord Jesus Christ. Jesus declared, "If you [really] love Me, you will keep (obey) My commands."[19] Obedience therefore comes through love.

2. *Personally glorify Christ by cooperating with the Holy Spirit.* Obedience to the Holy Spirit begins with receiving Him and continues with fully yielding to His promptings. Paul advised the church at Ephesus, "Do not grieve the Holy Spirit of God [do not offend or vex or sadden Him], by Whom you were sealed (marked, branded as God's own, secured) for the day of redemption (of final deliverance through Christ from evil and the consequences of sin)."[20]

We hinder the flow of living water by ignoring or resisting the leading of the Holy Spirit, or by subjecting the Holy Spirit within us to something that is offensive to Him. For instance, we may sense the discomfort of the Holy Spirit when we watch certain television shows or participate in certain conversations.

The hindrance may be sin or a weight. In this context, we'll consider sin to be any action or inaction, willful thinking, or motivation that deviates from the will of God. We know God's will through His written Word and also through His Holy Spirit. A weight is anything that is not sin that leads us away from conformity to the Word of God or distracts us from the leading and working of the Holy Spirit. The writer of the book of Hebrews encouraged early Christians, "Let us strip off and throw aside every encumbrance (unnecessary weight) and that sin which so readily (deftly and cleverly) clings to and entangles us, and let us run with patient endurance and steady and active persistence the appointed course of the race that is set before us."[21]

The indwelling of the Holy Spirit produces power within the believer in Christ. Paul prayed for the Ephesians, "May He grant you out of the rich treasury of His glory to be strengthened and reinforced with mighty power in the inner man by the [Holy] Spirit [Himself indwelling your innermost being and personality]."[22] Just as we can learn to breathe more deeply in the natural, we can learn to take in more of the Holy Spirit and become more sensitive to His guidance.

3. *Personally glorify Christ by honoring His headship.* We glorify Christ by allowing the Holy Spirit to empower us to yield to the headship of the Lord Jesus Christ. In the new covenant dimension, Christ is the head of the church, of which we are a part. As our physical head directs our physical body, Jesus Christ, our spiritual head, directs our lives. We must, however, voluntarily yield to Him for this headship to function. It is through Christ's headship that God exercises His authority and power through us.

Paul taught the church in Ephesus, "He [God] put all things under His [Jesus'] feet, and gave Him to be head over all things to the church, which is His body, the fullness of Him who fills all in all."[23] He also informed the Colossian church, "He is the head of the body, the church, who is the beginning, the firstborn from the dead, that in all things He may have the preeminence."[24] In other words, God exercises His authority over all things through us, His church, when we are fully yielded to the Lord Jesus Christ.

4. *Personally glorify Christ by keeping a pure heart.* Christ cannot be our head, however, unless we know what He is currently saying to us and what He wants to do in and through us. The author of the

book of Hebrews admonished believers, "The Holy Spirit says: Today, if you will hear His voice, do not harden your hearts, as [happened] in the rebellion [of Israel] and their provocation and embitterment [of Me] in the day of testing in the wilderness."[25] Hardening our hearts, as we discussed in chapter 5, greatly hinders God's communications to us, reducing our ability to receive the power He wants to exercise in and through us.

Purity of motive is imperative to glorify Christ. Improper motive nullifies our glorification of Him. Our motive should be void of pride and personal ambition. In the new covenant, the Holy Spirit should govern our inner motivations, our outward conduct, our relationships with other people, and our ministry to others.

Thirsting for the Living Christ to Be Revealed in Us

For streams of living water to flow from within us, we come to Jesus—who is revealed within us—and drink. Our thirst, then, is an intense desire to continually experience the indwelling presence of the glorified Lord Jesus Christ, our righteousness. Matthew records Jesus teaching the following in the Sermon on the Mount: "Blessed are those who hunger and thirst for righteousness, for they shall be filled."[26]

Coming to Christ and drinking spiritually transforms us from possessing mere knowledge of Christ to actually experiencing intimacy with Him. Through this intimacy, we truly enter into the presence of the Almighty. The Holy Spirit makes the way for us to know the Son through His inner working. And the Son opens our awareness to the presence of the Father. We perceive Christ living within us when we (1) realize that Christ lives within us, (2) recognize Jesus Christ is the Son of God, (3) disassociate ourselves from the world, and (4) allow Christ to diminish our inner darkness. Let's take a closer look at each one of these.

Realizing That Christ Lives within Us

The living Christ does not reveal Himself to us from without, through our minds; He reveals Himself to us in our hearts. When Judas (not Judas Iscariot, who betrayed Jesus) asked Jesus how He would manifest Himself to His disciples, Jesus replied, "If a person [really] loves Me, he will keep

My word [obey My teaching]; and My Father will love him, and We will come to him and make Our home (abode, special dwelling place) with him."[27] The apostle Paul testified that God "was pleased to reveal (unveil, disclose) His Son within me."[28]

Recognizing Jesus Christ Is the Son of God

Second, Christ reveals Himself to us when we recognize Him as the Son of God. Scripture identifies Jesus Christ as the Son of Man and the Son of God. We must not only know Jesus as the Son of Man, but also as the Son of God. If we know Him as the Son of Man, we may not necessarily know Him as the Son of God. If we know Him as the Son of God, we also know Him as the Son of Man. Remember from chapter 6, the post-incarnate Christ encompasses the preincarnate and incarnate dimensions of Christ.

According to the gospel of Matthew, Jesus once asked His disciples who other people were saying that He, the Son of Man, was. They replied that some said He was John the Baptist, some said He was Elijah, and some said He was Jeremiah or one of the other prophets. It would have been supernatural for Christ to be any one of these men returning from the grave, but each of these answers was intellectually conceived. Not one was spiritually discerned. Not one recognized Jesus as the Son of God. Not one was received by revelation.

Then Jesus asked the disciples who they said that He was. According to Matthew's gospel, "Simon Peter answered and said, 'You are the Christ, the Son of the living God.' Jesus answered and said to him, 'Blessed are you, Simon Bar-Jonah, for flesh and blood has not revealed this to you, but My Father who is in heaven. And I also say to you that you are Peter, and on this rock I will build My church, and the gates of Hades shall not prevail against it.'"[29] Jesus pointed out that Peter did not receive this answer by natural means. He then said, "On this rock I will build My church."

Christ builds His church on this revelation: Jesus Christ is the Son of the living God. The church is the *ecclesia*—the "called-out ones." Each of us is a part of His church. He builds each one of us on this revelation. In fact, we enter into eternal life by recognizing Jesus as the Son of the living God. In his first epistle, the apostle John explained that when we know Jesus as the Son of God, we know the Father and have eternal life: "God has given us eternal life, and this life is in His Son. He who has the Son has life; he who does not have the Son of God does not have life."[30]

Disassociating Ourselves from the World

The third qualification for Jesus to reveal Himself to us is to disassociate ourselves from the world. For Christ to be more fully revealed within us, we distance ourselves from the things of the world as the Word of God instructs and the Holy Spirit leads.

The less we are influenced by or conformed to the world—the ways of mankind apart from God and Christ—the more we can know and experience the Holy Spirit. Speaking of the Holy Spirit, Jesus told Philip, "The world cannot accept him, because it neither sees him nor knows him. But you know him, for he lives with you and will be in you."[31]

As we yield to the Holy Spirit in what we see, hear, think, say, and do, we disassociate ourselves from the world in greater measure. Our sensitivity to the Holy Spirit's gentle restraining differs for each one of us depending on our stage of spiritual growth and the nature of our assignment (the specific work God has for us to do). For instance, as I'm editing this manuscript, I'm sensing the Holy Spirit's gentle resistance, preventing me from reading further until I revise the wording in this paragraph. As we continue to disassociate ourselves from the world in these ways, the darkness within us diminishes.

Diminishing Inner Darkness

The last requirement we will discuss for Christ revealing Himself to us is our allowing Him to diminish the inner darkness that prevents us from perceiving the living presence of the Lord within us. This darkness diminishes as we surrender to Christ. John wrote in his first epistle, "I am writing you a new commandment, which is true (is realized) in Him and in you, because the darkness (moral blindness) is clearing away and the true Light (the revelation of God in Christ) is already shining."[32] Referring to Jesus, he also revealed in his gospel that "in Him was Life, and the Life was the Light of men. And the Light shines on in the darkness, for the darkness has never overpowered it [put it out or absorbed it or appropriated it, and is unreceptive to it]."[33]

Experience the Living Christ!

Paul noted, "Once you were darkness, but now you are light in the Lord; walk as children of Light [lead the lives of those native-born to the Light]."[34] As we realize that Christ lives within us, recognize Him as the Son of God, disassociate ourselves from the world, and diminish our inner darkness, Christ reveals Himself within us. We come to Christ, who is in us, to receive the flow of the Holy Spirit that never ceases.

Receive the Flow of the Holy Spirit That Never Ceases

God promises that if we are persistent, we will receive the Holy Spirit. We can have continual, intimate fellowship with God our Father if we diligently seek Him. When one of Jesus' disciples asked Him to teach them to pray, He taught them what we now know as the Lord's Prayer. He then continued to instruct them as follows: "Ask and keep on asking and it shall be given you; seek and keep on seeking and you shall find; knock and keep on knocking and the door shall be opened to you. For everyone who asks and keeps on asking receives; and he who seeks and keeps on seeking finds; and to him who knocks and keeps on knocking, the door shall be opened."[35]

Come to Jesus and drink. Remember Isaiah 55:1 in the Amplified Bible: "Wait and listen, everyone who is thirsty! Come to the waters; and he who has no money, come, buy and eat! Yes, come, buy [priceless, spiritual] wine and milk without money and without price [simply for the self-surrender that accepts the blessing]."

Only with the Holy Spirit can we receive the fullness of truth. Without Him, we are left to our natural comprehension. We therefore are wise to abandon our dependence on our intellect and instead depend on the Holy Spirit. Jesus exhorted His disciples: "I have much more to say to you, more than you can now bear. But when he, the Spirit of truth, comes, he will guide you into all truth."[36]

We are not capable of understanding or receiving the spiritual truths that the Lord Jesus Christ has in store for us without drinking in the Holy Spirit. The more of the Holy Spirit that we drink in, the greater our ability to receive what the Lord Jesus Christ has in store for us. We drink by waiting on God our Father and our Lord Jesus Christ.

Jesus proclaimed: "Whoever takes a drink of the water that I will give him shall never, no never, be thirsty any more. But the water that I will give him shall become a spring of water welling up (flowing, bubbling) [continually] within him unto (into, for) eternal life."[37] He responded to the Pharisees who were challenging Him: "The Bread of God is He Who comes down out of heaven and gives life to the world. . . . I am the Bread of Life. He Who comes to Me will never be hungry, and he who believes in and cleaves to and trusts in and relies on Me will never thirst any more (at any time)."[38] Jesus promises the flow of the Spirit that never ceases. We never have to be out of the blessed flow!

This flow, however, is not only for us; it's also for others. The apostle Paul taught the Corinthians that we are called to be companions and participants with our Lord Jesus Christ: "God is faithful (reliable, trustworthy, and therefore ever true to His promise, and He can be depended on); by Him you were called into companionship and participation with His Son, Jesus Christ our Lord."[39] As companions and participants with Christ, we awaken thirst not only in ourselves, but also in others.

Awakening Thirst in Others

To minister effectively, not only do we thirst and come to Jesus and drink ourselves, but we also (1) recognize the lack of thirst in others, (2) awaken thirst in them, and (3) lead them to Jesus to drink. We awaken thirst in others by ministering in the Spirit, because recognizing and awakening thirst are functions of the Holy Spirit.

Ministry of the intellect is responsible for much of the apathy in the church today. When people are taught the principles of the Bible without the accompanying power of the Holy Spirit, they try to believe and implement those principles in their own strength. Then, when they fail repeatedly, they become discouraged.

One time Jesus came upon a disabled man at the pool of Bethesda. Many sick people waited around this pool. When an angel periodically stirred the water, the first one to enter the water would be healed. John reports, "When Jesus noticed him lying there [helpless], knowing that he had already been a long time in that condition, He said to him, Do you want to become well? [Are you really in earnest about getting well?]"[40]

In the same way, Jesus is asking us today, "Do you thirst? Do you really thirst?" People who wish to receive but have no spiritual thirst hinder the ministry of the Holy Spirit. The absence of thirst in believers today retards spiritual growth in our churches. We should confront people as Jesus did, saying, "Are you really serious? Do you strongly desire to grow spiritually? Are you strongly motivated to seek Jesus? If you're not really serious, you need to get serious!" It's better to be cold or hot than to be lukewarm, as we will discuss in chapter 19.

Don't Be Deterred by Opposition

Unfortunately, not everyone is open to the flow of the Spirit of God. Some people not only reject it, but also actively oppose it. Mind-oriented religion instinctively opposes Spirit-oriented belief. When Jesus proclaimed, "Whoever believes in me, as the Scripture has said, streams of living water will flow from within him," John reports that people responded: "'Surely this man is the Prophet.' Others said, 'He is the Christ.' Still others asked, 'How can the Christ come from Galilee? Does not the Scripture say that the Christ will come from David's family and from Bethlehem, the town where David lived?' Thus the people were divided because of Jesus."[41]

Not a one of us has complete knowledge, no matter how knowledgeable we are. Regardless of our level of education or knowledge of the Scriptures, there is much we do not know. The most highly educated religious minds of His day opposed Jesus and put Him to death—not those who knowingly opposed God, but those who thought they were serving God! Let's not be like them.

Generally, when the true ministry of the Holy Spirit comes forth, religious people oppose it. People challenge the messenger of truth today just as some of the crowd challenged Jesus in His time on earth. Don't allow religious people to deter you!

At the same time, let's not be ignorant of the devil's devices. Let's strive to keep the unity of the Spirit in peace. Paul instructed the church at Ephesus: "Walk worthy of the calling with which you were called, with all lowliness and gentleness, with longsuffering, bearing with one another in love, endeavoring to keep the unity of the Spirit in the bond of peace. There is one body and one Spirit, just as you were called in one hope of your calling; one Lord, one faith, one baptism; one God and Father of all, who is above all, and through all, and in you all."[42] In spite of trial and opposition, continue to come to Jesus and drink.

Admonition to Come to Jesus and Drink

Thirst for more of Christ. Come to Jesus and drink. Believe. Glorify the Lord Jesus Christ by submitting yourself to Him. Be transformed from simply having knowledge about Christ to intimately fellowshiping with Him. Realize that Christ is in you. Recognize Him as the Son of God. Disassociate yourself from the world as the Word of God instructs and the Holy Spirit leads. Allow Christ to diminish your inner darkness. Activate continuous streams of living water flowing from within you by waiting on the Lord and listening to Him. Don't be surprised by opposition from mind-oriented, religious people—and refuse to be suppressed by it.

Recognize the lack of thirst in others, awaken thirst in them by the Holy Spirit, and lead them to Jesus to drink. Before ministering to others, ask yourself: Am I thirsty, truly thirsty? Have I come to Jesus to drink? Do I believe, truly believe? Is my true motive to glorify God the Father and the Lord Jesus Christ?

Pray to Thirst and to Come to Jesus and Drink

Father, I want to thirst, really thirst, for You. Please reveal my spiritual depravity to me. Please cause me to seek You with my whole heart. I desire to leave the confines of the natural realm and enter into supernatural fellowship with the glorified Lord Jesus Christ. I want to know Him as He really is—the Son of God—revealed within me. I want to earnestly seek to know and do Your will. I want to thirst, regularly come to Jesus and drink, believe, and glorify the Lord Jesus Christ. I want to recognize the lack of thirst in others, awaken thirst in them, and lead them to Jesus to drink. All this I ask, not only for my own spiritual growth, but also that our Lord Jesus Christ, in whose name I pray, may be glorified and exalted in and through me. Amen.

Where Do We Go from Here?

In part 2, we are learning to activate eight foundational spiritual truths that are essential for experiencing the living Christ, living our lives in the presence of God, and leading others to experience the living Christ and live in God's presence as well. We began in this chapter by recognizing that spiritual thirst is a prerequisite to experiencing the living Christ and living in the presence of God. Our glorifying Christ opens the way for the Holy Spirit to reside in us and minister through us. In the next chapter, we'll find that building the kingdom of God is a supernatural commission, that God builds His kingdom in us, and that it is God who adds people to the church. We'll realize that we are completely dependent on God to build His kingdom.

In the chapters that follow, we'll learn to receive revelation through grace in peace. We'll note that grace is the empowerment of God and that inner peace enables us to hear the Lord's voice on a routine and consistent basis. We'll discover that faith is giving Christ preeminence. We'll then learn to have faith in the person of the Lord Jesus Christ. After that, we'll see how our doctrine forms our perception of reality, which in turn defines the limits of our faith. We'll find out whether our doctrine is a stepping stone to greater faith or a stumbling block to unbelief.

Then we'll learn to view God's sovereignty in light of His nature, His character, His Word, and His covenant, and we'll allow God to exercise His wonderful sovereignty in our lives. Next, we'll enter into a lifestyle of fellowship with Christ. Finally, we'll see that Jesus Christ is *the leader*, and that true spiritual leadership is allowing Jesus Christ to lead through us.

Let's continue in the next chapter by noting that building the kingdom of God is a supernatural commission. We'll find that we are completely dependent on God to build His kingdom.

Chapter 10

Participate in God's Supernatural Commission

> The kingdom of God does not come with observation;
> nor will they say, "See here!" or "See there!" For indeed,
> the kingdom of God is within you.
> Luke 17:20–21

We have seen that thirst is a prerequisite for the Holy Spirit to actively live within us and effectively minister in and through us. We noted that for streams of living water to flow from within us, we thirst, come to Jesus and drink, believe, and glorify the Lord Jesus Christ. Next in our quest to experience the living Christ and live in the presence of God, we'll turn our attention to the formation of the kingdom of God in ourselves and in other people.

Our second foundational truth is this: building the kingdom of God has always been—and will always be—the supernatural work of the Lord Jesus Christ through the Holy Spirit. We will identify our primary purpose as knowing and loving God and, through this intimacy, allow God to do His work in and through us. In this way, we fulfill the Great Commission: making disciples. Before we can make disciples, though, we must first become disciples ourselves. We'll realize that making disciples is a spiritual rather than a natural process. We'll stress the importance of proper motivation and the denial of our flesh in building God's kingdom. We'll discuss the biblical way of forming the kingdom of God within ourselves and in other people.

Jesus Emphasized the Supernatural Aspect
of His Kingdom

In our opening scripture, Jesus informed the inquiring Pharisees, "The kingdom of God does not come with observation; nor will they say, 'See here!' or 'See there!' For indeed, the kingdom of God is within you." He also emphasized the supernatural aspect of His kingdom when the Jewish rulers brought Him before Pilate, the Roman governor at the time, accusing Him of claiming to be the king of the Jews. They wanted Pilate to condemn Jesus to death because they lacked the authority to do so.

In his interrogation, Pilate asked Jesus if He was the king of the Jews. "Jesus answered, 'My kingdom is not of this world. If My kingdom were of this world, My servants would fight, so that I should not be delivered to the Jews; but now My kingdom is not from here.'"[1] In other words, if Jesus' kingdom was of this world, His followers would use worldly methods to build and defend it. Because His kingdom is not of this world, they do not.

Jesus continued to answer Pilate's question by saying, "You say rightly that I am a king. For this cause I was born, and for this cause I have come into the world, that I should bear witness to the truth. Everyone who is of the truth hears My voice."[2] To hear Jesus' voice is supernatural. No one can build the kingdom of God through natural or worldly means. The Lord Jesus Christ builds it by the power of the Holy Spirit. Paul informed the Corinthian believers, "The kingdom of God is not in word but in power."[3]

What, then, is mankind's part? Mankind's primary purpose is knowing and loving God. In this intimacy, God works through ordinary people. Anointed work for God is the work of God. He works through those who know Christ intimately. Jesus illustrated this intimacy by teaching His disciples: "I am the vine, you are the branches. He who abides in Me, and I in him, bears much fruit; for without Me you can do nothing."[4] This is the way that God builds the body of Christ.

The Lord Jesus Christ Builds His Church

Jesus said that He, not others, would build His church. He told Peter, "On this rock I will build My church."[5] We—all believers together—make up the church. Jesus' building the kingdom of God in each of us builds the

Participate in God's Supernatural Commission

church. Each believer is responsible for facilitating the formation of the kingdom of God within himself or herself and for contributing to its formation in fellow members of the body of Christ.

Mankind can build organizations and societies, but only Christ can build His church. The church began when the Holy Spirit came to live in believers at Pentecost and continues to grow in like manner today. Sophisticated advertising campaigns cannot build the kingdom of God, nor can conforming ourselves or our churches to the world. God has not changed. He has not discontinued, deemphasized, or reduced the work of the Lord in building His kingdom in individuals or in His church as a whole.

Mankind is dependent on God to add to the church. After Peter's address on the day of Pentecost, God added three thousand people to the church. Following this event, Luke states in the book of Acts that "the Lord added to the church daily those who were being saved."[6] Paul emphasized this fact when he corrected believers in Corinth for some of them following Paul and others following Apollos: "Who then is Paul, and who is Apollos, but ministers through whom you believed, as the Lord gave to each one? I planted, Apollos watered, but God gave the increase. So then neither he who plants is anything, nor he who waters, but God who gives the increase."[7] Indeed, only the Lord adds to the church.

Christ builds His church through us when we recognize our spiritual impoverishment. Our pride resists recognizing our impoverished state, but God cannot fully use us until we acknowledge it. The apostle Peter, bold in his own strength, boasted that even if all the others deserted the Lord, he would not do so and that he would even die for Him. Nevertheless, while the chief priests, the elders, and the scribes interrogated and tortured Jesus before His crucifixion, Peter denied knowing and following the Lord. As a result, he suffered the recognition of his spiritual impoverishment.

Just before His betrayal by Judas Iscariot, Jesus told His disciples that they would all stumble that night according to the Scriptures, but after He had been raised, He would precede them to Galilee. Matthew gives this account of Peter asserting his self-confidence in spite of Jesus' declaration to the contrary:

> Peter answered and said to Him, "Even if all are made to stumble because of You, I will never be made to stumble."

>Jesus said to him, "Assuredly, I say to you that this night, before the rooster crows, you will deny Me three times."
>
>Peter said to Him, "Even if I have to die with You, I will not deny You!"
>
>And so said all the disciples.[8]

That night, when the Jewish rulers arrested Jesus, His disciples fled. But Peter followed and watched as the religious leaders interrogated and tortured Jesus. While this was taking place, Peter denied knowing Jesus to a servant girl. Later he denied knowing Jesus to another girl. Then others accused Peter of being with Jesus. He cursed and firmly asserted a third time that he did not know Him. At that moment, a rooster crowed. Peter, realizing his denial of Christ, broke down and grieved intensely.

Even though Peter denied Christ three times, the Lord later used him to preach on the day of Pentecost, and three thousand people were added to the church in one day! Only after Peter was spiritually broken, faced his spiritual impoverishment, and was baptized in the Holy Spirit could God use him mightily. So it is with us.

Forming and Worshiping Golden Calves

Unfortunately, some Christians ignore their spiritual impoverishment. They proceed in building their personal lives or ministries with natural methods. In so doing, they form their "golden calves."

The Bible speaks of people who worshiped idols—images or statues made by craftsmen. At one time, even the children of Israel formed and worshiped a golden calf.

When Moses was on Mount Sinai receiving the Ten Commandments from God, he was delayed in returning. The children of Israel, not knowing if he would return, became impatient. Aaron, Moses' second in command, led them in forming and worshiping a golden calf. The book of Exodus states: "He received the gold from their hand, and he fashioned it with an engraving tool, and made a molded calf. Then they said, 'This is your god, O Israel, that brought you out of the land of Egypt!'"[9]

When Moses returned from being with God on Mount Sinai, he found the people worshiping this golden calf. He confronted Aaron, who responded: "Do not let the anger of my lord become hot. You know the people, that they are set on evil. For they said to me, 'Make us gods that shall go before us; as for this Moses, the man who brought us out of the land of Egypt, we do not know what has become of him.' And I said to them, 'Whoever has any gold, let them break it off.' So they gave it to me, and I cast it into the fire, and this calf came out."[10] Ridiculous! Yet we find ourselves doing the same thing.

The children of Israel made four mistakes: (1) they related to God through Moses rather than relating to God themselves, (2) they became impatient, (3) they relied on their natural wisdom and abilities, and (4) they focused on natural rather than spiritual provision. If we are not careful, we too may enter into idolatry through the same four mistakes: relying on people instead of God, becoming impatient, relying on our human wisdom and abilities, and focusing on natural provision instead of spiritual provision.

Relying on People Rather Than God Weakens Faith

The children of Israel had Moses interact with God for them. As a result, they trusted Moses instead of God. Not having a relationship with God, they credited Moses with bringing them out of Egypt, making him an idol. When they thought Moses would not return from Mount Sinai, they turned to another idol—a golden calf.

We need to relate to God ourselves, not through other people. We cannot rely on our pastor, our mother or father, our husband or wife, or anyone else to relate to God for us. We must personally interact with God, hearing and obeying Him through individual fellowship with Him.

Impatience Leads to Idolatry

Referring to the children of Israel, the book of Acts states, "They made a calf in those days, offered sacrifices to the idol, and rejoiced in the works of their own hands."[11] In contemporary Christianity, our idols are no longer golden calves fashioned by human craftsmen. They are opinions formed with human reasoning.

Just like the children of Israel, some believers today enter into idolatry through impatience. They enter through (1) not taking the time or making the effort to hear from God, (2) forming doctrines with human reasoning, and (3) attempting to achieve spiritual objectives in natural ways.

First, some believers don't take the time or make the effort to hear from God. Not having heard from God about a matter of concern to them, they feel that they cannot wait any longer. They think they must do something rather than nothing, so they make a decision and proceed in their human wisdom and abilities—without the direction and empowerment of the Lord. Still, if they succeed, they say, "Look what the Lord has done!"

Second, some believers, not having the enlightenment of the Holy Spirit, form doctrines with human reasoning. They may reason, knowingly or unknowingly, that God is no longer active as He was in the Bible, and they adjust their beliefs to compensate for God's inactivity in their lives and ministries. When they form their doctrines with human reasoning they form their golden calves.

Third, some Christians attempt to achieve spiritual objectives in natural ways. They pray and minister in accordance with their humanly determined doctrines. When they pray and minister according to their humanly devised doctrines, they worship their golden calves. Again, if they experience success, they say, "Look what the Lord has done!"

By forming our impatient doctrines and methods, we misrepresent our work as being God's work. We thereby degrade God to our earthly limitations. And we wonder why we don't experience the power of God in our lives and ministries!

Human Wisdom and Abilities Build Golden-Calf Lives and Ministries

Sometimes we ignore God in making personal and ministry decisions. We may even build our churches with our human abilities—a social church rather than the spiritual church of the Lord Jesus Christ, who is alive and active and has never changed. When we do, we build an external kingdom, even though the kingdom of God is internal.

Focusing on Natural Provision Leads to Idolatry

The children of Israel focused on natural rather than spiritual provision. While in the wilderness, they complained about God's supernatural supply of manna and longed to return to the natural provision of Egypt. In so doing, they distanced themselves from God and fell into idolatry.

Even today, individuals, churches, and ministries sometimes focus on natural provision: increase in number of dollars or number of followers, extension of influence, and increase of personal possessions or the size and appearance of physical facilities. When they emphasize natural provision over spiritual provision, they likewise distance themselves from God. Their diversion becomes an idol, which they worship by devotion of focus, time, and resources.

We therefore must be cautious not to divert our focus from objectives of the Spirit. We must guard against (1) emphasizing the increase in our number of followers at the expense of making disciples, (2) elevating the increase of our finances or facilities to a higher priority than winning the lost and maturing the saints, and (3) increasing our public acceptance by not preaching repentance and holiness.

Making Disciples Builds the Body of Christ

The Lord's church is not a nursery school perpetually catering to baby Christians, but a training ground for making disciples. Making disciples brings people into fellowship with God the Father, the Lord Jesus Christ, and other believers.

Paul informed the church at Ephesus that Jesus Christ gave apostles, prophets, evangelists, pastors, and teachers to equip believers for the work of the ministry, for the edifying of the body of Christ, until the whole body comes "to the unity of the faith and of the knowledge of the Son of God, to a perfect man, to the measure of the stature of the fullness of Christ."[12] Therefore, our spiritual success is measured by these four criteria: (1) unity of the faith between believers, (2) unity of the knowledge of the Son of God between the members of the body, (3) oneness of spiritual maturity (the word *perfect* means "mature"), and (4) formation of the full stature of Christ in individuals and in the body as a whole.

Unity of the faith, however, is more than mental agreement, outward conformity, or the absence of expressed strife. Unity of the knowledge of the Son of God is more than agreement on biblical facts about Jesus. Oneness of spiritual maturity is more than individual spiritual growth. The measure of the full stature of Christ is deeper than outward conduct.

Unity of the faith is the knitting together of the hearts of the members of the body of Christ by the Holy Spirit. Unity of the knowledge of the Son of God is participation together in intimate fellowship with Christ. Oneness of spiritual maturity is the body of Christ growing into one mature, supernatural spirit-being. And the measure of the full stature of Christ includes all inner attitudes and motivations, and the formation of the genuine compassion of Christ within the believer, as well as outward conduct.

Unity of the faith, unity of intimate fellowship with the Son of God, oneness of spiritual maturity, and Christlikeness form the mature body of Christ, out of which comes numerical growth. Increasing the body of Christ numerically without first establishing this unity, oneness, intimate fellowship, and Christlikeness within its members builds a weak body without the bonding of true spiritual maturity. Such numerical growth without spiritual maturity, sooner or later, produces strife and division in the body of Christ.

Again, our objective in every Christian endeavor should be to become a companion and participant with Christ as Jesus was with the Father. We noted in the last chapter that Paul exhorted the Corinthian believers that "God is faithful (reliable, trustworthy, and therefore ever true to His promise, and He can be depended on); by Him you were called into companionship and participation with His Son, Jesus Christ our Lord."[13] Jesus said only what He heard the Father say, and He did only what He saw the Father do. In like manner, our being companions and participants with Christ begins with being intimate with Him and continues with hearing and obeying His instructions.

Our lives and ministries should be more like Moses' and less like Aaron's. To maintain our spiritual focus, our motivation should be pure before God.

Shun Worldly Motivation

In the Garden of Eden, when Eve "saw that the tree was good for food, that it was pleasant to the eyes, and a tree desirable to make one wise, she took of its fruit and ate. She also gave to her husband with her, and he ate."[14] Unfortunately, this same motivation is still causing Christians to fall today. Too many believers are motivated by their own natural needs and desires and disregard what the Lord Jesus Christ wants to do within and through them by the inner working of the Holy Spirit.

As Christians, what is our motivation for desiring the things of God? Is our motivation to feel good (the lust of the flesh), to look good (the lust of the eyes), or to appear wise in spiritual things (the pride of life)? What is our motivation when we go to church services? Do we desire to hear the preaching of the Word because it is entertaining, makes us feel good, or makes us appear spiritual?

As Christian leaders, what is our motivation for desiring success? Is it to increase the number of followers or to increase finances (the lust of the flesh), to build greater facilities (the lust of the eyes), or to appear successful (the pride of life)?

Are we motivated by our fallen nature or by our new nature? To be truly successful, we must have the right motivation.

Resist the Motivation of the World

The apostle John admonished believers: "Do not love the world or the things in the world. The love of the Father is not in those who love the world; for all that is in the world—the desire of the flesh, the desire of the eyes, the pride in riches—comes not from the Father but from the world. And the world and its desire are passing away, but those who do the will of God live forever."[15] James took John's admonishment one step further, strongly warning the early church: "You adulterous people, don't you know that friendship with the world is hatred toward God? Anyone who chooses to be a friend of the world becomes an enemy of God. Or do you think Scripture says without reason that the spirit he caused to live in us envies intensely? But he gives us more grace. That is why Scripture says: 'God opposes the proud but gives grace to the humble.'"[16]

Unfavorable Circumstances Reveal Our True Motivation

Our true motivation, the motivation of the heart, may only be revealed in unfavorable circumstances because our heart usually conceals it. The prophet Jeremiah proclaimed this truth: "The heart is deceitful above all things, and it is exceedingly perverse and corrupt and severely, morally sick! Who can know it [perceive, understand, be acquainted with his own heart and mind]? I the Lord search the mind, I try the heart, even to give to every man according to his ways, according to the fruit of his doings."[17]

Our true motivation is revealed in our innermost attitudes toward those who have mistreated us or the people we love. David, who was greatly mistreated, prayed, "Search me, O God, and know my heart; try me, and know my anxieties; and see if there is any wicked way in me, and lead me in the way everlasting."[18]

We know our motivation is pure when someone else's well-being is more important to us than our comfort or when someone else's eternal judgment is more important to us than our well-being. Few reach this purity of motivation, but it's a worthy goal.

Our self-nature is probably behind more of our motivation than we realize. But how do we change? We change by spending time with the Lord Jesus Christ. As He increases within us, the influence of our self-nature decreases. Jesus declared, "If anyone desires to come after Me, let him deny himself, take up his cross, and follow Me."[19]

Denying Self and Taking Up Our Cross

As God glorified Jesus because of His crucifixion, our pathway to spiritual effectiveness is the path of the crucified life. By the mind of Christ, we humble ourselves, take the form of a bond servant, and become uncompromisingly obedient to God.

The power of Christ is available to us through crucifying our flesh nature—our self-life. Paul implored the church at Philippi: "Let this mind be in you which was also in Christ Jesus, who, being in the form of God, did not consider it robbery to be equal with God, but made Himself of no reputation, taking the form of a bond servant, and coming in the likeness of men. And being found in appearance as a man, He humbled Himself and became obedient to the point of death, even the death of the cross."[20]

Humbling ourselves, taking the form of a bond servant, and becoming uncompromisingly obedient to God show the mind of Christ formed within us. God offers to form the mind of Christ in us, but we must submit to the inner working of His Spirit to receive and maintain it.

Each time we encounter an unfavorable occurrence in our lives, God offers us an opportunity to let Him form the mind of Christ Jesus within us. We receive and embrace the mind of Christ by choosing to respond to unfavorable events and mistreatment by others in a Christlike manner.

Determination of the flesh—self-discipline—cannot form the mind of Christ. The working of the Holy Spirit forges the mind of Christ within us.

Jesus told His disciples that He would suffer many things, be killed, and would be raised from the dead on the third day. Peter, being naturally minded, rebuked Him, saying this would never happen. Jesus scolded him: "Get behind Me, Satan! You are an offense to Me, for you are not mindful of the things of God, but the things of men."[21] He then told His disciples that those who want to come after Him must deny themselves, take up their cross, and follow Him.

To take up our cross is to disregard our own self-interest and be faithful and obedient to God regardless of the consequences. Jesus, sentenced to death and obedient to God, carried His cross to Golgotha, and in so doing, He carried out His death sentence. To follow Jesus, we consider our self-nature dead, deny its life and power, and are made alive instead by the Holy Spirit.

Building the Body of Christ

Having dealt with our own spiritual growth, let's turn our attention to making our contribution to the spiritual growth of other people. We build the body of Christ by first abiding in Christ ourselves. Jesus taught that He is the true vine and we are the branches. If He lives in us and we live in Him, we'll bear much fruit. Without Him, we can do nothing. We are merely fruit-bearing branches of the true vine. Christ builds His church through us, His branches. As He began building His church through His disciples on the day of Pentecost, the Lord continues to build the body of Christ through us today by our waiting on God in unity, exalting Christ crucified, and calling all to repentance.

Waiting on God in Unity

We prepare for God to add to the church by waiting on Him in unity. After His resurrection from the dead, Jesus appeared to His disciples many times, proving that He was alive and teaching them about the kingdom of God. Just before He ascended into heaven, Jesus strictly commanded His disciples to wait to be empowered by the Holy Spirit. Luke records in the book of Acts, "Being assembled together with them, He commanded them not to depart from Jerusalem, but to wait for the Promise of the Father, 'which,' He said, 'you have heard from Me; for John truly baptized with water, but you shall be baptized with the Holy Spirit not many days from now.'"[22]

On the day of Pentecost, Christ birthed the church by adding three thousand people in one day through followers who waited to receive God's power in unity. Christ has not changed. Today He continues to build His church in like manner, through unified, Holy Spirit–empowered believers.

Exalting Christ Crucified

The second part of building the body of Christ is exalting Christ crucified. On the day of Pentecost, after Jesus' followers had waited in unity, the sound of a mighty, rushing wind came into the house where they were waiting. Tongues like fire parted and came to rest on each person; they were all filled with the Holy Spirit, and they all began to speak in tongues, foreign languages that they did not know. The commotion was so great that a crowd assembled outside, wondering what was happening. People from many nations heard these uneducated, unsophisticated followers of Jesus praising God in the crowd's native languages. Peter then exalted Christ crucified when he addressed those who had gathered, saying:

> Men of Israel, hear these words: Jesus of Nazareth, a Man attested by God to you by miracles, wonders, and signs which God did through Him in your midst, as you yourselves also know—Him, being delivered by the determined purpose and foreknowledge of God, you have taken by lawless hands, have crucified, and put to death; whom God raised up, having loosed the pains of death, because it was not possible that He should be held by it. For David says concerning Him: "I foresaw the Lord always before my face, for He is at my right hand, that I may not be shaken."
>
> . . . He, foreseeing this, spoke concerning the resurrection of the Christ, that His soul was not left in Hades, nor did His flesh see corruption. This Jesus God has raised up, of which we are all witnesses. Therefore being exalted

to the right hand of God, and having received from the Father the promise of the Holy Spirit, He poured out this which you now see and hear.[23]

In his epistles, the apostle Paul emphasized the importance of relying on the Holy Spirit rather than on natural knowledge or abilities when preaching God's Word. He candidly wrote to the Corinthian church: "And I, brethren, when I came to you, did not come with excellence of speech or of wisdom declaring to you the testimony of God. For I determined not to know anything among you except Jesus Christ and Him crucified. I was with you in weakness, in fear, and in much trembling. And my speech and my preaching were not with persuasive words of human wisdom, but in demonstration of the Spirit and of power, that your faith should not be in the wisdom of men but in the power of God."[24]

Paul was well qualified to use "persuasive words of human wisdom." He was a former Pharisee, a former member of the Jewish religious elite. Educated by one of the foremost religious educators of his time, a man named Gamaliel, Paul confounded the Jews in Damascus by proving Jesus was the Messiah.

Instead of demonstrating his religious knowledge and persuasive ability, Paul chose to humble himself to make way for the demonstration of the Spirit and power of God. How many of us are willing to sacrifice our pride as Paul did—being in weakness, in fear, and in much trembling—so that the Word of God spoken through us will demonstrate the Spirit and power of God?

Calling All to Repentance

The third part of building Christ's church is calling all to repentance. When the crowd heard Peter's message that God had made Jesus, whom they had crucified, Lord and Christ, they were convicted in their hearts and asked what they should do. Peter instructed them: "Repent, and let every one of you be baptized in the name of Jesus Christ for the remission of sins; and you shall receive the gift of the Holy Spirit."[25]

Some Christians today lack the boldness to call all to repentance. For fear of offending people, some believers employ worldly methods in an attempt to draw people to the Lord. They fail to realize that building Christ's church is a supernatural commission.

Admonition to Participate in God's Supernatural Commission

Accept the Lord's supernatural commission. Become intimate with God so He may do His work in and through you. Rely on Jesus Christ to build His church. Abandon formulas to advance the kingdom of God. Come into the unity of the faith by knitting your heart together with those of the other members of the body of Christ. Become one mature, supernatural spirit-being with the other members of the body. Participate with other believers in intimate fellowship with Christ. Allow God to form the measure of the full stature of Christ in your inner attitudes and motivations and to form the genuine compassion of Christ within you. Make your motivation the compassion of Christ. Follow the path of the crucified life into spiritual maturity and spiritual effectiveness. Wait on the Lord; exalt Christ crucified; call all to repentance.

Pray to Supernaturally Build the Kingdom of God

Father, please forgive me for trying to build Your kingdom without being completely dependent on You. Forgive me for trying to build the body of Christ in my own strength. Forgive me for being unduly motivated to increase the number of followers, number of dollars, size and appearance of facilities, and span of influence. Please forgive me for the many times that I failed to allow You to form the mind of Christ within me by my inappropriate responses to unkind people and negative circumstances. Please forgive me for not disregarding my own self-interest and being faithful and obedient to You regardless of the consequences.

Please, Father, empower me by Your Holy Spirit to be completely dependent upon You and to allow You to do Your work in and through me rather than my trying to work for You in the way I think is best. Please bring me into the unity of the faith by knitting my heart together with the other members of the body of Christ. Form me into one mature, supernatural spirit-being with the other members of the body. Draw me into intimate fellowship with Christ, together with other believers. Forge in me the

Participate in God's Supernatural Commission

---

measure of the full stature of Christ in my inner attitudes and motivations, and form the genuine compassion of Christ within me.

I desire to be motivated by the compassion of Jesus Christ. I want to let You form the mind of Christ within me every time I'm faced with mistreatment and unfavorable situations. Please empower me to carry out Your death sentence on my self-life in Christ Jesus. Please prepare me to supernaturally build the kingdom of God. All this I ask, not only for my own spiritual growth, but also that our Lord Jesus Christ, in whose name I pray, may be glorified and exalted in and through me. Amen.

Where Do We Go from Here?

We have established that building the kingdom of God is a supernatural work that mankind cannot accomplish in its own power. Only Christ can build His church. Now we will turn our attention to two essential elements through which Christ empowers mankind for His service: grace and peace. We will see that we receive revelation in inner peace and carry out that revelation through God's power of grace.

Chapter 11

Receive Revelation through Grace in Peace

Grace to you and peace from God our Father and the Lord Jesus Christ.
Romans 1:7

We have recognized that building the kingdom of God is a supernatural commission. Christ has not changed. He still builds His church through disciples who wait on God in unity, exalt Christ crucified, and call all to repentance. We will now turn our attention to two supernatural gifts, grace and peace, through which Christ builds His church.

Our third foundational truth through which we experience the living Christ and live in the presence of God is this: we receive revelation through grace in peace. We will see how grace and peace form the foundation of spiritual effectiveness. We'll learn how inner peace is essential to hearing God's voice. And we'll discover that grace is the empowerment of God to live righteously and accomplish God's will.

Grace and peace give us supernatural spiritual perception of the Word of God, empower our faith in God, and form the foundation for our living supernatural Christian lives. They are two indispensable elements in successfully living the supernatural Christian life.

Paul began many of his books in the Bible by pronouncing grace and peace. Each pronouncement was not just a greeting, but a profound, purposeful prayer. Paul generally opened his letters with an impartation similar to this one in our opening scripture: "Grace to you and peace from God our Father and the Lord Jesus Christ."

Paul's written impartation of grace and peace prepared his readers to receive God's spiritual insight contained in his letters. Many of the revelations in Paul's letters exceeded the capacity of the natural mind to understand, because the things of God are spiritually discerned. The apostle Peter even wrote this to believers concerning Paul: "His letters contain some things that are hard to understand."[1]

Other people in the Bible imparted peace. Jesus imparted peace to His disciples, saying, "Peace I leave with you, My peace I give to you; not as the world gives do I give to you. Let not your heart be troubled, neither let it be afraid."[2]

Jesus also instructed His followers to impart their peace. One time He sent out seventy followers to go into many villages and heal the sick. They were to take no provisions with them and had no arrangements for where they would stay overnight. He told them that they would know the home in which they should stay in this way: "Whatever house you enter, first say, 'Peace to this house.' And if a son of peace is there, your peace will rest on it; if not, it will return to you. And remain in the same house, eating and drinking such things as they give."[3] From Paul's and Jesus' pronouncements of grace and peace, we see that grace and peace can be imparted by both the written and spoken word.

Peace Is Essential to the Christian Life

Peace is so essential to the Christian life that the Bible urges believers to earnestly seek peace within themselves and with other people. Peace opens people to spiritual change and produces righteousness, contentment, and assurance of salvation.

Peace Opens People to Profound Spiritual Change

When we speak of peace, we are speaking of spiritual peace within and between believers; we are not speaking of external circumstantial peace. This inner peace forms the environment in which revelation flows. Without it, we are too clamorous inside to notice the still, small voice of the Lord. There are at least two clear examples in the Bible where revelation came through peace. One example is when the Lord Jesus Christ confronted Saul, who was later called Paul, on the road to Damascus. At the time, Saul was traveling to the city of Damascus to arrest Christians and bring them to Jerusalem to be imprisoned. A bright light shined around him, and he fell to the ground blinded. The Lord asked Saul why he was persecuting Him and then told him to go to Damascus, where he would be told what to do.

Saul, waiting in Damascus, did not eat or drink for three days. Quieted by this Damascus road experience, Saul received direction from the Lord that radically changed his life. He immediately stopped persecuting the church, converted to Christianity, and became one of the great new covenant Christian leaders.

A second example of revelation coming through peace is when Peter had the revelation that the gospel could be preached to the Gentiles, people who were not Jews. One day Peter, while staying at the house of Simon the tanner, went up on the roof to pray. During this time, he fell into a trance and had a vision. While Peter was wondering what this vision meant, the Holy Spirit told him that three men were coming to the house where he was and that he should go with them. At that time, the men sent by a Gentile named Cornelius arrived. They asked Peter to return with them to Cornelius's house and speak to his household. Ordinarily, Jews would not go to a Gentile's home, because Jews considered Gentiles unclean.

As the result of this revelation, Peter did go to Cornelius's house. There the Holy Spirit fell on Cornelius's household as Peter was speaking. The leaders in the church then realized that God wanted the gospel preached to the Gentiles as well as to the Jews so that they too might be saved. When Peter heard the Holy Spirit in his time of quietness on Simon's roof and obeyed, God used him to open the preaching of the gospel to the Gentiles.

Peace Produces Righteousness, Contentment, and Assurance of Salvation

Righteousness comes out of peace. The apostle James taught the early Christians, "The fruit of righteousness is sown in peace by those who make peace."[4] This scripture in the Amplified Bible is a little difficult to follow, but the additional insight is well worth the effort. It reads, "The harvest of righteousness (of conformity to God's will in thought and deed) is [the fruit of the seed] sown in peace by those who work for and make peace [in themselves and in others, that peace which means concord, agreement, and harmony between individuals, with undisturbedness, in a peaceful mind free from fears and agitating passions and moral conflicts]."

Paul taught the Philippian believers that peace produces contentment and assurance of salvation among Christians: "God's peace [shall be yours, that tranquil state of a soul assured of its salvation through Christ, and so fearing nothing from God and being content with its earthly lot of whatever sort that is, that peace] which transcends all understanding shall garrison and mount guard over your hearts and minds in Christ Jesus."[5] Accordingly, peace not only gives us contentment and assurance of salvation, but it also protects our hearts and minds. Peace is essential, then, to Solomon's advice to his son: "Above all else, guard your heart, for it is the wellspring of life."[6]

The Bible Urges Us to Earnestly Pursue Peace

The apostle Peter instructed believers to actively seek peace with these words: "Let him search for peace (harmony; undisturbedness from fears, agitating passions, and moral conflicts) and seek it eagerly. [Do not merely desire peaceful relations with God, with your fellowmen, and with yourself, but pursue, go after them!]"[7]

We are to keep peace with other people as much as it depends on us. The writer of the book of Hebrews admonished believers, "Make every effort to live in peace with all men and to be holy; without holiness no one will see the Lord."[8] Paul listed peace as a fruit of the Spirit in Galatians 5:22. He also exhorted the Ephesian church: "Be completely humble and gentle; be patient, bearing with one another in love. Make every effort to keep the unity of the Spirit through the bond of peace."[9] The Amplified Bible offers this valuable additional insight: "Be eager and strive earnestly to guard and keep the harmony and oneness of [and produced by] the Spirit in the binding power of peace." Indeed, the body of Christ comes together as one through peace.

Unfortunately, living with inner peace seems to be a lost practice in much of contemporary Christianity. Many Christians are so busy that they do not regularly hear the voice of the Lord. Yet Jesus said that His sheep hear and listen to His voice. We cannot consistently hear the voice of the

Lord without living in peace, and we cannot receive ongoing revelation without hearing the voice of the Lord.

We can't achieve inner peace in our own strength. We receive inner peace through the empowerment of grace.

Grace Is the Empowerment of God

Grace, commonly defined as "unmerited favor," is also much more. Grace is the supernatural empowerment that God gives to believers that enables them to will and to do His good pleasure. It is the God-given intangible power that enables believers to overcome the difficulties or hardships that frequently hinder a God-given task or mission. Grace does not remove the need for diligence, dedication, determination, or sacrifice; neither does it necessarily remove the obstacles to successful completion of a God-given task. It does, however, produce supernatural ability to trust God, to endure hardship, to believe, to persevere, and to overcome obstacles, difficulties, and hardships.

Grace is active, not passive. It is strong, not weak. Indeed, grace is power. Grace empowers all miracles. Apart from grace, there would be no supernatural phenomena of God.

Grace is undeserved; it cannot be earned. If it were earned, it would not be grace. Grace may operate independently from human effort or in conjunction with human effort.

Unless grace is in operation, people are only performing works, because grace and works are mutually exclusive. Paul taught the church at Rome: "If by grace, then it is no longer of works; otherwise grace is no longer grace. But if it is of works, it is no longer grace; otherwise work is no longer work."[10]

Grace is a manner in which God makes His power, perseverance, and ability available to those who believe. Paul wrote to believers in Corinth, saying, "I thank my God at all times for you because of the grace (the favor and spiritual blessing) of God which was bestowed on you in Christ Jesus, [so] that in Him in every respect you were enriched, in full power and readiness of speech [to speak of your faith] and complete knowledge and illumination [to give you full insight into its meaning]."[11] He then continued, "You are not [consciously] falling behind or lacking in any special spiritual endowment or Christian grace [the reception of which is due to the power of divine grace operating in your souls by the Holy Spirit]."[12]

God made Paul a minister by His gift of grace and the exercise of His power. Paul wrote to the church at Ephesus, "Of this [Gospel] I was made a minister according to the gift of God's free grace (undeserved favor) which was bestowed on me by the exercise (the working in all its effectiveness) of His power."[13]

Grace is an indispensable, continuing, active, divine force in our everyday Christian lives. It is the ongoing, enabling empowerment of God.

What Grace Is Not

Now that we understand what grace is, we'll take a look at what grace is not. Grace is not (1) a one-time occurrence, (2) an excuse for spiritual laziness, (3) unlimited pardon or amnesty, (4) love, forgiveness, patience, or long-suffering, or (5) a measurement of spiritual maturity.

First, grace is not a power by which God set things in motion and then stepped back to see what would happen. It was not a one-time occurrence that God used to establish His church. Nor is it a one-time empowerment granting an individual salvation, then leaving him or her to continue without it.

Grace is also not an excuse for spiritual laziness. It does not short-circuit God's requirements. Grace does not displace a person's effort but magnifies that effort through submission to God.

Then third, grace is not unlimited pardon or amnesty. God's forgiveness and salvation are attained through grace. Grace does not, however, release us from individual or group accountability to God or to fellow believers. Grace does not release us from the consequences of known, unconfessed sin. In other words, we should not presume, on the basis of grace, that God will work in our lives and ministries if we willfully disregard our wrongdoing, wrong motives, or wrong attitudes.

Fourth, grace is not love, forgiveness, patience, or long-suffering, although it is the gateway to God's love, forgiveness, patience, and long-suffering toward us. Receiving more grace does not mean God loves, forgives, has more patience, or is more long-suffering toward one individual than toward another.

And fifth, grace is not a measure of spiritual maturity. God grants His grace without direct or inverse relationship to spiritual maturity. Let's look deeper into the working of grace.

Grace Enables the Believer in Christ to Walk by Faith

Having focused on what grace is and also what it is not, let's look at four essential aspects of grace: (1) salvation comes by grace, (2) grace works through surrender and submission, (3) God gives grace in differing measures, and (4) grace does not abandon us to our own abilities.

Salvation Comes by Grace

Grace is the means by which God provides salvation through the atonement of Jesus Christ. God's grace is a gift; it cannot be earned. We are saved by grace through faith, not saved by faith alone. Without grace, there can be no faith. Paul taught the Ephesian church:

> It is by free grace (God's unmerited favor) that you are saved (delivered from judgment and made partakers of Christ's salvation) through [your] faith. And this [salvation] is not of yourselves [of your own doing, it came not through your own striving], but is the gift of God; not because of works [not the fulfillment of the Law's demands], lest any man should boast. [It is not the result of what anyone can possibly do, so no one can pride himself in it or take glory to himself.][14]

Grace Works through Surrender and Submission

Grace enables mankind's surrender to God yet operates strongly through people surrendered to God. It is inseparably linked to submission to God's will. By surrendering to God, believers give Him the authority to release His power of grace into their lives to accomplish His will.

Grace is indispensable to willing and doing all that God would have us to will and to do. This does not mean that if we are not in God's will, then we are not under grace. It means that grace only produces God's will. It operates according to His pleasure and His purpose. People cannot initiate or manipulate it.

God Gives Grace in Differing Measures

Grace comes through surrender and submission, but God also gives people grace in differing measures for other reasons. Grace can be associated with a specific calling or assignment. It may be associated with a gift: apostle, prophet, evangelist, pastor, teacher, working of miracles, gifts of healings, helps, administrations, varieties of tongues, prophesying, serving, encouraging, giving, leading, or governing (Eph. 4:11; Rom. 12:6–8; 1 Cor. 12:28). God extends grace to all believers for receiving salvation, walking in the Spirit, and growing into spiritual maturity. Paul taught the Ephesian church, "Grace (God's unmerited favor) was given to each of us individually [not indiscriminately, but in different ways] in proportion to the measure of Christ's [rich and bounteous] gift."[15]

It may appear that God grants more grace to new believers than to older believers. More likely, God's grace changes in character and application as believers proceed in their spiritual development. God rightfully expects progress in the spiritual growth of His saints over time and changes the type or application of grace according to His expectations.

Grace Does Not Abandon Us to Our Own Abilities

Grace never abandons earnest believers to do the best that they can on their own. Paul informed the Corinthian church that he had been given a thorn in the flesh—a messenger of Satan—to keep him from becoming proud because of the extraordinary revelations God was giving him. After he asked God to take this messenger of Satan away three times, God told him, "My grace is sufficient for you, for my power is made perfect in weakness."[16]

When God said, "My grace is sufficient," does it mean the messenger of Satan could not be defeated? Does it mean that God left Paul to deal with this messenger of Satan by his own natural strength and abilities? Does "My grace is sufficient" mean that Paul was to allow this messenger of Satan to control him? Most certainly not! Paul did not have to deal with this messenger of Satan in his own strength any more than he had to achieve his salvation through his own strength.

Paul told the Corinthian church, "Three times I pleaded with the Lord to take it away from me."[17] He was looking for the Lord to come and take the messenger of Satan away from him. Instead, God told him that His grace, which was resident within him, was sufficient to contend with this messenger of Satan.

This is not bad news; this is good news! God had already given Paul the power of grace that was more than enough to resist the messenger of Satan. Paul did not need God's help from without, because he already had God's power to overcome within him. He informed the Philippian church, "I have strength for all things in Christ Who empowers me [I am ready for anything and equal to anything through Him Who infuses inner strength into me; I am self-sufficient in Christ's sufficiency]."[18]

Learning to Rely on Grace and Peace

The impartation of grace and peace that we receive from God is directly related to the Sabbath rest of God. The old covenant required the Jews to rest the entire seventh day of every week—the Sabbath day. On that day, they were forbidden to do any work at all. The writer of the book of Hebrews admonished new covenant believers:

> There is still awaiting a full and complete Sabbath-rest reserved for the [true] people of God; for he who has once entered [God's] rest also has ceased from [the weariness and pain] of human labors, just as God rested from those labors peculiarly His own. Let us therefore be zealous and exert ourselves and strive diligently to enter that rest [of God, to know and experience it for ourselves], that no one may fall or perish by the same kind of unbelief and disobedience [into which those in the wilderness fell].[19]

We should therefore be diligent to enter into the rest of God. Not entering into God's rest opens us to the danger of falling into unbelief and disobedience. Entering God's rest is therefore imperative for all believers. Under the new covenant, we enter God's rest, a state of not exerting human labor, through grace-empowered effort. Grace empowers effort, or else effort becomes works; peace enables rest.

Implementing God's principles in our lives requires effort on our part, but not struggle. The difference between effort and struggle is that effort is empowered by grace and struggle is empowered by the flesh. The empowerment of grace makes struggle unnecessary. Jesus offers to give us rest. He proclaimed: "Come to Me, all you who labor and are heavy laden, and I will give you rest. Take My yoke upon you and learn from Me, for I am gentle and lowly in heart, and you will find rest for your souls."[20]

If we are struggling to implement God's principles in our lives, we are operating in the flesh rather than in the Spirit of God. We have not entered into God's rest. We need to spend time quietly in God's presence to know the works that He prepared ahead of time for us to do (Eph. 2:10) and to prepare us to do His works in His power. In this way, God works through us in prayer and ministry by faith.

Faith Normally Comes by Grace in Peace

As believers in Christ, our duty is to seek God in quietness (wait upon God), to hear the Lord's voice, and to obey Him. Our actions of obedience require effort that is exerted in the power of His grace, not in the strength of our flesh.

Peace is the environment in which revelation, supernatural enlightenment from God, flows; grace is the force that activates revelation as faith. Faith is the trust, reliance, confidence, and assurance that come out of intimate fellowship with God through the Lord Jesus Christ—personal revelation of God as Father and Jesus as Savior and Lord. We'll take a close look at faith in the next chapter.

Admonition to Receive Revelation through Grace in Peace

Enter into the environment in which God's revelation flows by waiting quietly on the Lord to receive His peace. Read Paul's epistles, taking a moment to receive his impartation of grace and peace to experience greater revelation from his teaching. Earnestly pursue inner peace and peace with other people. Receive spiritual change, righteousness, contentment, and assurance of salvation through peace.

Rely on the power of grace that God has placed within you, and surrender to its powerful, life-changing work. Look to the power of grace within you to meet your own needs and to help meet the needs of other people around you.

Pray to Receive Revelation through Grace and Peace

Father, I thank You for Your grace and peace. Please enable me to spend time quietly waiting before You. Please lead me into Your inner peace that enables me to receive Your revelation. Help me to earnestly pursue inner peace and peace with other people. I desire to receive spiritual change, righteousness, contentment, and assurance of salvation through Your peace.

I want to surrender to the powerful, life-changing work of Your grace within me. Please open the eyes of my understanding so that I may know the power of grace that You have placed within me. Thank You that Your grace does not leave me alone to solve my problems with my own abilities. Please teach me to look to Your power of grace within me to meet my own needs and to help meet the needs of people around me. All this I ask, not only for my own spiritual development, but also that our Lord Jesus Christ, in whose name I pray, may be glorified and exalted in and through me. Amen.

Where Do We Go from Here?

We have seen that peace is the environment in which revelation flows and that grace is the force that activates revelation as faith. Next, we will see that faith is giving Christ preeminence. It is the God-given ability to believe Him beyond our natural comprehension. Faith is giving Christ preeminence. It is based in surrender, comes from the heart, works by love, is activated by obedience, and produces supernatural change. The measure of our faith is the measure of the rule of Christ within us.

Chapter 12

Give Christ Preeminence

> I have been crucified with Christ; it is no longer I who live, but Christ lives in me; and the life which I now live in the flesh I live by faith in the Son of God, who loved me and gave Himself for me.
> Galatians 2:20

We have seen that grace and peace are essential for living a supernatural Christian life. They provide the receptivity and empowerment for the Christian to walk by faith. Peace provides the atmosphere in which believers receive revelation, and grace produces the power to enact revelation received in peace. Now that we understand the role of grace and peace in our spiritual lives, we are ready to turn our attention to the next foundational truth that enables us to experience the living Christ and live in the presence of God.

This is our fourth foundational truth: faith is giving Christ preeminence. We will see that God is the source of our faith and that faith exceeds natural understanding. We'll also find that faith comes from the heart, works by love, and is activated by obedience. We'll discover that specific faith begins with knowing the revealed will of God, that faith produces supernatural change, and that strong new covenant faith is knowing Christ personally. We'll find that great faith recognizes and submits to the authority of the Lord Jesus Christ and that Christ's rule within us is the measure of our faith.

In preparation for our study of faith, let's review a few key points from previous chapters. We know that Adam and Eve originally communed directly with God. But they separated themselves and all their descendants from Him when they ate the forbidden fruit of the tree of the knowledge of good and evil. God later sent His Son Jesus Christ as the only sacrifice worthy to bring mankind back into fellowship with Him.

We know that human beings are made of spirit, soul, and body. The human spirit and soul are eternal, and the body is temporal. People relate to the realm of God's presence with the heart, and they relate to the world with the mind. Faith, being of the supernatural realm, is not known naturally with the mind but is discerned spiritually with the heart.

We have recognized the importance of knowing Christ as He really is—in His supernatural dimension as well as in His natural dimension. We have also seen that the new covenant brings the spirit-being of believers together with the Spirit-being of Christ. Faith in Christ is the means by which God brings these two supernatural beings together.

According to the new covenant, all our provision from God is in Christ. Therefore, whatever we seek from God, we seek through faith in Christ. God provides all our needs—healing, deliverance, provision, protection, or anything else—by faith in Christ. All these needs are met in the person of Jesus Christ because they are the very essence, or nature, of Christ. As we concluded in chapter 8, we cannot separate Christ from His blessings, His atonement, His promises, His anointing, or His authority. The more we experience the person of Christ, the more we will experience these aspects of Christ.

We can therefore say that the role of faith is to allow Christ full preeminence in our hearts so that He lives within us and freely expresses Himself through us. Paul put it this way: "I have been crucified with Christ; it is no longer I who live, but Christ lives in me; and the life which I now live in the flesh I live by faith in the Son of God, who loved me and gave Himself for me."[1] The role of faith is to establish the preeminence of Christ in us so fully that His very nature shines through us without restriction and He can do whatever He pleases in and through us at any time.

Since the role of faith is to allow the preeminence of Christ in our hearts, the objective of faith is to achieve unconditional surrender to the Lord Jesus Christ, allowing Him free expression in and through us at all times. This faith cannot be attained by human effort. It is a gift from God.

God Is the Source of Our Faith

Faith originates with God. Paul informed the church in Rome, "God has dealt to each one a measure of faith."[2] Faith is an intangible gift from God that enables us to believe in Him as He reveals Himself to us in His Word and by His Spirit.

Preparing mankind to receive faith is the work of the Holy Spirit. Paul prayed for church at Ephesus "that He [God] would grant you, according to the riches of His glory, to be strengthened with might through His Spirit in the inner man, that Christ may dwell in your hearts through faith."[3] Our source of faith is God the Father. Our preparation to receive faith is the work of the Holy Spirit. And the development and completion of our faith is the work of the Lord Jesus Christ. The writer of Hebrews identified Jesus as "the author and finisher of our faith."[4]

Faith cannot be obtained or increased through the work of the flesh; it comes by hearing. Paul revealed how faith comes in his letter to the church at Rome: "Faith comes by hearing [what is told], and what is heard comes by the preaching [of the message that came from the lips] of Christ (the Messiah Himself)."[5] Faith comes by *spiritually* hearing *Spirit-empowered* words from Christ with *spiritual* ears. Faith, being supernatural, surpasses our natural understanding.

Faith Exceeds Natural Understanding

Faith exceeds our natural understanding. We cannot understand or exercise faith through our natural minds. Instead, we comprehend faith through the illumination of the Holy Spirit and experience faith through trust in an unseen supernatural being—the Lord Jesus Christ. Solomon gave us wise counsel when he exhorted his son, "Trust in the Lord with all your heart, and lean not on your own understanding; in all your ways acknowledge Him, and He shall direct your paths."[6]

When we rely on our natural understanding, we tend to pray for results that are not clearly identifiable and measurable. We retreat into areas of faith where results are more naturally attainable. Some Christians, reluctant to pray for supernatural healing, will pray for the doctors to have wisdom instead. The answer to the prayer for supernatural healing is truly extraordinary. The answer to the prayer for the doctors to have wisdom is not so extraordinary.

It's time for us to stop relying on our limited understanding. It's time to begin trusting in the Lord with all our heart beyond the limitations of our natural intellect.

Faith Comes from the Heart

Our faith is predominantly heart-based or mind-based, relationship-based or knowledge-based. We cannot truly believe in God without knowledge; neither can we truly believe in God based on knowledge alone. Knowledge of the Word reveals the promises that we can believe for; Jesus Christ is the one we believe in.

Building faith is cooperating with the author and finisher of our faith, Jesus Christ our Lord. Growing in faith is an activity of the Spirit, not of the flesh. Developing faith is far different from developing the intellect. Trying to build faith through the intellect is futile because the quickening of the Spirit, not the retention of facts, produces faith. For example, people can hear the message of salvation repeatedly, but they cannot receive salvation unless the message is quickened to them by the Holy Spirit. Accordingly, many people today know a lot about God but have little or no faith in God.

We believe with the heart. Paul taught the Roman church: "If you confess with your mouth the Lord Jesus and believe in your heart that God has raised Him from the dead, you will be saved. For with the heart one believes unto righteousness, and with the mouth confession is made unto salvation."[7]

We grow spiritually in the same way that we receive salvation—by believing in our hearts. Paul admonished the church at Colossae, "As you have therefore received Christ Jesus the Lord, so walk in Him."[8] Please take note: spiritual growth is not accumulating biblical knowledge, but progressively coming to know Christ more intimately.

Faith Works by Love

Above all, believers are to love God with all their hearts, souls, and minds and to love one another as they love themselves. When a Pharisee asked Jesus which commandment in the law was the greatest, Jesus replied:

"'You shall love the Lord your God with all your heart, with all your soul, and with all your mind.' This is the first and great commandment. And the second is like it: 'You shall love your neighbor as yourself.' On these two commandments hang all the Law and the Prophets."[9] At another time, Jesus declared, "This is My commandment, that you love one another as I have loved you."[10]

We love the Lord by obeying Him—not only conforming to the requirements of the written Word, but also by hearing and obeying His voice. Jesus instructed His disciples, "If you love Me, keep My commandments."[11] He also revealed these two truths: "He who has My commandments and keeps them, it is he who loves Me,"[12] and "You are My friends if you do whatever I command you."[13]

Paul taught the church at Galatia, "In Jesus Christ neither circumcision availeth anything, nor uncircumcision; but faith which worketh by love."[14] Faith works by love because faith comes from relationship. It's personal. It's intensely personal. God reveals His will to us through fellowship with Jesus Christ. Obedience to Christ activates our faith.

Obedience Activates Faith

Even Jesus did not speak on His own initiative. He declared: "I have not spoken on My own authority; but the Father who sent Me gave Me a command, what I should say and what I should speak. And I know that His command is everlasting life. Therefore, whatever I speak, just as the Father has told Me, so I speak."[15] Jesus was not speaking of a command written in an ancient text. He was speaking of a command spoken to Him personally by the Father. Jesus proclaimed, "My sheep hear My voice, and I know them, and they follow Me."[16] To obey Christ's commands, we must first hear His voice.

Therefore, faith begins with hearing and is activated by obedience. Again, Paul wrote to the church at Rome, "Faith comes by hearing [what is told], and what is heard comes by the preaching [of the message that came from the lips] of Christ (the Messiah Himself)."[17] James explained, "Faith, if it does not have works (deeds and actions of obedience to back it up), by itself is destitute of power (inoperative, dead)."[18] We do the works of God in the same way that Jesus did. As Jesus heard and obeyed the Father's commands, we hear and obey Christ's commands.

New Covenant Faith Produces Supernatural Change

New covenant faith produces what is naturally impossible. The writer of Hebrews revealed, "Now faith is the substance of things hoped for, the evidence of things not seen."[19] New covenant faith is confidence that Christ produces supernatural change according to His revealed will on a routine and consistent basis.

Faith in the person of the Lord Jesus Christ produces supernatural change. Faith in the promises alone does not consistently produce change; faith in the one who promised them does. The writer of Hebrews admonished believers, "Without faith it is impossible to please Him, for he who comes to God must believe that He is, and that He is a rewarder of those who diligently seek Him."[20] Trying to obtain God's promises does not necessarily please Him; seeking God Himself definitely pleases Him.

Believers hinder their faith by relying too much on their natural reasoning. Jesus proclaimed: "Most assuredly, I say to you, he who believes in Me, the works that I do he will do also; and greater works than these he will do, because I go to My Father. And whatever you ask in My name, that I will do, that the Father may be glorified in the Son. If you ask anything in My name, I will do it."[21]

As Christians, we believe other statements Jesus made, like, "If I go and prepare a place for you, I will come again and receive you to Myself, that where I am, there you may be also."[22] Why can't we believe, "I assure you, most solemnly I tell you, if anyone steadfastly believes in Me, he will himself be able to do the things that I do; and he will do even greater things than these, because I go to the Father"?[23] Why is the second scripture more difficult to believe than the first? In the second one, Jesus says, "I assure you, most solemnly I tell you." It is more emphatic and assuring than the first! One reason may be that we need to know God's will in a specific situation.

Specific Faith Begins with Knowing the Revealed Will of God

Faith for a specific outcome begins with knowing the revealed will of God. Until the will of God is revealed, there can be no faith for a specific outcome. Every prayer that is not praying the expressed will of God is so prayed because we have not taken the time and made the effort to discern the will of God first.

Jesus revealed the principle that God the Father *initiates* and the believer *imitates*. We see this principle at work in the ministry of Jesus, because Jesus Himself could do nothing without the Father. In fact, when the Jews criticized Jesus for healing a man on the Sabbath, He told them, "Most assuredly I say to you, the Son can do nothing of Himself, but what He sees the Father do; for whatever He does, the Son also does in like manner."[24]

We can similarly do nothing without Christ. Remember, Jesus taught His disciples: "I am the vine, you are the branches. He who abides in Me, and I in him, bears much fruit; for without Me you can do nothing."[25] We accomplish Jesus' works by being obedient to Him in the same way that He accomplished God's works by being obedient to the Father.

Strong New Covenant Faith Is Knowing Christ Personally

We begin to trust the Lord by getting to know Christ personally. The apostle Paul shared his faith with Timothy with these words: "*I know whom I have believed* and am persuaded that He is able to keep what I have committed to Him until that Day."[26] Paul did not write, "I know *what* I have believed"; he wrote, "I know *whom* I have believed." He continued, "I . . . am persuaded that He [Jesus] is able." Paul placed his faith, not in the Scriptures, but the person of Christ who fulfilled the Scriptures. Paul did not know Christ in human form like the other apostles did. Yet Paul believed in the person of the Lord Jesus Christ, not merely in what had been written or said about Him—and so should we.

Paul considered his religious heritage, accomplishments, strengths, triumphs, adherence to religious principles, religious affiliation, and credentials as worthless compared to knowing Christ personally. He shared this with the Philippian church in these words:

> I count everything as loss compared to the possession of the priceless privilege (the overwhelming preciousness, the surpassing worth, and supreme advantage) of *knowing Christ Jesus my Lord and of progressively becoming more*

> *deeply and intimately acquainted with Him* [of perceiving and recognizing and understanding Him more fully and clearly].... [My determined purpose is] that I may know Him [that I may progressively become more deeply and intimately acquainted with Him, perceiving and recognizing and understanding the wonders of *His Person* more strongly and more clearly].²⁷

Paul counted all things as loss compared to knowing Christ Jesus and "progressively becoming more deeply and intimately acquainted with Him." We, like Paul, should count all that we know, all that we are, all that we have accomplished, and all religious opinions as loss so that we may know Christ personally.

The essence of our faith is to hear the voice of our Lord and obey Him. Our position in the church, the doctrines of our denominations, and our retention of biblical facts are all secondary to hearing and obeying the Lord. Our knowledge of the Word of God is essential to validate the voice of the Lord, but it cannot substitute for hearing the Lord's voice.

We should not rely on our perceived advantages: our own righteousness, our carnal knowledge of the Word, our formulas and methods, our good conduct, or the good works that we have done. We should give up our attempts to manipulate the Word of God to achieve our objectives.

Many of us have spent a large portion of our lives learning the principles of God's Word, attempting to live by them, and attempting to activate them in our lives and in the lives of others. This is not how we want our children to relate to us as parents, and it is not how God wants us, as His children, to relate to Him. It's not wrong to ask God to fulfill His promises. But for believers in Christ, our desire to obtain God's benefits should be secondary to our desire to progressively know Christ more intimately.

God desires that we progressively come to know Christ more intimately. Knowing Christ intimately is not an instant event. Like coming to know anyone, knowing Christ intimately requires time spent in close proximity and openness with Him. Like Paul, we "progressively become more deeply and intimately acquainted with Him, perceiving and recognizing and understanding the wonders of His Person more strongly and more clearly".

To have strong new covenant faith, we depend upon knowing Christ personally rather than depending on our knowledge of the Bible or our standing in the religious community. Paul encouraged the Corinthian believers, "Imitate me, just as I also imitate Christ."[28] Paul's intimate fellowship with Christ, not his religious knowledge or standing in the religious community, produced great feats of faith. We should seek to imitate Paul, not in his exploits, but in his quest to know Christ more intimately. When we know Christ more intimately, the exploits will follow.

Great Faith Comes under the Authority
of the Lord Jesus Christ

We know Christ more intimately by being obedient to Him. Therefore, the work of faith is the work of surrender to the glorified Lord as we described Him in chapter 6. What we mean by this is that a person of great faith comes under the Lord's authority as a bond servant comes under the authority of his or her master. When we have great faith, we choose to do the Lord's will over doing our own will, and we choose to put the Lord's interest ahead of our self-interest.

One time a Roman military leader, a centurion, went to Jesus, asking Him to heal his servant who was seriously ill at home. Jesus said He would go and heal him, but the centurion replied that he was not worthy for Jesus to come into his home. He told Jesus that as his soldiers obeyed his commands, if Jesus would speak the word without going to his house, his servant would be healed. Jesus told the centurion to go and it would be done as he believed, and the servant was healed (Matt. 8:5–9, 13). Referring to this incident, Jesus told those who were following Him, "I have not found such great faith, not even in Israel!"[29]

God has given the Lord Jesus Christ all authority in heaven and on earth as we described in detail in chapter 6. Great faith recognizes and submits to His authority. This is a spiritual truth: the absence of submission to Jesus' authority is the absence of great faith. Our faith is not fully developed until we are completely dependent on the Lord Jesus Christ. The measure of our submission to the glorified Lord within us is the measure of our faith.

Christ's Rule Is the Measure of Our Faith

The measure of our faith is the measure of the rule of Christ within us. Christ's ruling within us transforms us increasingly into His image. As we allow Christ greater rule, the intensity of His presence increases. His presence permeates and shines through our being as Moses' face shined from his having been in the presence of God. The glory that is shining through us, however, comes from within rather than from without.

Christ lives in our hearts by faith. As we mentioned previously, Paul prayed for those in the Ephesian church "that Christ may dwell in your hearts through faith."[30] Through Christ ruling in our hearts, His kingdom is established within us. Jesus informed inquiring Pharisees: "The kingdom of God does not come with observation; nor will they say, 'See here!' or 'See there!' For indeed, the kingdom of God is within you."[31] We become more like Christ through His rule within us.

The work of faith is not obtaining the promises, but it is yielding to Christ who promises. We should seek God's promises in order to become more like Christ, not seek to be more like Christ in order to obtain God's promises. God gives us His promises so that we may be partakers of the divine nature. As Peter explained in his second epistle, God has "given to us exceedingly great and precious promises, that through these you may be partakers of the divine nature."[32] The purpose of God's promises is to conform us to the image of Christ.

The strength of our faith is not measured by the number of answers to prayers for God's promises that we possess, but by how much of us Christ possesses. Likewise, our spiritual success is not the accomplishments we have achieved, but the accomplishments Christ has achieved in us. This working of Christ within us generates faith that produces supernatural change in us and in the lives of others.

Paul wrote to the Colossian church, "As you therefore have received Christ Jesus the Lord, so walk in Him."[33] Just as we received Christ by the enlightenment of the Holy Spirit, we also grow spiritually. Paul wrote to the church at Galatia, "Are you so foolish? Having begun in the Spirit, are you now being made perfect by the flesh?"[34]

Admonition to Enter Fully into Faith in God

Cooperate with the author and finisher of your faith. Allow your faith to exceed your natural understanding. Allow Christ to rule in your heart. Ground your faith in love. Activate your faith with obedience. Seek to know the expressed will of God before you pray. Imitate the apostle Paul, not in his exploits, but in his quest to know Christ more intimately. Put your trust, not merely in the promises of the Bible, but in the Lord Jesus Christ who promised them. Surrender unconditionally to our Lord Jesus Christ.

Pray for Faith in the Person of Christ

Heavenly Father, please take me out of the realm of mere knowledge into the realm of the inner working of Christ. Please release me from the captivity of my five senses and my natural-reasoning mind. May my faith be in the person of the Lord Jesus Christ and be strengthened through intimate fellowship with Him. All this I ask, not only for my own spiritual growth, but also that our Lord Jesus Christ, in whose name I pray, may be glorified and exalted in and through me. Amen.

Where Do We Go from Here?

Our faith is either increased or decreased by our doctrine, our opinion of what God's Word means; there is no middle ground. In the next chapter, we'll enhance our experiencing the living Christ and living in the presence of God by learning that our doctrine forms our perception of reality, and our perception of reality determines our future. We'll see that our doctrine is either a stepping stone to greater faith or a stumbling block to unbelief.

Chapter 13

Embrace Living Doctrine

*Now we have received, not the spirit of the world,
but the Spirit who is from God, that we might know the things
that have been freely given to us by God.*
1 Corinthians 2:12

We have seen that the role of faith is to allow Jesus Christ unrestricted expression in and through us at all times, and we have learned to put our faith in the person of the Lord Jesus Christ, not just in what has been written about Him. Next, we will address what is probably the greatest deciding factor in whether or not Christians experience the living Christ and live in the presence of God—doctrine.

Our fifth foundational truth is this: our doctrine is either a stepping stone to greater faith or a stumbling block to unbelief. We will find that sound doctrine is determined by the Word of God and the Spirit of God, not by the Word or the Spirit alone. Our doctrine forms our perception of reality, and our perception of reality determines our destiny in this world and the next. Sound doctrine empowers our faith, but unsound doctrine undermines our faith.

People generally think of doctrine as a series of concepts or principles—what we should think or the position we should take on a given issue. Just as we realized that grace is more than unmerited favor, we will see that doctrine is more than the teaching of concepts or principles. Doctrine is more than what we think in our minds; it is what we live in our hearts.

A doctrine is not an academic statement that we dutifully conform to outwardly; it is a holy statement of divine truth expressed in living words formed by the Holy Spirit that conforms us inwardly. Doctrine rephrases the Spirit of truth expressed in the Bible.

Doctrine is not the justification of mankind's limitations; it is not the reason Scripture does not mean what its words express. Doctrine should not justify our natural comprehension or our lack of spiritual understanding, but instead, it should take us beyond our natural understanding.

Doctrine is the expression of God's principles of boundless provision for mankind—the enlightenment of the transference of life from God to mankind and the hindrances to that transference. Doctrine is spiritually discerned, defines our understanding of Scripture, and is the outward expression of our inner beliefs. Doctrine is much more than a listing of statements that we believe; it forms our perception of reality.

Doctrine Forms Our Perception of Reality

Doctrine is the lens through which we view the Christian faith. It forms our perspective, thereby forming our perception of spiritual reality. As the glass through which we view Scripture, it either magnifies or obscures our perception of the truth. Doctrine either enhances, retards, or disables the influence of the living Word in, through, and around us.

Our doctrine will either lead us into or lead us away from being who God has created us to be. We become who God created us to be by adopting and adhering to sound doctrine.

We form our personal doctrine and our personal doctrine forms us, not only in this life, but for eternity. Any doctrine that is not sound doctrine becomes a prison, limiting who we are and what we can accomplish for Christ. Unsound doctrine can cost us our lives and our eternal destinies. How then can we know that the doctrines we believe are sound and will produce effective, energizing faith within us?

What Is Sound Doctrine?

Sound doctrine is consistent with Scripture, but doctrine based on knowledge of Scripture alone is not necessarily sound. Sound doctrine is determined by the Word and the Spirit of God, not by the Word or the Spirit alone. It is understood by illumination. While sound doctrine is taught, it must at the same time be imparted, communicated by the Holy Spirit, because "the things of the Spirit of God . . . are spiritually discerned."[1]

The soundest doctrine is Scripture simply stated. As human reasoning is added to Scripture to form doctrine, it becomes less sound. As human interpretation increasingly modifies Scripture, doctrine becomes progressively less sound until it progresses into false doctrine. False doctrine contradicts Scripture simply stated. As we will discover, sound doctrine originates with God, is spiritually discerned, provides stability, is spiritually empowering, reveals supernatural reality, energizes the supernatural dimension, and produces spiritual authority.

Sound Doctrine Originates with God

Sound doctrine originates with God. Paul taught Timothy, "All Scripture is given by inspiration of God, and is profitable for doctrine."[2] Jesus proclaimed, "My doctrine is not Mine, but His who sent Me."[3]

Our doctrine must not be our own; it must come from God. We obtain sound doctrine by the Holy Spirit illuminating Scripture.

Sound Doctrine Is Spiritually Discerned

Jesus taught many parables. The value of His teaching was not in the factual information He presented, but in the spiritual truth His teaching illustrated. In the parable of the sower, Jesus explained how the condition of the soil affects the growth of the seed that was sown, as recorded in chapter 4 of Mark's gospel. The agricultural information Jesus presented, while factually accurate, had no spiritual significance. Only the Holy Spirit's illumination of the parable revealed its meaningful application.

Relating factual information without the illumination of the Holy Spirit is spiritually ineffective. Christian teaching is far more than sharing factual knowledge; it's imparting the Spirit of truth. After teaching the parable of the sower, Jesus proclaimed, "He who has ears to hear, let him hear!"[4]

This is the meaning of Jesus' statement: those who have *spiritual* ears *spiritually* receive *spiritual* truth. This hearing is different from natural hearing. While preparing His disciples for His imminent crucifixion, Jesus told them, "He [the Holy Spirit] will teach you all things."[5] Just as mankind witnesses and God saves souls, mankind teaches and the Holy Spirit illuminates and empowers truth in the hearts of those being taught.

In the world, knowledge is power, because the world does not have the Holy Spirit. Any "power" received through mere Spiritless knowledge, however, is clearly inferior to knowledge empowered by the Holy Spirit. Unless doctrine is enlightened by the Holy Spirit, it is mere intellectual precept.

Jesus is the Word, the embodiment of the entire knowledge of God. He lives in our hearts. He is living doctrine. This living doctrine is the foundation of spiritual teaching—teaching that not only provides natural knowledge to the minds of the listeners, but also imparts the Spirit of God in their hearts to activate the message within them.

Accordingly, doctrine is not complete until it is brought to life—transformed into spiritual enlightenment. This transformation takes place through personal illumination initiated and empowered by the Holy Spirit. Sound doctrine is generally received through the illumination of the Holy Spirit when we read or meditate on the Word of God, wait quietly on the Lord, or hear a Holy Spirit–empowered message.

As the apostle Paul explained to the Corinthian church, supernatural truth is not communicated with natural words but is revealed and quickened by the Holy Spirit (1 Cor. 2:13). Enlightened doctrine brings people into contact with the living Christ. It introduces them to or enhances their relationship with the Godhead.

Sound Doctrine Provides Stability

This supernatural relationship with the Godhead then provides the believer with spiritual stability. Establishing sound doctrine in our lives protects us from the dangers of unsound doctrine. Christ gave us His ministry gifts (apostles, prophets, evangelists, pastors, and teachers) to teach and instruct us so that "we should no longer be children, tossed to and fro and carried about with every wind of doctrine."[6]

Doctrine received from Christ anchors us in the truth and stabilizes our faith. When we are well grounded in sound doctrine, we are less susceptible to being deceived by unsound doctrine. Sound doctrine protects us from human reasoning that contaminates our core beliefs. The stability provided by sound doctrine leads believers into spiritual empowerment.

Sound Doctrine Is Spiritually Empowering

Sound doctrine is supernaturally empowering. Paul stated this truth by enlightenment of the Holy Spirit: "All Scripture is given by inspiration of God, and is profitable for doctrine, for reproof, for correction, for instruction in righteousness, that the man of God may be complete, thoroughly equipped for every good work."[7]

To be thoroughly equipped for every good work is not just the mental preparation of retaining biblical facts. To be thoroughly equipped for every good work is also to be spiritually enlightened and empowered by the Holy Spirit. When we receive doctrine by illumination, we receive a transfer of life from God.

Sound doctrine, being enlightened and empowered by the Holy Spirit, enables us to give ourselves to Christ for Him to work in and through us, rather than our doing our works for Christ. This spiritual equipping by Christ is one aspect of supernatural reality.

Sound Doctrine Reveals Supernatural Reality

Words spoken or written by the Holy Spirit have a supernatural dimension that natural words do not have. When we perceive that dimension, we receive the divine resource that exceeds the meaning of the words themselves. One example of this is the doctrine of divine healing. We cannot logically explain how divine healing takes place, but we can receive divine healing if we believe.

This spiritual dimension is beyond the ability of the human mind to comprehend. Paul put it this way: "We are setting these truths forth in words not taught by human wisdom but taught by the [Holy] Spirit, combining and interpreting spiritual truths with spiritual language [to those who possess the Holy Spirit]."[8]

God's reality exceeds our natural understanding. His reality is infinite, yet we are finite. It is impossible for the finite to encompass the infinite. Our human minds cannot grasp the full dimension of God's infinite reality. How do we, who are finite, perceive God's infinite, supernatural reality? If we relate to God with our hearts and human spirits, the limitations of our minds do not restrict the infinite dimension of God to us.

Sound Doctrine Energizes the Supernatural Dimension

This relating to God beyond the limitations of the natural mind is a function of the supernatural dimension. Sound doctrine energizes the supernatural nature of the ministry gifts of Jesus Christ: apostle, prophet, evangelist, pastor, and teacher. In other words, those energized by sound doctrine conduct these ministries out of the presence of God and the illumination and power of the Holy Spirit, rather than out of the mind and a system of man. Clearly, God intends the ministries of evangelists, pastors, and teachers to be supernaturally inspired and empowered by the Lord Jesus Christ. Consider these words of apostles Paul and John:

> Faith comes by hearing [what is told], and what is heard comes by the preaching [of the message that came from the lips] of Christ (the Messiah Himself).[9]

> The substance (essence) of the truth revealed by Jesus is the spirit of all prophecy [the vital breath, the inspiration of all inspired preaching and interpretation of the divine will and purpose, including both mine and yours].[10]

Teaching or preaching the prophetic message from the Lord divides the soul and spirit, as we discussed in chapter 5. It releases the human spirit from the dominating influence of the soul and enables the hearers to be more sensitive to the realm of God's presence.

Sound doctrine also empowers the supernatural ministry of every believer. Luke quoted Jesus as saying, "You shall receive power when the Holy Spirit has come upon you; and you shall be witnesses to Me in Jerusalem, and in all Judea and Samaria, and to the end of the earth."[11] Mark quoted Jesus as saying, "These signs will follow those who believe: In My name they will cast out demons; they will speak with new tongues; they will take up serpents; and if they drink anything deadly, it will by no means hurt them; they will lay hands on the sick, and they will recover."[12] Jesus proclaimed, "Most assuredly, I say to you, he who believes in Me, the works that I do he will do also; and greater works than these he will do, because I go to My Father."[13] Christ equips believers, who recognize and embrace this dimension of sound doctrine, with spiritual authority.

Sound Doctrine Produces Authority

Sound doctrine produces spiritual authority. When Jesus taught in the synagogue in Capernaum, Mark observed, "They were astonished at His teaching, for He taught them as one having authority, and not as the scribes."[14] In the synagogue, a man with an unclean spirit drew attention to himself by becoming loud and boisterous. Jesus commanded the spirit to come out of him. Mark reported: "When the unclean spirit had convulsed him and cried out with a loud voice, he came out of him. Then they were all amazed, so that they questioned among themselves, saying, 'What is this? What new doctrine is this? For with authority He commands even the unclean spirits, and they obey Him.'"[15]

We cannot maintain mere intellectual doctrine (doctrine established by the mind without the enlightenment and empowerment of the Holy Spirit) and have spiritual authority. If we establish doctrine by our human reasoning, we are limited to mere human authority. All authority is in Christ. When we are in Christ and our doctrine is from Christ by illumination of the Holy Spirit, Jesus Christ activates His spiritual authority through us.

Now that we understand sound doctrine, let's turn our attention to identifying unsound doctrine.

What Is Unsound Doctrine?

All doctrine that deviates from the Word of God is unsound doctrine. It includes substituting the work of the flesh for the work of the Spirit and the reasoning that people use to justify their natural thinking, their personal experiences, or their lack of spiritual authority.

Unsound doctrine is rooted in human logic, is perpetrated through philosophies and rules devised by mankind, and produces hypocrisy. Jesus rebuked the Pharisees, "You are nullifying and making void and of no effect [the authority of] the word of God through your tradition, which you [in turn] hand on."[16] Unsound doctrine is void of the Spirit, emphasizes outward conduct over inner purity, emphasizes works over grace, and rationalizes the Word of God.

Dead Doctrine Is Unsound

Doctrine without the Spirit does not have the life of the Spirit, and without the life of the Spirit, it is dead. It has no power and is therefore spiritually ineffective. Natural effort cannot produce supernatural results.

Mentally understanding a principle and applying it with natural abilities cannot transform doctrine into biblical faith. Without illumination by the Holy Spirit, doctrine is dead and ineffective. The teaching of dead doctrine may be biblically correct, but it has no power to produce spiritual growth or permanent change in conduct. Dead doctrine may define what conduct should be, but it cannot empower change.

The natural application of dead doctrine is the source of much hypocrisy in the church. Modification of outward conduct through natural abilities is insufficient to produce change that will remain under pressure. This is one reason Christians who appear to be strong in the faith succumb to the temptations of the flesh and the devil, making Christianity appear hypocritical to persons outside of the faith. Genuine spiritual growth and permanent change come from the heart. Any other change is superficial and lacks spiritual strength.

Improving external conduct without receiving the internal empowerment of the Holy Spirit deceptively masquerades as spiritual maturity. In other words, some people may act as though they are spiritually mature but lack the internal strength of true spiritual maturity. We must not lose sight of this fact: spiritual maturity is the internal work of the Holy Spirit. Holiness is not an end in itself, but the means to an end: entering into personal, communal fellowship with God the Father and the Lord Jesus Christ.

Unsound Doctrine Emphasizes Outward Conduct over Inner Purity

In Jesus' time, the Pharisees were zealous and diligent in their pursuit of the things of God, but they did not have an intimate relationship with Him. Void of direct contact with God, they devised rules that replaced communication with Him.

Some Christians today are finding themselves in a similar posture. Not being in contact with God, they pursue Him through a religious system. They conform to codes of conduct and reach out to God through formulas or religious tradition. They may speak to God in prayer but rarely listen to Him in return. By justifying their spiritual shortcomings, they distance themselves from the Son of God.

Our character and manner of living must run much deeper than mere outward conduct. They should manifest sound doctrine lived out of a pure heart.

Unsound Doctrine Emphasizes Works over Grace

Conforming to Spiritless knowledge by natural abilities is works, void of the power of God; being conformed to Spirit-illuminated knowledge by the inner working of the Holy Spirit is grace, the power of God in operation. Paul warned the Colossian church that when people outwardly comply with the doctrines of men, they have an appearance of wisdom, but they are actually void of spiritual power. He wrote:

> If you died with Christ from the basic principles of the world, why, as though living in the world, do you subject yourselves to regulations—"do not touch, do not taste, do not handle," which all concern things which perish with the using—according to the commandments and doctrines of men? These things indeed have an appearance of wisdom in self-imposed religion, false humility, and neglect of the body, but are of no value against the indulgence of the flesh.[17]

Teaching that is not the expression of the Spirit of God leads people into a false sense of spiritual maturity. Thinking they are wise, they become opinionated, unteachable, and hardened into religious arrogance. They unknowingly oppose the teaching and working of the Holy Spirit. They become victims of the doctrines of the scribes and Pharisees. Their doctrines, while appearing biblically accurate, lack the life-empowering dimension of the Holy Spirit and are accordingly invalid.

Unsound doctrine is embraced by the intellect. Intellectualizing the gospel opens people to being deceived by various and strange doctrines. The intellect not enlightened by the Holy Spirit rationalizes the Word of

God, changing its meaning to something entirely different from the truth revealed by its Spirit-empowered words.

Unsound Doctrine Rationalizes the Word of God

When we say unsound doctrine rationalizes the Word of God, we mean any doctrine that deviates from the Holy Scriptures is unsound, regardless of how reasonable it seems to the natural mind or how well it conforms to life's experiences. The Word of God is supernatural and, as such, exceeds natural reasoning.

Unsound doctrine subordinates the Word of God to mankind's natural reasoning. Let's look again at the doctrine of divine healing. We cannot comprehend how divine healing takes place with our natural minds. We may know and highly respect a committed Christian who believed for healing but was not healed, or even died. We may have prayed for people to be healed, and they were not. We may have believed for divine healing for ourselves, and it did not occur. None of these occurrences invalidate God's Word! None justify our forming or believing a doctrine that does not fully embrace the fact that Jesus Christ still heals people by grace through faith today.

We must not form, believe, or preach doctrine that denies the supernatural aspect of God's Word. Paul sternly stated, "Even if we, or an angel from heaven, preach any other gospel to you than what we have preached to you, let him be accursed."[18] Neither should we live unsound doctrine.

Living Sound Doctrine

Doctrine becomes effective when we live sound doctrine from our hearts, not merely know it in our minds. Sound character comes from a heart that has been prepared by sound doctrine; it cannot be achieved through self-discipline or carnal effort alone. Living sound doctrine from our hearts is not external conformity to a set of rules but is being internally conformed to the image of Christ. We adhere to sound doctrine through fellowship with Christ and by the working of the Holy Spirit. The apostle John admonished the early Christians, "Let that abide in you which you heard from the beginning. If what you heard from the beginning abides in you, you also will abide in the Son and in the Father."[19] Jesus taught

His disciples, "It is the Spirit who gives life; the flesh profits nothing. The words that I speak to you are spirit, and they are life."[20]

To be effective, our doctrine must be personal and real, not merely conceptual. Doctrine becomes actively effective when we live it from the heart. By living sound doctrine from the heart, we translate doctrine into faith and transfer living doctrine to other believers.

Jesus said only what He heard the Father say, and He did only what He saw the Father do. He saw and heard the Father, not with physical eyes and ears, but with spiritual eyes and ears. What Jesus said and did came directly from His fellowship with the Father.

In Christianity, our ministry comes out of fellowship with Christ; we say what we hear Him say and do what we see Him do. Spiritual productivity is therefore relationship-oriented rather than task-oriented. Being relationship-oriented is focusing on the one who does the work through us; being task-oriented is focusing on the work being done. Task orientation produces mere works, good deeds performed without the leading and enabling of the Spirit of God.

Consider Christ's command to love. It is not an outward task, a theory, or a principle; it's the outward expression of a pure, internal state of being. The greatest commandment is "Love the Lord your God with all your heart and with all your soul and with all your mind."[21] The second is "Love your neighbor as yourself."[22] All that we do for God without the true, inner motivation of love is worthless (1 Cor. 13:1–3). Jesus declared, "A new command I give you: Love one another. As I have loved you, so you must love one another."[23]

Jesus does not love us with a superficial love that is no deeper than outward conduct. He loves us with compassionate, unconditional, self-sacrificing love. Since Jesus commanded us to love others as He has loved us, we cannot obey this command by outward conduct alone. We must obey His command to love with our hearts, souls, and minds.

As we mature spiritually, we progress from merely knowing doctrinal concepts with our minds to actually living doctrine from our hearts. Living, not just knowing, sound doctrine is a very serious matter. The apostle John warned:

> Whoever transgresses and does not *abide in* the doctrine of Christ does not have God. He who *abides in* the

doctrine of Christ has both the Father and the Son. If anyone comes to you and does not bring this doctrine, do not receive him into your house nor greet him; for he who greets him shares in his evil deeds.[24]

Living sound doctrine is a stepping stone to greater faith in Christ. Rationalizing unsound doctrine is a stumbling block to our faith.

Is Our Doctrine a Stepping Stone or a Stumbling Block to Our Faith?

We have seen that doctrine is not an intellectual precept or a task. More than something we conform to outwardly, doctrine is something we live. Doctrine becomes ours when we live it.

Any doctrine that deviates to any degree from the words clearly stated in the Bible becomes a stumbling block to our faith. This doctrine, formed by our intellect without our understanding being enlightened by the Holy Spirit, imprisons us in false perceptions. We therefore must not limit our doctrine to our conventional understanding. Our faith must exceed our natural comprehension, or it will rationalize the Word of God, believing something entirely different from the truth that its Spirit-empowered words actually convey.

To the degree that our doctrine is consistent with the Word of God and not modified by human reasoning, it is a stepping stone increasing our faith from glory to glory. To the degree that it is inconsistent, it becomes a stumbling block producing unbelief.

The Lord Jesus Christ is faithful to work sound doctrine in and through us. The writer of Hebrews encouraged believers, saying: "Every house is built by someone, but He who built all things is God. And Moses indeed was faithful in all His house as a servant, for a testimony of those things which would be spoken afterward, but Christ as a Son over His own house, whose house we are if we hold fast the confidence and the rejoicing of the hope firm to the end."[25]

Admonition to Live Sound Doctrine

Form your doctrine by illumination of the Word by the Spirit of God. Live doctrine from your heart; don't just learn principles with your mind. Allow your doctrine to transform you inwardly into the image of Christ; don't merely conform your conduct to a set of rules. Believe and live doctrine that becomes a stepping stone from glory to glory rather than a stumbling block producing unbelief.

Pray to Believe Doctrine Not Compromised by Human Reasoning

Father, please reveal to me all doctrine formed within me that is not of You. Please cleanse me inside so that I may be pure. I desire to live the pure doctrine of the Word of God enlightened by the Holy Spirit and to be free from the imprisonment of all else. I want to perceive beyond my human reasoning. Please deliver me from the restrictions of my natural mind by the power of Your Holy Spirit. All this I ask, not only for my own spiritual growth, but also that our Lord Jesus Christ, in whose name I pray, may be glorified and exalted in and through me. Amen.

Where Do We Go from Here?

We have seen that believing and living sound doctrine is probably the greatest determining factor in whether or not we experience the living Christ and live in the presence of God. Our personal doctrine forms our perception of the Christian faith, including our perception of the goodness of the Father. Next, we'll view God's wonderful sovereignty in the light of His nature, His character, His Word, and His covenant. We'll ask the question, what is our problem with God's sovereignty? And we'll learn how to allow God to exercise His wonderful sovereignty in our lives.

Chapter 14

Come to Know the Father's Goodness

> What shall we say then? Is there unrighteousness with God?
> Certainly not! For He says to Moses, "I will have mercy on whomever
> I will have mercy, and I will have compassion on whomever I will have
> compassion." So then it is not of him who wills, nor of him who runs,
> but of God who shows mercy.
> Romans 9:14–16

We have seen how doctrine shapes our faith, our lives on this earth, and our eternal destinies. After the importance of our doctrine, probably the next most influential factor in experiencing the living Christ and living in the presence of God is knowing the Father's goodness.

Our sixth foundational truth is this: God exercises His sovereignty in conformity with His nature, His character, His Word, and His covenant. The sovereignty of God is one of the most crucial doctrines of the Christian faith. Our perception of God—of His nature, His character, and His conduct—profoundly defines our faith, our relationship with God, and even our eternal destinies. Yet there is probably no doctrine that suffers more damage from well-meaning Christians than the sovereignty of God.

Let's examine this sovereignty. First, we'll give the sovereignty of God a definition. Then we'll turn our attention to accurately discerning the sovereignty of God. We'll view God's sovereignty in light of His nature and His character, and we'll reveal our problem with God's sovereignty. Finally, we'll see how we allow God to exercise His wonderful sovereignty in our lives.

Accurately Discerning God's Sovereignty

We can define the sovereignty of God in this way: God's sovereignty is His right and ability to set aside the normal course of natural and human events. He can do anything in conformity with His nature, His character, His Word, and His covenant at any time. God's nature is love; His character is faithful; His Word is true; His covenant is reliable. Early in our Christian life, we learn that God is love. When it comes to our concept of His sovereignty, however, some of us don't really believe it.

To accurately discern God's sovereignty, we must recognize that (1) grace is the sovereignty of God and that (2) God, in His sovereignty, chose to bind Himself by His covenant.

Grace Is the Sovereignty of God

Grace is the sovereignty of God. And God's greatest act of grace was exercising His sovereignty to redeem mankind from eternal destruction. In sending Jesus to the cross, God set aside the normal course of human events, asserting His sovereignty to save mankind from certain, self-imposed destruction. In the normal course of human events, we would all be dead in our sins and eternally separated from God.

As we discussed in chapter 4, Adam rebelled against God by eating the forbidden fruit of the tree of the knowledge of good and evil. In so doing, he brought death upon all humanity, eternally separating mankind from God. Everyone was doomed to eternal destruction. God intervened by sending His Son to pay the penalty for all sin. God's sovereignty set aside the course of human events to redeem all who believe through His new covenant.

God Chose in His Sovereignty to Bind Himself by His Covenant

God, in His sovereignty, has chosen to bind Himself by His covenant. The sovereignty of God cannot violate His covenant because God is the supreme covenant keeper. Moses instructed the children of Israel, "Know that the Lord your God, He is God, the faithful God who keeps covenant and mercy for a thousand generations with those who love Him and keep His commandments."[1] If God breaks His covenant, we have no assurance of salvation because salvation comes only through the new covenant. According to the book of Hebrews, Jesus is "the mediator of a new covenant, that those who are called may receive the promised eternal inheritance."[2]

We who are born again are in a covenant with God. Paul explained to the Galatian church: "Now to Abraham and his Seed were the promises made. He does not say, 'And to seeds,' as of many, but as of one, 'And to your Seed,' who is Christ. . . . And if you are Christ's, then you are Abraham's seed, and heirs according to the promise."[3] We are Abraham's seed and heirs according to the promise.

Viewing God's Sovereignty in Light of His Nature and His Character

God's sovereignty is consistent with His loving nature and His faithful character, but some Christians have trouble accepting this. Believers should recognize the following three points: (1) all that we don't understand is not the sovereignty of God, (2) our unfulfilled expectations are not necessarily the sovereignty of God, and (3) negative and undesirable occurrences are not necessarily the sovereignty of God.

All That We Don't Understand Is Not the Sovereignty of God

What we do not understand is not always the sovereignty of God; it is usually the ignorance of man. It is extreme arrogance to label our ignorance as God's sovereignty. We should never confuse the two.

God's sovereignty is not the explanation for occurrences that are contrary to our doctrine. It is not an excuse for what we do not understand or for those events that we think should not have happened. Instead of blaming what we don't understand on the sovereignty of God, we should have the courage and integrity to say, "I don't know why . . ." To exalt self by blaming what we don't understand on God's sovereignty is to distort God's image and to misrepresent Him to others—a grievous sin.

Men and women who have not experienced God's supernatural works in their lives and ministries often justify the undeniable fact that their prayers have not been answered and their ministry has not produced supernatural results by asserting God's inactivity is due to the sovereignty of

God. They erroneously claim that the responsibility for the absence of supernatural activity in their lives and ministries is not theirs, but God's.

Unfulfilled Expectations Are Not Necessarily the Sovereignty of God

Some believers try to manipulate God. They attempt to get what they want by finding a promise and doing what the Bible says will produce that result. Their motivation is to get what they want. James advised believers, "You ask and do not receive, because you ask amiss, that you may spend it on your pleasures."[4]

When God does not allow people to manipulate Him, some defile His character by blaming not getting what they want on the sovereignty of God. One common example is the belief that the sovereignty of God makes a person sick. Sickness is part of the curse (Deut. 28:58–61). Jesus redeemed us from the curse of the law, becoming a curse for us (Gal. 3:13). We were healed by the stripes of Jesus (Isa. 53:5 and 1 Pet. 2:24). Why would God undo the work He accomplished at such a terrible price?

Receiving healing from God should be normal for all Christians. Believers should have more faith in God to heal them than they have in the medical community's drugs and surgeries. When they experience sickness or pain, they should seek God's healing first. God's healing should not take second place to the practice of medicine.

God's pattern for living is not selecting a promise and manipulating Him to receive it. His pattern for living is surrendering to Him, hearing His voice, and obeying what He says. As we noted in chapter 12, God wants us to receive His promises. But His promises are not an end; they are a means to an end—becoming like Christ. Peter explained in his second epistle that God has "given to us exceedingly great and precious promises, that through these you may be partakers of the divine nature."[5]

Our motivation should be to glorify God the Father and the Lord Jesus Christ by being conformed to the image of Christ. When being partakers of the divine nature becomes our true motivation, we will surely see more of God's promises fulfilled.

Negative and Undesirable Occurrences Are Not Necessarily the Sovereignty of God

The sovereignty of God is positive and not negative, desirable and not undesirable. By His sovereignty, God sets aside the routine laws of nature and the consequences of human misconduct. Notice that our opening scripture is positive, not negative. God says He will have mercy and compassion on whomever He pleases. To receive God's unmerited mercy and compassion is good, not bad. Let's not take something good and make it bad. God did not say that He would condemn anyone He pleases. Mercy and compassion are blessings, not curses.

God exercises His sovereignty in conformity to His Word; His sovereignty does not violate His Word. The psalmist wrote by inspiration of the Holy Spirit, "You have exalted above all else Your name and Your word and You have magnified Your word above all Your name!"[6]

According to the book of James, "Every good gift and every perfect gift is from above, and comes down from the Father of lights, with whom there is no variation or shadow of turning."[7] The writer of Hebrews states, "Without faith it is impossible to please Him, for he who comes to God must believe that He is, and that He is a rewarder of those who diligently seek Him."[8] We would be wise to view God's sovereignty in light of these scriptures.

We may one day discover that many negative or misunderstood occurrences in our lives were not the result of the sovereignty of God, but the consequences of our flesh. The greatest obstacles to our faith are not caused by God's sovereignty, but by the flesh and the devil. To have strong faith in God, we must accurately discern God's sovereignty.

What Is Our Problem with God's Sovereignty?

Mankind tends to blame unexplained negative occurrences on God's sovereignty. They blame Him for events that He has not caused and for omissions that are not His fault.

Our problem is not God exercising or failing to exercise His sovereignty. Our problem is fourfold: (1) we resist God's sovereignty, (2) we are inattentive to God's sovereignty, (3) we misunderstand God's sovereignty, and (4) we deny God His sovereignty.

First, we resist God's sovereignty. When Adam ate the fruit of the tree of the knowledge of good and evil, he chose to live independently from God. He chose to be sovereign, and by so doing, he rejected God's sovereignty. By asserting our own sovereignty, we challenge God's sovereignty, making God's sovereignty difficult for us to accept.

Second, we are inattentive to God's sovereignty. We lead our lives in such busyness that we become insensitive to the Holy Spirit. To put it another way, our minds are so preoccupied with our own thoughts and activities that we cannot hear the Lord when He speaks to us. Through inattention, we ignore the promptings of the Holy Spirit and then blame God for the consequences.

Third, we do not understand God's sovereignty. We tend to confuse the sovereignty of God and the sovereignty of mankind. We may choose to believe or not believe God's Word, and we may choose to obey or disobey His commands. We are free to make our own decisions in our sovereignty, but we incur the consequences of our decisions according to God's superior sovereignty.

Through individual sovereignty, what a person believes becomes reality to him or her. In this way, many people will live forever outside of the presence of God. We who believe in Jesus Christ also form our own reality of life by recognizing or not recognizing God's goodness. By not fully recognizing God's goodness, we live our lives without much of His abundant, supernatural provision.

Fourth, we deny God His sovereignty. We refuse to give God access to our human affairs and then blame Him for not participating in them. We also resist God's sovereignty by denying Him His rights of initiation and implementation. We deny God these rights when we initiate our own works for Him and carry them out in our own strength.

This is how we refuse God's sovereignty. Now let's take a look at how we can allow Him to exercise His sovereignty in our lives.

Allowing God to Exercise His Sovereignty

We allow God to exercise His sovereignty in our lives by waiting on Him. God exercises much of His sovereignty as we spend quiet time before Him. We can best hear and obey the voice of the Lord when our hearts, souls, and minds are not otherwise engaged. If we consistently give

God His rightful place, we will see a great increase in God exercising His wonderful sovereignty in our lives and ministries.

Jesus submitted Himself to God's rights of initiation and implementation. He proclaimed: "I have not spoken on My own authority; but the Father who sent Me gave Me a command, what I should say and what I should speak.... Therefore, whatever I speak, just as the Father has told Me, so I speak."[9] He also revealed, "The Son can do nothing of Himself, but what He sees the Father do; for whatever He does, the Son does in like manner."[10] Jesus admonishes us: "I am the vine, you are the branches. He who abides in Me, and I in him, bears much fruit; for without Me you can do nothing."[11] This is allowing God to exercise His sovereignty.

As we emphasized in chapter 8, there is a great difference between what we do for God and what God does through us. What God does through us He does in His sovereignty and empowers by His life and Spirit. What we do for God we do in our sovereignty, which often lacks God's life and Spirit.

Admonition to Seek God's Sovereignty

Desire God's wonderful sovereignty. Keep your heart open to God's goodness. Embrace God's sovereignty that exceeds natural understanding. Invite God to exercise His sovereignty by waiting on Him and giving Him His rights of initiation and implementation.

Pray to Accurately Discern God's Sovereignty

My Father, please forgive me for misjudging Your sovereignty, for labeling my lack of spiritual understanding as Your sovereignty, for calling my failures to manipulate You Your sovereignty, and for imposing my individual sovereignty over Yours. Please give me wisdom to discern Your sovereignty. I invite You to exercise Your wonderful sovereignty without limitation in my life. I desire to change according to Your will and for Your good pleasure—and not for my own. All this I ask, not only for my own spiritual growth, but also that our Lord Jesus Christ, in whose name I pray, may be glorified and exalted in and through me. Amen.

Where Do We Go from Here?

Having discerned and sought God's sovereignty, we will now turn our attention to conducting our lives in light of God's sovereignty. We'll move closer to experiencing the living Christ and living in the presence of God by learning to recognize and cooperate with God's sovereignty. We'll enter into a lifestyle of fellowship with Christ, a lifestyle that is relationship-oriented rather than task-oriented. We will find that spiritual tasks come out of fellowship with Christ. And we'll return to our first love—the Lord Jesus Christ.

Chapter 15

Live a Lifestyle of Fellowship with Christ

"Martha, Martha," the Lord answered, "you are worried and upset about many things, but only one thing is needed. Mary has chosen what is better, and it will not be taken away from her."
Luke 10:41–42 NIV

We have seen that God's sovereignty conforms to His nature, His character, His Word, and His covenant. We learned that we allow God to exercise His wonderful sovereignty in our lives by waiting on Him and by giving Him His rights of initiation and implementation. We will now turn our attention to recognizing and cooperating with God's sovereignty.

This is our seventh foundational truth: we can choose a lifestyle of listening to Jesus, or we can choose a lifestyle that is too busily distracted to hear His voice. Our next step in experiencing the living Christ and living in the presence of God is to face the fact that our ability to hear the voice of Jesus and to know the specific will of God depends upon our lifestyle.

Mary and Martha Exemplify Two Different Lifestyles

The story of Mary and Martha illustrates these two lifestyles. Luke recounts the story of Jesus visiting Mary and Martha in their home in the tenth chapter of his gospel. As Jesus was speaking, Mary was listening at

His feet and Martha was busily making natural preparations. Martha urged the Lord to require Mary to help her in her busyness, but Jesus responded, "Only one thing is needed. Mary has chosen what is better, and it will not be taken away from her."[1]

This account illustrates two types of believers: those who focus on *working for* Jesus and those who focus on *waiting on* Jesus. Like Mary and Martha, believers today have welcomed Jesus into their houses—into their hearts. Sadly, some believers today, like Martha, are too busy working for Jesus to sit at His feet and listen to Him. He is speaking, but they are otherwise engaged.

Does this mean we should not spend time making physical preparations for ministry? Of course it doesn't. It does mean, though, that listening to the Lord is imperative and almost always takes precedence over physical preparations.

Every day we choose how much time we spend working in the natural and how much time we spend listening at Jesus' feet. We choose between preparing for the expected move of God in the natural and preparing for the expected move of God in the Spirit. We choose between works and grace.

Remember from chapter 7 that new covenant ministry imparts the Spirit of the Lord, but old covenant ministry follows Spiritless routines. Mary was receiving impartation, the spiritual benefit and empowerment of the Lord. Martha was too busy to receive the Lord's impartation. Afterwards, how much of the Lord did Martha have to impart to others compared to Mary?

As we've said, Mary and Martha represent two distinct lifestyles. Each one produces a different spiritual level of life and ministry. Mary exemplifies the way of the Spirit—the new covenant spiritual dimension. Martha exemplifies the way of the flesh—the old covenant spiritual dimension. Martha was task-oriented; Mary was relationship-oriented. Let's take a look at one person in the Bible who lived the Mary lifestyle—the apostle Peter.

Peter Lived the Mary Lifestyle

Peter's ministry to Cornelius's household is an example of the Mary style of life and ministry. Luke records in Acts 10 that Peter went up on the roof of Simon the tanner's house to pray. He fell into a trance and saw a sheet coming down from heaven with various kinds of animals on it. A voice said, "Come and eat." Peter's natural-realm response was "No, those things are unclean." However, this response was only momentary. Here again is what followed.

In Peter's time of quietness, the Holy Spirit told him that three men were looking for him and that he should go with them. The three messengers sent by a Gentile named Cornelius then arrived and requested Peter to go and speak to Cornelius's household. Cornelius was a God-fearing Roman military leader who prayed regularly. He had received a vision in which an angel of God told him to send for a man named Peter who was staying at the home of Simon the tanner.

Jewish religious law prohibited all Jews from associating with—or even visiting—a Gentile, and Peter faithfully conducted his life accordingly. This time, however, Peter chose to travel to Cornelius's house because he had been in prayer and was receptive to the Holy Spirit.

After arriving there, Peter addressed Cornelius's household telling them how God sent Jesus of Nazareth to the people of Israel to be crucified, to die, and to rise again from the dead so that everyone who believes in Him would receive forgiveness of sins through His name. Luke reports: "While Peter was still speaking these words, the Holy Spirit came on all who heard the message. The circumcised believers who had come with Peter were astonished that the gift of the Holy Spirit had been poured out even on the Gentiles. For they heard them speaking in tongues and praising God."[2]

Had Peter been living the Martha lifestyle, he would have been too busy to hear the Holy Spirit, and he would have refused to preach the gospel to Cornelius's household. He would have missed this powerful ministry of the Holy Spirit. Peter chose to live his life in close relationship to God like Jesus did. Sadly, however, some Christians today relate to God more like Moses did.

Moses and Jesus Had Differing Relationships with God

In breaking away from the religious law, Peter moved from the old covenant way of following prescribed rules into the new covenant way of personally receiving communication from God and obeying His directives. Along the same lines, the book of Hebrews contrasts Moses' and Jesus' relationships with God.

Moses served God as a servant, following prescribed rules according to the law; Jesus served God through intimacy with His Father. The writer of Hebrews explained: "Moses was faithful as a servant in all God's house, testifying to what would be said in the future. But Christ is faithful as a son over God's house. And we are his house, if we hold on to our courage and the hope of which we boast."[3]

Again, Moses was faithful as a servant, and Jesus was, and still is, faithful as a son. Both Moses and Jesus interacted directly with God. They accurately heard God's voice. They were obedient and did supernatural works of God.

Moses had an old covenant relationship with God, but Jesus had, and still has, intimate fellowship with the Father. Moses followed God's directives as a servant; Jesus expressed God's compassion to mankind as a son. Moses did God's work; Jesus enacted God's infinite love. Moses was task-oriented, but Jesus was, and still is, relationship-oriented.

Unfortunately, some believers who once had close, personal relationships with Jesus have lost their closeness with Him over time.

Leaving Our First Love

As we said, some Christians today relate to God more like Moses than like Jesus. They, like the Ephesian believers, may have labored intensely, endured hardship, persevered in trials and assignments, had accurate spiritual discernment, and been intolerant of evil. Yet they lack intimacy with Christ. Jesus sternly rebuked the church at Ephesus for not being intimate with Him. The apostle John received this message from Christ to be given to the church at Ephesus, as recorded in the second chapter of Revelation:

> I know your works, your labor, your patience, and that you cannot bear those who are evil. And you have tested those who say they are apostles and are not, and have found them liars; and you have persevered and have patience, and have labored for My name's sake and have not become weary. Nevertheless I have this against you, that you have left your first love. Remember therefore from where you have fallen; repent and do the first works,

or else I will come to you quickly and remove your lampstand from its place—unless you repent.⁴

Like the church at Ephesus, some believers today have lives and ministries that outwardly appear successful, but they have strayed from intimacy with their Lord. They have turned from a relationship-oriented lifestyle to a task-oriented lifestyle. Sincere believers are sacrificing intimacy with Christ on the altar of "justifiable" religious works. In other words, they don't spend the time necessary to be intimate with Christ because they are so busily engaged in Christian activity!

The Amplified Bible quotes Jesus as saying, "I have this [one charge to make] against you: that you have left (abandoned) the love that you had at first [you have deserted Me, your first love]."⁵ What is a first love? Do you remember meeting that someone special, and all you wanted to do was to be with him or her and let the rest of the world go by? It was so edifying to be together with that precious someone! Remember how you wanted to know everything about him or her? It's a wonderful season of life.

But what happens to many married couples? The world enters in and takes its toll. After a season, a couple's interest becomes less focused on each other and more focused on meeting the demands of the day.

How wonderful it was to bask in Jesus' presence and let the rest of the world go by when we first received salvation! What happened to our spiritual first love? The pressures of life left little time for intimate fellowship with our Lord. We grew distant. We left our first love. It may be a little uncomfortable to admit it, but we allowed the world—and at times even allowed our church activities—to distract us from having intimacy with Christ.

The church at Ephesus, as we just read, was in danger of having its lampstand removed. What does this mean? It means that God would remove His assignment, with its accompanying mantle and anointing, leaving the church without His specific direction.

We know that a lampstand gives light. Without light, people cannot see, and without seeing, they have no direction. As we have pointed out, some denominations today are mere shadows of their former glory. Leaders in these denominations have lost their sense of spiritual direction. They boldly proclaim teachings condoning behavior that is clearly in violation of Scripture—and even participate in such behavior! Churches that once ministered the anointing and presence of God now teach Spiritless knowledge and involve themselves in mere religious rituals and social activities. Likewise, some Christians who once heard and obeyed the voice of the Lord are no longer sensitive to His Holy Spirit. We each should ask, "Am I in danger of having my lampstand removed?"

Christ strongly admonished the Ephesian church, "Remember therefore from where you have fallen; repent and do the first works."[6] He's speaking that same word to us today. When was the last time that you enjoyed being with the Lord Jesus Christ so much that you wanted to let the rest of the world go by? It's time to do it again—and again!

How do we do this? It takes time, quiet time alone with Him. Let Jesus restore the intimacy that busyness has stolen. Come back to Him in quietness and humility. Intimacy with Jesus is not reestablished in a group setting; nor is it regained in activity. It is restored by being alone with Him.

Spiritual Tasks Flow from Intimacy with Christ

We normally think of intimacy as romantic involvement between two adults of the opposite sex. But there are other kinds. There is intimacy between a mother and her child and between the Lord and His worshiper.

Under the new covenant, spiritual tasks originate in intimacy with Christ and are an expression of His intimacy. We have repeatedly quoted Jesus' teaching to His disciples: "Abide in Me, and I in you. As the branch cannot bear fruit of itself, unless it abides in the vine, neither can you, unless you abide in Me. I am the vine, you are the branches. He who abides in Me, and I in him, bears much fruit; for without Me you can do nothing."[7] Unless our ministry tasks are initiated and empowered by Christ, they are only dead works or, at best, good works.

We must return to our first love. Our ministry tasks must flow out of our intimacy with Christ. We need to be more like Mary and less like Martha, more like Jesus and less like Moses.

Jesus told His disciples, "No longer do I call you servants, for a servant does not know what his master is doing; but I have called you friends, for all things that I heard from My Father I have made known to you."[8] He told the Jews, "My sheep hear My voice, and I know them, and they follow Me."[9] Paul, one of the more stable and spiritually productive people in the Bible, shared his desire to know Christ with the Philippian church: "[My determined purpose is] that I may know Him [that I may progressively become more deeply and intimately acquainted with Him, perceiving and recognizing and understanding the wonders of His Person more strongly and more clearly]."[10]

Admonition to Enter into First-Love Relationship with Jesus Christ

Return to your first love. Become intimate with Jesus by (1) sitting at His feet and listening to what He imparts to you, (2) avoiding the busyness that leaves little time alone with your first love, Jesus Christ, and (3) refraining from being so inwardly preoccupied that you cannot hear Jesus' voice. The Lord frequently asks for your attention when you're not prepared, not ready, not at your best, or pressed for time. Will you listen at His feet, or will you be distracted by your busyness?

Pray to Enter into a Lifestyle of Fellowship with Christ

Father God, I desire to, like Mary, do the one thing needed—listen at Jesus' feet. I want to stop busying myself so much in the natural that I don't take time to listen to the Lord. I want to return to my first love and enter into intimacy with Him. I desire to wait on the Lord and listen to Him. All this I ask, not only for my own spiritual growth, but also that our Lord Jesus Christ, in whose name I pray, may be glorified and exalted in and through me. Amen.

Where Do We Go from Here?

Just as the story of Mary and Martha represents two distinct lifestyles, it also represents two distinct leadership styles. In the next chapter, we'll look at how we lead others to experience the living Christ and live in the presence of God. We will see that not all human effort produces spiritual progress; Christ-initiated, Spirit-empowered effort produces spiritual progress. We will ask if we are so busy making outward preparations that we are missing the inner move of God.

Chapter 16

Allow Jesus Christ to Lead

> [God] put all things under [Christ's] feet, and gave Him
> to be head over all things to the church, which is His body,
> the fullness of Him who fills all in all.
> Ephesians 1:22–23

> In Him dwells the fullness of the Godhead bodily; and you are complete
> in Him, who is the head of all principality and power.
> Colossians 2:9–10

We just identified two opposing lifestyles in the last chapter: the Mary lifestyle centered on listening to Jesus and the Martha lifestyle focused on working for Jesus. We saw that sincere believers are sacrificing intimacy with Christ on the altar of "justifiable" religious works, and we responded to Jesus' call to return to our first love. In light of these two opposing lifestyles, let's turn our attention to leading others to experience the living Christ and live in the presence of God.

The eighth and last foundational truth we will discuss is this: to be leaders in the body of Christ, we must first understand that we are not *the Leader*. We'll now consider what it means to be a spiritual leader in the body of Christ, and we'll examine two distinct styles of leadership. We'll ask the question, Despite our best efforts, have we been missing the current move of God? We will then pray to lead others by Christ influencing them through us.

God expects new believers in Christ to become leaders through the normal progression of spiritual growth. The writer of Hebrews chastised carnal Christians, saying, "Though by this time you ought to be teachers, you need someone to teach you."[1] The purpose of making disciples is to make disciples who then make other disciples. We all should, therefore, not only be committed followers of those who are in spiritual authority, but also lead people into fellowship with God the Father and the Lord Jesus Christ ourselves. We must realize, though, that making disciples is a spiritual task that the Lord does through us.

Jesus Christ Is the Leader

True leadership in the body of Christ is not fulfilled in the flesh, but in the Spirit. It is not a role that we play or a position that we fill. Genuine Christian leadership is a person, the Lord Jesus Christ, living fully and unreservedly through us. Authentic spiritual leadership is when a person influences others by (1) being led by the Holy Spirit, (2) imparting the Holy Spirit, and (3) demonstrating the Holy Spirit (1 Cor. 2:1–5).

To be leaders in the body of Christ, we must first understand that we are not the Leader. As we have noted repeatedly, Jesus revealed, "The Son can do nothing by himself; he can do only what he sees his Father doing"[2]; and He informed His disciples, "Apart from me you can do nothing."[3]

Jesus, in His life and ministry, took time to be alone to hear the Father's voice and receive His instructions. Mark observed, "Very early in the morning, while it was still dark, Jesus got up, left the house and went off to a solitary place, where he prayed."[4] Paul exhorted the Corinthians, "Follow my example, as I follow the example of Christ."[5] Paul recognized that he was not the Leader. Jesus Christ was the Leader. Just as Jesus did only what He saw the Father doing, we should do only what we discern that Christ is doing. In order to do this, we, like Mary, must spend time listening at His feet.

In the kingdom of God, we are all followers, especially the leaders. Jesus commanded His disciples to go and make disciples—followers of Christ. Leaders in the body of Christ should train disciples to be led by the Spirit of God, to relate to God themselves rather than depending on their leaders to relate to God for them.

A Christian leader is a companion and participant with Christ. Christ leads and does the work; leaders accompany Him and participate with Him, allowing Him to do His work in and through them. Again, Paul taught the Corinthian church: "God is faithful (reliable, trustworthy, and therefore ever true to His promise, and He can be depended on); by Him you were called into companionship and participation with His Son, Jesus Christ our Lord."[6] Notice that being a companion with Christ comes before being a participant with Him. We may assume we are working with Jesus when we have neither taken the time nor made the effort to hear what He is saying to us. To be spiritual leaders, we must allow Christ to lead through us.

Christ Leads through Spiritual Leaders

A spiritual leader continually listens to the Lord and is responsive and obedient to Him. The Lord Jesus Christ leads through those who possess these qualities: attentiveness, responsiveness, and obedience. Remember, God reserves the right of initiation for Himself. We give Him this right by waiting on the Lord. It is He who uses us, not we who use Him.

In the Old Testament, Moses was one of God's great leaders. He ascended Mount Sinai, communed with God, and returned in the presence of God to lead the children of Israel. When he returned, his face shone so brightly that the children of Israel had him wear a veil because they could not look on his face.

The role of Christian leaders is (1) to enter into the presence of God in Christ, (2) to return, not only with direction, but also in God's presence, and (3) to lead people into His presence. In the body of Christ, we lead from within, not from without. Leadership starts with the leader's intimacy with Christ and proceeds with Christ's inward development of the leader. This intimacy with Christ and Christ's inward development then extends to fellow leaders and ultimately to followers.

Everything of spiritual value comes out of intimacy with Christ and is achieved by Christ working in and through us. Our degree of intimacy with Christ determines our degree of spiritual productivity.

As spiritual leaders, we must realize that not all religious activity produces spiritual progress. Natural activity, at best, produces natural progress. Christ-initiated, Holy Spirit–empowered activity produces progress toward genuine spiritual maturity. Any activity that draws people away from their relationship with Christ does not contribute to true spiritual growth.

We can appear successful and still be spiritual failures. Any church without the active ministry of the Lord Jesus Christ through the Holy Spirit is a good example, regardless of its size. The size of a church is not an indicator of the spiritual maturity of its members or even of its leaders. The image of Christ in individuals and in the body as a whole is the indicator.

Mary and Martha Depict Two Styles of Leadership

In the last chapter, we saw that Mary and Martha represented two different lifestyles. Mary and Martha also represent two distinct leadership styles. Let's review their interaction with the Lord.

According to the gospel of Luke, Jesus was teaching at Mary and Martha's house. Mary was listening at Jesus' feet, while Martha was busily distracted with making natural preparations. (Several Bible versions say that Martha was busily distracted with much serving.) Martha appealed to Jesus to require Mary to help her. Luke quoted Jesus' response: "'Martha, Martha,' the Lord answered, 'you are worried and upset about many things, but only one thing is needed. Mary has chosen what is better, and it will not be taken away from her.'"[7]

While Mary and Martha may not have been leaders in the early church, the story of Mary and Martha illustrates two distinctly different styles of leadership. Martha depicts leadership guided by natural reasoning, and Mary depicts leadership guided by listening to Jesus.

The difference between these two styles is not determined by personality but is found in varying depths of intimacy with Christ and sensitivity to the Holy Spirit. The Martha style of leadership leads people away from the presence of God; the Mary style leads people into His presence.

While it's helpful to divide leaders into two distinct leadership styles, please note that not a one of us is wholly a Martha leader or a Mary leader. We're all somewhere in between. Our fallen tendency, however, is to be more like Martha. We all must guard against becoming entangled in busyness in our lives and ministries. Let's examine these two leadership styles.

The Martha Leadership Style Relies on Natural Reasoning

Martha was making natural preparations after the Lord was already present and active. The Martha style of leadership becomes so immersed in the natural activities of ministry that it has little time for intimate fellowship with Christ.

In the book of Acts, the leaders of the early church recognized this truth at a time when the number of followers was growing extremely rapidly. As a result, one group was not receiving its fair share of food. The time required for the apostles to adequately oversee the natural aspects of ministry had increased to the point that it would compromise their spiritual pursuits. The twelve apostles observed, "It is not desirable that we should leave the word of God and serve tables."[8]

Busyness with natural affairs like those just mentioned frequently renders the Martha-style leaders spiritually ineffective. Being so preoccupied, they typically do not take sufficient time to enter into, return with, and minister to others the revelation, life, and power of God. They usually place so much emphasis on engaging people in activities that they cannot achieve intimacy with Christ or facilitate inner spiritual growth in themselves or in others.

Martha attempted to lead Mary away from Christ and into her natural distraction. Likewise, those who immerse themselves in natural religious activities frequently try to enlist and even compel those who are spiritually engaged to assist them in their busyness.

Martha-style leaders may be extremely knowledgeable of biblical facts. A thorough knowledge and understanding of the Word of God is essential. But this knowledge and understanding cannot substitute for regularly listening at Jesus' feet. Study and analysis of the written Word can never substitute for receiving revelation from the living Word—Jesus Christ. New covenant ministry is more than dispensing Spiritless knowledge, as we discussed in chapter 8. New covenant ministry is Jesus Christ actively ministering through believers.

Martha leaders generally surround themselves with excessive natural activity. They are usually uncomfortable being still and quiet. They calm themselves through activity rather than through quietness. They frequently miss direction from God and generally are void of the presence and power of God.

The Mary Leadership Style Relies on Revelation

Mary-style leaders value the quietness of being alone with Jesus. They are comfortable in silence, although they may at times also struggle to enter into the presence of God. These leaders may appear to be inactive to undiscerning followers, because they emphasize inner spiritual growth. Therefore, carnally minded persons may become discouraged by not seeing external progress in the early stages of growth.

This style of leadership is not characterized by indecision, inactivity, or immobility, as some may think. Mary-style leaders have the spiritual sensitivity and patience necessary to be led by the Holy Spirit rather than by human reasoning. They spend time quietly before the Lord, but they also quietly wait on Him simultaneously with performing ministry tasks.

It has been commonly taught that leaders should duplicate themselves in others. Instead of trying to reproduce ourselves in others, however, we should be imparting Jesus in others. This impartation is a supernatural work of the Holy Spirit.

Our waiting on Jesus allows Him to impart Himself into us so that He can later impart what is in us into others. We cannot impart Jesus in others until we first take the time for Jesus to impart Himself into us. We do this by living a lifestyle of waiting on the Lord. The apostle Paul lived this lifestyle.

Consider Paul's Journey to Macedonia

Paul was a Mary-style leader. He was sensitive to the Holy Spirit. The following passage from the book of Acts discloses one occasion when Paul allowed the Holy Spirit to override his intellectual knowledge of the Word of God. As he and Silas were going into all the world to preach the gospel, this is what happened:

> Now when they had gone through Phrygia and the region of Galatia, they were forbidden by the Holy Spirit to preach the word in Asia. After they had come to Mysia, they tried to go into Bithynia, but the Spirit did not permit them. So passing by Mysia, they came down to Troas. And a vision appeared to Paul in the night. A man of Macedonia stood and pleaded with him, saying, "Come over to Macedonia

and help us." Now after he had seen the vision, immediately [they] sought to go to Macedonia, concluding that the Lord had called [them] to preach the gospel to them.[9]

Notice that the apostle Paul did not receive the Holy Spirit's guidance on where to go until after he had received His guidance on where not to go two times. If Paul had persisted in going to Asia, he would have been out of the will of God. As a result, he would have preached to the wrong people in the wrong place at the wrong time. He therefore would have preached a gospel void of the life and power of the Holy Spirit.

Some well-intentioned Martha-style leaders "go to Asia," believing that they are obeying Christ's commandment to "go therefore and make disciples of all nations."[10] Unaware of specific direction from the Holy Spirit, they blindly assume Christ's command to go is without ongoing individual guidance.

Through impatience or by insensitivity to the Holy Spirit, they venture beyond the revealed will of God. In other words, they do not wait for the ongoing specific direction of the Holy Spirit. They accordingly venture out of the will and timing of God. They lead the wrong people in the wrong place at the wrong time. They preach a gospel void of the life and power of God. They stray from the Lord's provision and may even employ manipulative practices to fund their cause.

If we have acted upon the written Word only to be puzzled by apparent failure, we may not have received the ongoing specific direction of the Holy Spirit. We may have strayed into "Asia" instead of following the Holy Spirit into "Macedonia." We should all pray as David prayed: "Keep back Your servant also from presumptuous sins; let them not have dominion over me. Then I shall be blameless, and I shall be innocent of great transgression."[11] Like Paul, we should follow the leading of the Holy Spirit in making disciples of Christ.

Go and Make Disciples of All Nations

Jesus' disciples were His most earnest followers. They lived with Him, ate with Him, traveled with Him, assisted Him, and even suffered persecution and died for Him. Jesus taught them, instructed them, trained them, mentored them, and empowered them.

Jesus also had many converts who were not disciples. Multitudes followed Him to hear His teaching and to receive or observe His miracles. These people had neither the fellowship with Jesus nor the strong commitment to Jesus that His disciples had. Discipleship requires intimacy and strong commitment. Without these qualities, followers are not disciples—they are merely converts.

Jesus commanded His disciples to go and make disciples of all nations. He did not command them to make mere converts. Disciples follow Jesus; converts follow theological concepts. Disciples make other disciples, but converts do not. Today Jesus' command to the church is the same: go and make disciples, not converts. Every salvation creates the obligation to make a disciple; every conversion creates the obligation to bring the new convert into fellowship with God the Father and the Lord Jesus Christ.

At the time of Jesus' ministry on earth, many other religious leaders also had committed followers called disciples. For instance, John the Baptist had disciples. When Jesus commanded His disciples to go and make disciples, He intended them to make disciples *of* Jesus, not to make disciples of Peter, James, John or the others *for* Jesus. We make disciples *for* Jesus when we teach them to follow us. But we make disciples *of* Jesus when we teach them to follow Jesus themselves.

We make disciples of Jesus, not just by leading people into salvation, but also by leading those who have received salvation into a life lived in His presence, under His direction, and subject to His work within them. We bring them into intimacy with Christ.

Jesus is alive and still disciples His followers. As Jesus taught, instructed, trained, mentored, and empowered His disciples when He walked this earth, He now teaches, instructs, trains, mentors, and empowers His disciples through the Holy Spirit. Jesus' present-day disciples still eat with Him, travel with Him, assist Him, suffer persecution for Him, and die for Him. All suffer death of self; some also suffer martyrdom. Followers of Jesus who are not disciples are likely to miss the coming move of God.

Don't Miss the Coming Move of God

Preparation for the coming move of God does not solely involve building facilities and training personnel. It is, first and foremost, preparing the hearts of believers. Once again, spiritual preparation produces spiritual growth; natural preparation produces natural growth.

We tend to find ourselves preparing outwardly for the coming move of God. But the present move of God is here! The Lord is continually working within us, but some leaders are too busy preparing for the coming move of God on the outside to recognize, cooperate with, or even be aware of the present move of God on the inside. Like Martha, they find themselves busily distracted in religious tasks while the Lord is already ministering.

Admonition to Allow Jesus Christ to Be the Leader

Don't miss the coming move of God by not perceiving the present move of God. Allow Jesus Christ to be the Leader. Lead from revelation rather than from natural reasoning. Follow Jesus' example of saying what He heard the Father say and doing what He saw the Father do.

Build the body of Christ by leading people into the presence of God. Enter into God's presence, return in God's presence, and lead people into His presence. Produce Christ-initiated, Spirit-empowered progress—not just natural activity. Don't miss the present move of God by being distracted by a ministry of good works.

Pray to Live and Minister in God's Presence

Our Father in heaven, I come to You clothed in the righteousness of our Lord Jesus Christ. Nothing compares with You, yet my busyness often draws me away from You. Have mercy on me. Strengthen me in my weaknesses. Draw me into You by the power of Your love. Come into me in such a way that I am also in You. I desire to worship You with every fiber of my being. I want to come into the glory of Your presence by Your grace.

My Father, I want the Lord Jesus Christ to come into me and work in me with His Spirit in such measure that I would enter into the presence of God, return in the presence of God, and lead people into the presence of God. I desire to live and minister in the presence of God continually. I want to make disciples and not mere converts. I sincerely desire that Jesus Christ be the Leader in and through me. All this I ask, not only for my own spiritual growth, but also that our Lord Jesus Christ, in whose name I pray, may be glorified and exalted in and through me. Amen.

Part 2 Summary

In this second part, we activated eight foundational truths that are essential to our experiencing the living Christ, living in the presence of God, and leading other people to experience the living Christ and live in the presence of God as well. We began by recognizing that thirst is a prerequisite to the ministry of the Holy Spirit flowing through us. For this ministry to flow, we thirst, come to Jesus and drink, believe, and glorify Christ. We then recognized that building the kingdom of God has always been, and will always be, the supernatural work of the Lord Jesus Christ through the Holy Spirit. We learned that we receive revelation through grace in peace. We then found that faith is giving Christ preeminence. After that, we learned to live sound doctrine—doctrine determined by the Word and the Spirit of God, not by the Word or the Spirit alone.

We then came to know the Father's goodness by accepting that God exercises His sovereignty in conformity with His nature, His character, His Word, and His covenant. Next, we learned to live a lifestyle of listening to Jesus, rather than one of being too busily distracted to hear His voice. Lastly, we found that we are completely dependent on the Lord Jesus Christ to lead through us. We are not the Leader; Jesus Christ is the Leader.

Where Do We Go from Here?

In part 2, we have activated eight foundational truths that are essential for experiencing the living Christ, living our lives in the presence of God, and leading other people to experience the living Christ and live their lives in God's presence as well. In part 3, we will yield ourselves to five maturing processes that God uses to enable us to intimately fellowship with God the Father and the Lord Jesus Christ and to offer this same lifestyle to others.

We will begin in the next chapter by recognizing the importance of encountering the living Christ. We'll learn that crucial decisions that we make in response to certain occurrences in our lives take us from the life and ministry of the intellect into the life and ministry of the Spirit of God.

Part 3

Yielding to God's Maturing Processes

Chapter 17

Encountering the Living Christ

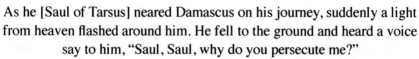

> As he [Saul of Tarsus] neared Damascus on his journey, suddenly a light from heaven flashed around him. He fell to the ground and heard a voice say to him, "Saul, Saul, why do you persecute me?"
> "Who are you, Lord?" Saul asked.
> "I am Jesus, whom you are persecuting," he replied. "Now get up and go into the city, and you will be told what you must do."
> Acts 9:3–6 NIV

In part 1 and part 2, we embraced spiritual realities and activated foundational truths that are essential to experiencing the living Christ, living in the presence of God, and leading others to experience the living Christ and live in the presence of God as well. In this third and last part, we will yield ourselves to five maturing processes through which God enables us to enter into true, intimate fellowship with God the Father and the Lord Jesus Christ.

Our first maturing process is leaving the realm of the intellect and entering into the realm of God's presence through our personal encounters with Jesus Christ. We will review Saul of Tarsus's personal encounter with Jesus on the road to Damascus and see how changing from knowledge without the Holy Spirit to knowledge with the Holy Spirit changed the course of his life and ministry. We'll recognize the place of knowledge in ministry and define ministry in the Spirit. We'll then describe our personal Damascus road encounters and the effect they have on our lives and ministries. Let's begin with Saul's encounter with the Lord.

Saul's Damascus Road Encounter Changed His Life and Ministry

According to the book of Acts, Saul of Tarsus (later called the apostle Paul) obtained authority from the chief priest to travel to the city of Damascus to capture men and women who believed in Jesus Christ and return them to Jerusalem for imprisonment. As he was approaching Damascus, the Lord Jesus Christ encountered Saul with a bright light, knocking him to the ground and blinding him. Saul then heard a voice that asked him, "Why are you persecuting Me?" Upon Saul's inquiry, Jesus said it was He whom Saul was persecuting and instructed him to continue to Damascus, where he would be told what he must do after arriving there. Those who were traveling with Saul led him to Damascus, where his blindness continued and he did not eat or drink for three days.

The Lord sent a disciple named Ananias to minister to Saul. When Ananias laid his hands on Saul, Saul was filled with the Holy Spirit, received his sight, and then was baptized. Saul immediately began to proclaim that Jesus was the Son of God in the local synagogues. What a transformation!

Saul's Damascus road encounter with Christ dramatically changed him. Let's look at the characteristics of Saul before and after his Damascus road encounter. The following table compares Saul's characteristics before and after his encounter with the Lord Jesus Christ.

Before Saul's Encounter	After Saul's Encounter
Zealous	Zealous
Exceptionally well educated	Exceptionally well educated
Dedicated	Dedicated
Angry	Peaceful
Prideful/arrogant	Humble
Legalistic	Extending grace
Merciless	Merciful
Self-centered	God-centered
Motivated by the law/works	Motivated by the Holy Spirit/grace
Had only natural understanding	Possessed natural and spiritual understanding
Submitted to man's authority	Submitted to God's and man's authority

Note that God changed all of Saul's negative characteristics but none of his positive characteristics! We therefore need not fear God changing us. We will be the same person after His change, only better—much better! Until God changes us, like Saul, we may be misguided by relying on knowledge of the Scriptures not tempered by the Holy Spirit.

Religious Knowledge Void of the Spirit Is Dangerous

Knowledge of God without the Spirit of God frequently leads to opposition to God. The Pharisees' system of religious education, void of the Spirit, produced Saul's misguided aggression. Saul of Tarsus—knowledgeable of the Scriptures, well trained in religious tradition, and foremost in his zeal for God—actually thought he was serving God by ferociously persecuting followers of Christ. He disclosed to Timothy, however, that he persecuted the church out of ignorance and unbelief (1 Tim. 1:13).

After Saul's encounter with the living Christ, he no longer relied on his Spiritless knowledge and religious training. He informed the brethren in Philippi, "If anyone else thinks he may have confidence in the flesh, I more so: circumcised the eighth day, of the stock of Israel, of the tribe of Benjamin, a Hebrew of the Hebrews; concerning the law, a Pharisee; concerning zeal, persecuting the church; concerning the righteousness which is in the law, blameless."[1] Luke quoted the apostle Paul in the twenty-second chapter of Acts: "I am indeed a Jew, born in Tarsus of Cilicia, but brought up in this city at the feet of Gamaliel, taught according to the strictness of our fathers' law, and was zealous toward God as you all are today. I persecuted this Way to the death, binding and delivering into prisons both men and women, as also the high priest bears me witness, and all the council of the elders, from whom I also received letters to the brethren, and went to Damascus to bring in chains even those who were there to Jerusalem to be punished."[2]

Saul's misguided aggression before his encounter with the Lord was largely due to his serving God from his intellect without the enlightenment of the Holy Spirit. Not having personally encountered the Spirit-realm Christ, he was unknowingly opposing God—whom he thought he was fervently serving! He had vision, initiative, zeal, and knowledge, but he had not come face-to-face with the living Christ. Unfortunately, this is true of some Christians, ministries, and churches in our day as well.

Today religious education without the inner working of the Holy Spirit still generally produces either legalistic aggression toward the truth of the Spirit or excessive tolerance toward the fallen nature. Remember from chapter 13, teaching biblical facts without the enlightenment of the Holy Spirit leads people into a false sense of spiritual maturity, making them opinionated, unteachable, and arrogant.

To produce spiritual growth, religious education must be accompanied with the inner working of the Holy Spirit. Jesus admonished the Pharisees in Matthew's gospel, "First cleanse the inside of the cup and dish, that the outside of them may be clean also."[3] Spiritual maturity comes out of actual fellowship with Jesus Christ, which is developed by waiting in quietness before Him. Holiness, developed through intimacy with Christ, is also essential to spiritual maturity and productivity.

Unfortunately, some contemporary Christians have lost sight of the importance of actual ongoing personal fellowship with God the Father and the Lord Jesus Christ. They have substituted education for the inner work of the Holy Spirit. A remarkable number of Christians, ministries, and churches are unknowingly opposing God by teaching mere religious knowledge without also leading their followers into intimate ongoing fellowship with Christ.

Surely, exercising biblical knowledge void of the enlightenment of the Holy Spirit is presumptuous. By being presumptuous, we mean that we overstep our bounds by asserting that our unenlightened interpretation of Scripture is true, when we should know by the illumination of the Holy Spirit that it's not. Let's not be guilty of unknowingly opposing God through exercising biblical knowledge not enlightened by the Spirit of God! We should all pray as David prayed in the book of Psalms: "Keep back Your servant also from presumptuous sins; let them not have dominion over me. Then I shall be blameless, and I shall be innocent of great transgression."[4]

What Is the Place of Knowledge in Ministry?

Accurate knowledge of God's Word is, of course, essential to ministry in the Spirit. As the Old Testament is the foundation of the New Testament, knowledge of God's Word is the foundation of new covenant ministry in the Spirit. Ministry in the Spirit includes knowledge, but it is not limited to knowledge. Ministry in the Spirit imparts the Spirit of the Word as well as teaching the natural knowledge of the Word.

Ministry can be divided into two spheres: knowledge and Spirit. Both are necessary. Knowledge must be in and of the Spirit to be profitable, and ministry of the Spirit must be biblically correct to be profitable. Each is incomplete and ineffective without the other.

Likewise, truth has two dimensions: mental (knowledge) and Spirit (Spirit-empowered enlightenment). The mental dimension is necessary to communicate truth, but only the Spirit dimension is capable of revealing revelation and releasing the power of truth. True ministry of the Spirit teaches the mental dimension of the Word *and also* imparts the Spirit dimension of the Word.

The ministry of the Spirit works something like this: One person communicates truth to another through language. As we stated in chapter 3, though, ordinary words are insufficient to communicate the Spirit dimension of truth. Therefore, the spiritual person communicates revelation to another with Spirit-empowered words. The spiritual hearer receives this revelation when the Holy Spirit reveals the spiritual meaning hidden in these words to him or her. The unenlightened person notices only the natural meaning of the language and does not benefit from the Spirit of the message.

The unenlightened knowledge of the Old Testament, upon which Saul based his persecution of the church, was not altogether faulty. He later used the same knowledge to declare Jesus was the Son of God. Paul never substituted this knowledge with something else; he subordinated it to the Holy Spirit. The knowledge itself was not defective; the intellectual interpretation was defective.

Knowledge without the Spirit is at best ineffective and at worst is dangerously misleading. It is imperative that we live and minister in the Spirit, not in and through the intellect alone.

Teaching biblical facts is not a substitute for ministry in the Spirit. It performs a different function and yields different results. Knowledge of biblical facts *informs* us of what we ought to be. Ministry in the Spirit *transforms* us into what we ought to be. Teaching biblical facts alone is no more effective in changing lives than eating soup with a fork. It's simply not designed or intended for that purpose and loses a lot in the process!

In the ministry of the Spirit, the written Word validates the accuracy of the revelation of the Spirit. The Spirit confirms the appropriateness of the message. Accuracy speaks to content. Appropriateness also includes motivation, timing, and delivery. Let's take a closer look at ministry in the Spirit.

This Is Ministry in the Spirit

Once again, after Saul was struck blind on the road to Damascus, he was taken to the city. The Lord told a disciple named Ananias to go to Saul, and that Saul had seen a vision of a man named Ananias coming and laying his hands on him to restore his sight. Even though Ananias was reluctant to go because of Saul's vicious persecution of believers, he was obedient. Upon entering the house where Saul was, Ananias placed his hands on Saul and told him that the Lord had sent him to restore his sight and to fill him with the Holy Spirit. Immediately Saul could see again. He was baptized, ate, and regained his strength. He stayed with the disciples in Damascus several days and declared in the local synagogues that Jesus was the Son of God (Acts 9:17–20).

Ananias's ministry—hearing and obeying the voice of the Lord—transformed Saul from basing his life and ministry on knowing Spiritless knowledge to receiving the full benefit of Spirit-empowered knowledge. This transformation enabled Saul to prove that Jesus was the Son of God so conclusively that he confounded the Jews (Acts 9:22). This ministry of Ananias is an example of the new covenant ministry of the Spirit.

As we noted in chapter 7, Paul reveals in the book of Romans that the old covenant was weakened by the flesh. The ministry of knowledge without the new covenant impartation of the Spirit of God is accordingly limited to the weakness of the flesh. Knowledge without the Spirit builds the intellect; impartation and inner working of the Holy Spirit change the inner man. The measure of ministry is, therefore, not in its factual content, but in its life-changing power that builds the image of Christ in the inner man.

Receiving a message from God and relating its knowledge does not constitute ministry in the Spirit. Ministry in the Spirit is impartation of the Spirit, not merely presenting mental knowledge of a message from the Lord. Genuine ministry in the Spirit is (1) initiated by God, (2) received from the living Christ, (3) developed by the Holy Spirit within the heart of the ministering believer, (4) presented and imparted by the Holy Spirit through the ministering believer, and (5) received through the Holy Spirit in the hearts of the hearers.

We should live and minister out of the Spirit and validate our ministering with knowledge of the Word of God. We should minister the Word by the Spirit, with God confirming His message through the ministry of His Spirit.

To minister in the Spirit usually requires a life lived in fellowship with Christ. It frequently begins with a personal encounter with the living Christ.

Experiencing Our Personal Damascus Road Encounter

As religious education without the Spirit adversely influenced Saul, it has affected nearly all of us to some degree. Most of us need a personal Damascus road encounter with Christ to transform us from the life and ministry of the intellect into the life and ministry of the Spirit. This type of encounter changes our perspective from natural to spiritual. It is indeed our opportunity to enter into the Spirit realm with the living Christ. Although we may experience many encounters with the Lord, there is usually one extraordinarily traumatic encounter that sets the course of our lives. In this one, we come to the end of ourselves.

We enter the Spirit-dimension life and ministry through this personal Damascus road encounter with Christ. This encounter generally has five stages: (1) confrontation by the living Christ, (2) recognition of helplessness, (3) awakening to the realm of God's Spirit, (4) season of one-on-one training with the Lord, and (5) life and ministry operating in the power of God. Let's discuss each one.

First, our Damascus road encounter normally occurs through crisis. The crisis, however, is not the encounter. Our Damascus road encounter is the mutually exclusive conflict between God's Word and our intellectual reasoning. It confronts us with choosing either the truth of God's Word or the apparent reality of our personal experience, but not both. This encounter forces us to choose between rationalizing the Word of God and surrendering completely to the living Christ.

Second, our Damascus road crisis stretches us beyond our ability to cope with the crisis we are facing. It brings us to the point of breaking. Through this brokenness, our internal defenses are weakened, and Jesus Christ enters deeply into us to do His work. Through this access, Christ begins to forge us into His image.

At this time, it's imperative to turn to the Lord, not turn away from Him. We must not retreat into our intellect. The choice we make at this juncture sets the course of our lives and ministries. We either turn to the living Christ, or we turn to rationalization. There is no middle ground.

Many times we miss the opportunity to benefit from our Damascus road encounter by intellectually justifying our unbelief. Something brings us to our knees, like the death of a loved one. We may have believed for healing, which did not occur. At this point, the Lord requires us to choose between believing our personal experience or believing the Word of God.

Third, the living Christ desires to lead us out of the natural realm and into the realm of His Spirit. But if we choose to believe our personal experience over the Word of God, we turn away from Him. We miss our opportunity to come into supernatural fellowship with the living Christ.

Fourth, when we refuse to compromise in our Damascus road encounter, we experience supernatural love and closeness to God the Father and the Lord Jesus Christ. The living Christ receives us, comforts us, and reassures us in His presence.

As we proceed from this crisis, however, we tend to lose this closeness. That's why it's so important to surrender completely to Christ in our brokenness and to take time to remain in close fellowship with Him. This is a tremendous opportunity to be transformed from the realm of the flesh into the realm of God's presence.

The fifth stage of our Damascus road encounter is experiencing Spirit-dimension life and ministry. We enter this Spirit dimension by traveling the "road to Zion."

We Journey between Damascus and Zion

Damascus represents *the life and ministry of the flesh*; Zion represents *the life and ministry of the Spirit*. The road extends between Damascus and Zion. Each rationalization we make takes us closer to Damascus (the life and ministry of the flesh) and farther from Zion (the life and ministry of the Spirit). We cannot have a Zion life and ministry while on the road to Damascus. We must turn around to go to Zion. We will discuss entering into the supernatural realm called Zion in chapter 21. For now, we'll just determine whether we are headed toward Damascus (the flesh) or Zion (the Spirit) by the criteria in the following chart:

Moving toward Damascus	Moving toward Zion
Intellect based	Spirit based
Rationalization of the Word	Faith in the Word
Natural sight	Spiritual sight

When Saul experienced his Damascus road encounter, he had to reevaluate everything he had learned. He had to subordinate it all to the Spirit reality of knowing Christ personally. He had to discard what he had intellectually believed and substitute the truth of the realm of God's presence. He could no longer rely on his intellect but could rely only on Christ. It required him to change his entire mode of life and ministry. Subordinating his intellectual learning to the Spirit did not invalidate his knowledge. Yet it produced a fundamental change in his life and ministry.

We have seen that Saul of Tarsus persecuted Jesus by persecuting the church. When we persecute the church, we are also guilty of persecuting Jesus. We might think we haven't persecuted the church, but we all have. We persecute the church when we criticize our brother or sister or other parts of the body of Christ (denominations) with whom we disagree. We all need our own individual Damascus road encounter with Christ to transform us out of this intellectual realm and into the realm of God's presence.

Admonition to Look to the Spirit in Your Damascus Road Encounters

Look to the Spirit when your personal experience or natural reasoning conflicts with the Word of God. Choose the truth of the Word over rationalization of the Word. Abandon living and ministering from a mere intellectual interpretation of the written Word. Allow Christ to actively live and minister in and through you. Turn to the living Christ instead of to doctrines of man in your times of decision. Advance from the powerless realm of the intellect into the power of the realm of God's presence.

Pray to Turn to the Spirit of God

Father, in facing my Damascus road encounters, I want to choose the truth of the Spirit of the Word over the rationalization of the Word. I desire to turn to the Lord Jesus Christ and not turn away from Him. I want to completely surrender to You so You can form the image of Christ more fully in me. Please enable me to do so by Your Spirit. All this I ask, not only for my own spiritual growth, but also that our Lord Jesus Christ, in whose name I pray, may be glorified and exalted in and through me. Amen.

Where Do We Go from Here?

In part 3, we are yielding ourselves to five of God's maturing processes through which we enter into true, intimate fellowship with God the Father and the Lord Jesus Christ. We began in this chapter by noting how confrontation by the living Christ sets the spiritual direction of our lives. We found that what we believe when our life experiences contradict the Word of God determines whether we enter into the realm of God's presence or restrict our perception of reality to our natural understanding.

In the next chapter, we will evaluate our strength. We'll find that true strength is reliance on God without having to rely on our own abilities and that spiritual strength comes out of acknowledged weakness. The realization that natural strength is weakness accordingly opens the power of the Spirit to every believer.

In subsequent chapters, we'll discover that we obtain ultimate freedom through genuine surrender. We'll see how surrendering who we are to God, and submitting our will to His, produces true freedom. Then we'll learn that we grow spiritually through intimacy with Christ, realizing that how well we know Christ determines the true level of our spiritual maturity. We will come to know Christ within us, instead of knowing Christ from afar.

After that, we'll enter into the supernatural dimension of true Christianity. Finally, we will enter into Zion through the tearing of our inner veil, learn that eternal life is knowing God the Father and the Lord Jesus Christ, and find out that we already have eternal life.

Let's continue in the next chapter, where we'll find that true strength is reliance on God without having to rely on ourselves and that spiritual strength comes out of acknowledged weakness. The realization that natural strength is weakness accordingly opens the power of the Spirit to every believer.

Chapter 18

Increasing Spiritual Strength by Embracing Weakness

He said to me, "My grace is sufficient for you, for my power is made perfect in weakness." I will all the more gladly boast of my weaknesses, that the power of Christ may rest upon me. For the sake of Christ, then, I am content with weaknesses, insults, hardships, persecutions, and calamities; for when I am weak, then I am strong.
2 Corinthians 12:9–10 RSV

We have seen how the personal encounter of Saul of Tarsus by the living Christ transformed him from persecuting the followers of Jesus to devoting his life to Jesus Christ and declaring that Jesus of Nazareth is the Son of God. We noted our need for a personal encounter with the living Christ that transforms us from the life and ministry of the intellect into the life and ministry of the Spirit, and we realized the futility of relying on our natural reasoning.

Our second maturing process by which we enter more deeply into fellowship with God the Father and the Lord Jesus Christ is increasing spiritual strength by embracing our weakness. In the following pages, we will discover that true strength is spiritual strength. We'll acknowledge and embrace our weaknesses, obtain true strength, and learn to rely on God's strength.

When we think of strength, we normally think of natural strength: strength of body, personality, character, will, or wealth. However, there is a greater strength than these: spiritual strength.

First, let's look at two men in the Bible to whom God gave extraordinary natural strength and at one man to whom God gave spiritual strength. In Judges 14–16, God gave Samson supernatural physical strength, and in 1 Kings 3, He gave Solomon two extraordinary strengths: wisdom and wealth. In the book of Acts, God gave Paul spiritual strength. Strength must be accompanied by obedience to God. Paul was obedient to God; Samson and Solomon were not.

God Gave Samson Supernatural Physical Strength

According to the book of Judges, Samson was born to a barren woman to whom the angel of the Lord appeared and foretold that he would be a Nazirite, was never to cut his hair, and would begin to deliver Israel from the Philistines. Samson, to whom God gave extraordinary physical strength, became a ruling judge in Israel and a great warrior. One time when his enemies, the Philistines, attacked him, he killed a thousand men with the jawbone of a donkey. However, he became involved with a seductive woman named Delilah and confided in her that his strength was in his hair. She then weakened him by cutting his hair and delivered him into the hands of the Philistines.

The Philistines gouged out his eyes, enslaved him, and mocked him. In the end, however, his hair began to grow back, and he pushed against two columns holding up a building where there was a great assembly of the Philistines, causing it to collapse on himself and all the people assembled there. Tragically, he killed more of Israel's enemies in his death than in his life.

God Gave Solomon Extraordinary Wisdom and Wealth

Solomon, a son of King David, succeeded him as king of Israel at a young age. According to 1 Kings 3, God appeared to young King Solomon in a dream and asked him what He should give him. When Solomon asked for an understanding heart so that he could judge Israel rightly, God gave him a wiser and more understanding heart than anyone before or after him. Because Solomon did not ask for riches, God also gave him more riches and honor than any other king of his day.

However, contrary to God's command, Solomon married women from other nations and worshiped their gods. He continued worshiping other gods even after God appeared to him twice, commanding him to stop. God therefore raised up adversaries who took ten of the twelve tribes from under his rule in 1 Kings 11:30–35.

God Gave Paul Spiritual Strength

In contrast, God gave the apostle Paul (formerly Saul of Tarsus) spiritual strength. Paul wrote a large portion of the New Testament, endured tremendous hardship, made numerous disciples, and performed many miracles. In fact, Acts 19 tells us that God worked extraordinary miracles through Paul. In our opening scripture Paul disclosed to the Corinthians, "I will all the more gladly boast of my weaknesses, that the power of Christ may rest upon me." The apostle Paul maintained spiritual strength through his obedience to God.

True Strength Is Spiritual Strength

When we finally come to the point that we know we can do nothing unless the Lord does it through us, God can begin to build His strength within us. Until we reach that point, our intellect primarily rules our faith. To enter into God's strength, we abandon our apparent strength by believing Him beyond the limitations of our intellect.

True strength is spiritual strength—reliance on God without reliance on natural abilities. Solomon admonished his son in the book of Proverbs, "Trust in the Lord with all your heart, and lean not on your own understanding."[1]

Realizing That Our Natural Strength Is Weakness

In our Damascus road encounter, we realize that our natural strength is not strength at all. Our natural strength is frequently nothing more than an obstacle that keeps God from exercising full control and free expression in our lives and ministries. The realization that natural strength is truly weakness opens the power of the Spirit to every believer. In other words, by recognizing our strength as weakness, we rely on God's strength instead of our own and place more reliance on the Spirit than on the flesh.

When the apostle Paul pleaded with God to take away the thorn in his flesh (a messenger of Satan), God told him, "My power is made perfect in weakness."[2] Paul then acknowledged, "When I am weak, then I am strong."[3] If we embrace our weakness instead of our strength, we will surely rely more on God and less on ourselves.

Embracing Our Weakness

We embrace our weakness by realizing that we do not have the capacity to perform spiritual tasks with our natural abilities or to understand spiritual truths through our natural reasoning. Paul wrote to the Corinthian church: "I resolved to know nothing (to be acquainted with nothing, to make a display of the knowledge of nothing, and to be conscious of nothing) among you except Jesus Christ (the Messiah) and Him crucified. And I was in (passed into a state of) weakness and fear (dread) and great trembling [after I had come] among you."[4]

Through the realization that our natural strength is weakness, we enter into true strength—not our own strength, but God's strength. We have true spiritual strength when we can rely completely on God without having to depend on our natural abilities.

Obtaining True Strength

We human beings, even born-again believers, are naturally weak, even if we are physically strong or highly intelligent. Compared to God's strength, our natural strength is weakness.

To rely on our natural strength is to refuse God's strength. Even so, most of us are so accustomed to relying on our own strength, having lived that way for so long, that we are fearful of abandoning our natural strength in order to receive God's vastly superior strength. We feel secure in our unnoticed feebleness and limited reasoning.

Changing from primarily relying on our natural abilities to relying on the Spirit of God is a significant departure from ordinary reasoning. But when we make this change, the abandonment of our own strength catapults us into the realm of God's power. Paul confided to the Corinthians, "I will all the more gladly boast of my weaknesses, that the power of Christ may rest upon me."[5] We too obtain true strength by acknowledging our weaknesses.

Instead of being discouraged when we come face-to-face with our weaknesses, we should become encouraged. We should rejoice and allow God to encourage us, because we can no longer rely on ourselves. We must rely on God.

It usually takes a crisis to shake us out of the deception of our natural strength. For Paul, it was his encounter with the Lord Jesus Christ on the road to Damascus. For Peter, it was his denial of Christ. We don't have to experience a crisis to shake us out of the deception of our natural strength. We can receive the recognition by revelation if we wait on the Lord.

Here is a portion of Scripture from the book of Isaiah that addresses surrendering our strength and receiving God's strength. Speaking of God, he proclaims:

> He gives power to the faint and weary, and to him who has no might He increases strength [causing it to multiply and making it to abound]. Even youths shall faint and be weary, and [selected] young men shall feebly stumble and fall exhausted; But those who wait for the Lord [who expect, look for, and hope in Him] shall change and renew their strength and power; they shall lift their wings and mount up [close to God] as eagles [mount up to the sun]; they shall run and not be weary, they shall walk and not faint or become tired.[6]

As this passage tells us, true strength is not the strength and vitality of those who are young. To quote the prophet Isaiah again, "Even youths shall faint and be weary, and [selected] young men shall feebly stumble and fall exhausted." True strength comes to those who wait on the Lord. According to Isaiah, "Those who wait for the Lord [who expect, look for, and hope in Him] shall change and renew their strength and power."

When we remove ourselves from the busyness of life and wait upon the Lord, He exchanges our natural strength and power for His supernatural strength and power. He brings us into His very presence: "They shall lift their wings and mount up [close to God]." He changes and renews our strength and power so that we do not become disheartened: "They shall run and not be weary; they shall walk and not faint or become tired." He will help us to confront our weakness.

Confronting Our Weakness

Our natural strength does not determine our spiritual success. Whether we rely on our natural strength determines our spiritual success. Reliance on our strength leads to spiritual failure. Reliance on God's strength leads to spiritual success.

God wants to mature us and do extraordinary works through us. Paul encouraged the Philippian church, "It is God who works in you both to will and to do for His good pleasure."[7] We grow in God and do His works, not by our strength, but by surrender and submission to the Holy Spirit.

When we rely on our own abilities, we become weary in our attempts to achieve spiritual results. The solution is to allow Jesus Christ to set our goals and work through us to attain them. Remember, Jesus proclaimed: "Come to Me, all you who labor and are heavy laden, and I will give you rest. Take My yoke upon you and learn from Me, for I am gentle and lowly in heart, and you will find rest for your souls. For My yoke is easy and My burden is light."[8] When we take Christ's yoke upon us, we allow Him to provide for us and do His work through us.

Anything short of dependence on God is pride. Before the fall, Adam was dependent upon God and enjoyed intimate fellowship with Him. He fell when he decided to rely on himself. Unfortunately, we all fell with him. God wants to restore us to relying on Him, but we must be willing to give up our self-reliance.

When Paul appealed to God to remove the messenger of Satan, also known as his thorn in the flesh, God told Paul, "My grace is sufficient for you." God wants to encourage us with the same truth. As we learned in chapter 11, grace never abandons us to our own devices; it is the empowerment of God. Paul wrote, "By grace you have been saved through faith, and that not of yourselves; it is the gift of God"[9]; and "As you therefore have received Christ Jesus the Lord, so walk in Him."[10] We walk in Christ, not in our own strength, but by grace, God's supernatural enablement.

Paul relied on his own strength prior to his Damascus road encounter with Christ. He stated in Philippians 3:4–6 that he had more reason to have confidence in himself than any of his contemporaries because of his education, his religious heritage, his diligence in following the law, and his zeal in persecuting the church. After his Damascus road encounter, Paul learned the true value of his own strength. We see this in the following verses, where he explained:

> We are the circumcision, who worship God in the Spirit, rejoice in Christ Jesus, and have no confidence in the flesh. ... But what things were gain to me, these I have counted loss for Christ. Yet indeed I also count all things loss for the excellence of the knowledge of Christ Jesus my Lord, for whom I have suffered the loss of all things, and count them as rubbish, that I may gain Christ and be found in Him, not having my own righteousness, which is from the law, but that which is through faith in Christ, the righteousness which is from God by faith; that I may know Him and the power of His resurrection, and the fellowship of His sufferings, being conformed to His death, if, by any means, I may attain to the resurrection from the dead.[11]

We, like Paul, should refuse to rely on our own persuasiveness and wisdom. Paul wrote in his first letter to the Corinthians, "My speech and my preaching were not with persuasive words of human wisdom, but in demonstration of the Spirit and of power, that your faith should not be in the wisdom of men but in the power of God."[12]

Jesus openly prayed: "I thank You, Father, Lord of heaven and earth [and I acknowledge openly and joyfully to Your honor], that You have hidden these things from the wise and clever and learned, and revealed them to babies [to the childish, untaught, and unskilled]. Yes, Father, [I praise You that] such was Your gracious will and good pleasure."[13] We should earnestly seek to rely on God's strength instead of our own.

Admonition to Rely on God's Strength instead of Your Natural Strength

Rely on God's strength instead of your natural abilities. Embrace your weakness instead of depending on your natural strength. God's strength is made perfect in your weakness. Wait upon the Lord to exchange your natural strength and power for God's supernatural strength and power.

Pray for True Spiritual Strength

Father, I want to rely on You without having to rely on my natural abilities. Please help me to wait on You so that You can change my strength and power into Your strength and power. Usher me into Your very presence and refresh me with Your strength and power so that I can do Your works and not be disheartened. I desire to run and not be weary, to walk and not faint or become tired. I choose not to depend on my natural strength so that You can catapult me into the realm of Your power. All this I ask, not only for my own spiritual growth, but also that our Lord Jesus Christ, in whose name I pray, may be glorified and exalted in and through me. Amen.

Where Do We Go from Here?

Next in yielding ourselves to God's maturing processes, we'll see that in the realm of God's presence, surrender is strength and victory. We'll learn that surrender begins with yielding ourselves to God for Him to remake us and continues with our subordinating our wills to God's will. We will discover that the believer in Christ finds true freedom in surrender.

Chapter 19

Obtaining Ultimate Freedom through Genuine Surrender

*Live as free men, but do not use your freedom as a cover-up for evil;
live as servants of God.*
1 Peter 2:16 NIV

We have seen that true strength is reliance on God without having to depend on our natural abilities. We discovered that we attain real spiritual strength by facing and embracing our weakness. We became secure in knowing that we achieve spiritual success by exchanging our natural strength and power for God's supernatural strength and power while waiting on Him.

The third maturing process through which we enter into fellowship with God the Father and the Lord Jesus Christ is obtaining ultimate freedom through genuine surrender. We will define genuine surrender, examine Jesus' example of submission to the Father, evaluate our degree of surrender, look at two biblical patterns of yielding to God, count the cost of surrender, and enter the lifestyle of a surrendered believer.

Our first act of surrender is receiving Jesus Christ as our Savior and Lord. In our initial surrender, we may offer only a shallow and somewhat superficial yet sincere subordination of ourselves to God. When we do, we become frustrated because we cannot attain the life and benefits of the Spirit in this limited submissiveness.

We eventually come to the realization that we cannot attain this life and these benefits by our human efforts. We face the fact that the only way to attain the life and benefits of the Spirit and to enter into active, personal fellowship with God the Father and the Lord Jesus Christ is by genuine surrender.

This deeper surrender is relinquishing our actual self, our innermost being, the essence of who we are to God for Him to re-form us according to His pleasure and His purpose. It begins with the renewing of our minds and progresses to Jesus abiding in us and freely expressing Himself through us by the Holy Spirit.

Genuine surrender to the Lord is joyous trust in the Lord beyond the comfort of the flesh and the false security of the natural mind. It is looking to Jesus for all comfort, protection, and provision. This absolute submission is the outward expression of our inner adoration of Him. It is in love joyously giving all that we are and all that we have, all that we ever will be and all that we ever will have, to Jesus.

This devotion to God begins with offering our bodies with all their faculties as a living sacrifice. Paul urged the church at Rome, "Make a decisive dedication of your bodies [presenting all your members and faculties] as a living sacrifice."[1] Our faculties include our hearts, souls, minds, and all that we are. This sacrifice is our "reasonable (rational, intelligent) service and spiritual worship."[2]

In this surrender, we transfer everything that concerns us into God's control; we hold nothing back. As the scripture we just quoted tells us, this is our reasonable service and spiritual worship. Paul confronted the believers at Corinth: "Do you not know that your body is the temple of the Holy Spirit who is in you, whom you have from God, and you are not your own? For you were bought at a price; therefore glorify God in your body and in your spirit, which are God's."[3] He informed the Galatian church, "I have been crucified with Christ; it is no longer I who live, but Christ lives in me; and the life which I now live in the flesh I live by faith in the Son of God, who loved me and gave Himself for me."[4]

Jesus made the way for us to surrender to God by completely surrendering Himself to God. Earlier in human history, however, Adam chose not to submit himself to God.

Contrasting Two Adams in Two Gardens

In the Garden of Eden, the first Adam ate the fruit of the tree of the knowledge of good and evil in spite of God's instruction to the contrary. He chose to make his own decision based on his own reasoning. He asserted his God-given right to judge for himself. In the Garden of Gethsemane, the last Adam (Jesus) subordinated His own will to the will of God and deferred all judgment to the Father.

In the Garden of Gethsemane, Jesus prayed, "Father, if you are willing, take this cup from me; yet not my will, but yours be done."[5] He knew the Father's will. He knew His own will, which differed from the Father's will. And He chose the Father's will over His own. Jesus told His disciples on the day before His crucifixion, before praying in the Garden of Gethsemane, "You know that after two days is the Passover, and the Son of Man will be delivered up to be crucified."[6] Without question, Jesus knew that He was going to be crucified.

Notice that Jesus did not ask that His will be conformed to the Father's will. While we should desire that our will be conformed to the Father's will, we should also ask that, despite our will being different, God's will be done.

Even though Jesus' will differed from the Father's will, the Father and the Son were in perfect unity. Our will can be different from the Father's will, yet we can be in unity with Him as long as our will is truly subordinated to His. Likewise, we can be in unity with the body of Christ even though our will is different from leaders in the body, as long as our will is subordinated to the will of leaders who are in rightful spiritual authority under Jesus Christ.

God has given all people the right to choose, to exercise their sovereign will. Our sovereignty is to obey or not obey God—and to receive the blessings of our obedience or the consequences for our disobedience. We may choose to disobey God as Adam did, but when we do, we too will incur the consequences of disobedience.

We should never relinquish our right to choose. Any spirit that overrides our will, regardless of how good it seems, is not of God and is necessarily in opposition to God.

Every day God gives each of us opportunities to choose between being like the first Adam or like the last Adam (Jesus). Will we reserve judgment for ourselves, or will we defer all judgment to the Lord and surrender our will to God's will?

Surrendering to the Lord Brings Victory!

In the world, to surrender to something implies weakness and defeat. In the realm of God's presence, however, surrender brings strength and victory. Our surrender makes the triumphant entry of Christ into our lives possible. Scripture tells us to lift up our heads in celebration; we lift up our heads in victorious surrender! David proclaimed:

> Lift up your heads, O you gates! And be lifted up, you everlasting doors! And the King of glory shall come in. Who is this King of glory? The Lord strong and mighty, the Lord mighty in battle. Lift up your heads, O you gates! Lift up, you everlasting doors! And the King of glory shall come in. Who is this King of glory? The Lord of hosts, He is the King of glory.[7]

Wait and listen in jubilant, victorious surrender! Celebrate your surrender to our Father God and to our Lord Jesus Christ. Enter into Christ through victorious surrender. Surrender to Christ brings victory over self.

Identifying Degrees of Surrender

Not all surrender is complete surrender. We can identify seven degrees of surrender and describe them as follows:

1. Actively cooperative	Aggressively seeking to know and do God's will
2. Passively cooperative	Desiring to do God's will without actively seeking it
3. Reluctantly cooperative	Doing God's will because it is the right thing to do and knowing that not obeying will probably result in negative consequences
4. Coercively cooperative	Seeking God's will when under pressure

5. Indifferent	Not seeking or resisting God's will
6. Passively resistant	Delaying or reasoning why not to immediately obey the leading of the Holy Spirit; outwardly cooperative but inwardly resistant
7. Actively resistant	Knowingly resisting the leading of the Holy Spirit

Where is the dividing line between being fully cooperative with God and being partially resistant to God? The dividing line is between number one, being actively cooperative, and number two, being passively cooperative. By not actively seeking to do God's will, we reveal a hidden reluctance that exposes at least a degree of uncooperativeness within us. God wants us to be fully committed to Him. When asked which commandment was the greatest, Jesus replied, "You shall love the Lord your God with all your heart, with all your soul, and with all your mind."[8]

Christ sent word to the church at Laodicea: "I know your works, that you are neither cold nor hot. I could wish you were cold or hot. So then, because you are lukewarm, and neither cold nor hot, I will vomit you out of my mouth."[9] To be hot is to be actively cooperative, number one. To be cold is to be actively resistant, number seven. Numbers two through six are lukewarm. Let's be actively cooperative!

Being actively cooperative includes (1) relinquishing self, who we are, to God and (2) subordinating our will to God's will. In relinquishing self to God, we give our entire being to Him to re-form us according to His purpose. In subordinating our will to God's will, we choose to do God's will rather than our own.

Before we can do what God has created us to do, we must become who God created us to be. We accordingly surrender to the Lord in two distinct ways. First, we yield our total being to God for Him to remake us into a vessel suitable for His will and purpose. Second, we submit our will to His to do what He has for us to do. The Bible illustrates this first type of surrender as a potter re-forming a clay vessel and illustrates the second type as a beast taking on the yoke of its master. Let's take a closer look at each one.

Yielding to the Potter's Hands

In the book of Jeremiah, God told Jeremiah to go to the potter's house, and He would speak to him there. Jeremiah went and observed the potter forming a vessel of clay. The vessel became disfigured, so the potter started over, re-forming the clay into a different vessel. God then spoke to Jeremiah, saying, "Look, as the clay is in the potter's hand, so are you in My hand, O house of Israel!"[10]

When our surrender is actively cooperative, we become workable clay in the potter's (God's) hands. We no longer restrict God to making selective or superficial changes in our lives. He is then able to make profound, permanent changes in us.

At this level of surrender, we stop struggling to produce the life and benefits of the Spirit. We learn to obtain genuine, complete, and permanent change through absolute reliance on God. We wait on God on a regular basis. In the words of the prophet Isaiah, "O Lord, You are our Father; we are the clay, and You our potter, and we all are the work of Your hand."[11]

As long as the clay is struggling to form itself, it is not workable in the potter's hands; only when the clay stops its efforts entirely is it fully pliable. Instead of exerting effort to change, it yields to the potter. The clay's effort changes from forming itself to being pliable. The clay relinquishes all self-will, self-direction, and self-effort. It focuses solely on submitting to the potter's vision and form. All initiative is with the potter. The clay conforms to the image formed through the pressure of the potter's hands.

When we try to change through self-effort, we are like a hardened lump of clay in the potter's hands. The potter cannot re-form or reshape the hard lump of clay until it is softened. The clay becomes softened through submissiveness to the will and actions of the potter. The potter cannot form the clay into His image as long as the hardened lump of clay is self-directed. Partial surrender by the lump of clay does not allow the potter to form the lump into His image. Isaiah reasoned: "You turn things upside down, as if the potter were thought to be like the clay! Shall what is formed say to him who formed it, 'He did not make me'? Can the pot say of the potter, 'He knows nothing'?"[12]

One reason God has not made some of the changes that we have asked Him to make in our lives may be that we have not surrendered sufficiently to be pliable in the potter's hands. We may be expecting God to re-form us into *our* image—what *we* think we should be. If we are, we are a hardened lump in the potter's hands.

Let's completely, unconditionally, permanently, and perpetually relinquish our innermost being to God our Father—all that we are and ever will be—with nothing held back.

Now that we have yielded our total being to God for Him to remake us into a vessel suitable for His will and purpose, we are ready to subordinate our will to God to do His will instead of our own.

Submitting to the Master's Yoke

Re-formation by the potter deals with who we are and who we will become. The yoke of Christ speaks to what we do for God and how we do it. Jesus declared:

> Come to Me, all you who labor and are heavy-laden and overburdened, and I will cause you to rest. [I will ease and relieve and refresh your souls.] Take My yoke upon you and learn of Me, for I am gentle (meek) and humble (lowly) in heart, and you will find rest (relief and ease and refreshment and recreation and blessed quiet) for your souls. For My yoke is wholesome (useful, good—not harsh, hard, sharp, or pressing, but comfortable, gracious, and pleasant), and My burden is light and easy to be borne.[13]

Let's look at the meaning of the yoke, the role of the master, the place of the beast, and the lifestyle of yoke bearing.

The Yoke Defines the Relationship

In Jesus' time, a yoke was a large collar-like device that people put on a beast of burden, such as an ox, and attached to an implement, such as a plow. It enabled them to use the ox to pull the plow at their direction.

The yoke is accordingly an instrument of productivity. It gives the master control of the beast, and it gives the beast the benefit of the owner's intelligence and direction. The master, through the yoke, enlists the beast to accomplish the *master's* task. The master does not ask the beast for input in performing the desired task or the timing of that task; nor does the master ask the beast if it feels like working!

In our illustration, the relationship is between a person and a beast of burden. But in His discussion, Christ is actually defining the relationship between Himself and the believer. Surrendering to the yoke of Jesus brings peace, rest, and productivity.

We take His yoke upon us through humility. Our relationship with the Lord Jesus Christ is like that between the master and the beast of burden. The beast is clearly inferior to the master and can never become the master. God is our creator, and we are His created. Being created by God, we are clearly inferior to God and can never take His place.

At the same time, God has created us to be much more than mere beasts. God made us in His own image (Gen. 1:27). When we are born again, we become children of God (John 1:12). And we may become friends with Christ through our obedience to Him (John 15:14).

We can say that Jesus' yoke is similar to the Holy Spirit in three ways. First, as the master exercises his authority through the beast by the yoke, so the Lord exercises His authority through the believer by the Holy Spirit. Second, as the yoke is "wholesome (useful, good—not harsh, hard, sharp, or pressing, but comfortable, gracious, and pleasant)", so the fruit of the Spirit is love, joy, peace, longsuffering, kindness, goodness, faithfulness, gentleness, and self-control (Gal. 5:22). Third, as the beast might resist the master's command through the yoke, so the believer might grieve the Holy Spirit by resisting the Lord's command. And as the beast might refuse to obey the master's command through the yoke, so the believer might quench the Holy Spirit by refusing to obey Him.

Jesus does not impose His right as master over anyone in this life. Instead, He draws us to Himself by His love.

The Master Is Responsible for the Welfare of the Beast

The yoke places the responsibility on the master to provide for the beast. The master provides food, water, shelter, and care. The beast provides none of these or any other necessity for itself. In return, the beast is submissive to its master.

The Beast Is Submissive to the Master

The beast does the master's work—in the master's time, in the master's way, and at the master's pace. The beast accordingly takes on the characteristics of the master. The beast and the master are like Jesus and the Father. Jesus explained, "The Son can do nothing by himself; he can do only what he sees his Father doing, because whatever the Father does the Son also does."[14]

The beast and the master work as one. The beast provides motion solely on the impetus and direction of the master. For the beast to move without the master's impetus and direction would be unruly. The headstrong, unruly, or rebellious beast is not suitable to yoke.

Just as a beast must be trained to accept its yoke, so our Adamic nature must be subdued. The beast has the choice to obey or not to obey, but its original nature is to go its own way. The beast's nature must be changed from being independent to being compliant so that the master and the beast can work together as one. So it is with us.

The beast is productive only when working together with the master and completely under the master's control. Only tasks directed by the master and performed in active participation with the master are productive. A beast roaming in a field without the yoke and direction of the master is not plowing a field or otherwise being productive.

The same is true for the believer in Christ. Energy that believers expend outside of the yoke of the Lord is spiritually unproductive. Paul admonished the Corinthian believers, "You were called into companionship and participation with His Son, Jesus Christ our Lord."[15] Jesus admonished His disciples, "Apart from me you can do nothing."[16] Productivity flows from fellowship with Christ. Tasks done in response to Christ's initiative and at His direction are spiritually productive. Taking on the yoke of Christ is not a periodic commitment—it's a lifestyle.

Wearing the Yoke of Jesus Is a Lifestyle

Wearing the yoke of Jesus is not a part-time job; it's a lifestyle. The lifestyle of the yoke-wearer is one of productivity resulting from regular times of waiting. Just as a thoroughbred racehorse must wait for the command from the jockey to run at top speed to win a race, so the yoke-wearer must wait upon the Lord. As a racehorse waits for its jockey's command, so we are to wait on the Lord. As the trainer prepares the thoroughbred for the race, so the Lord prepares us for His work.

In Christianity, we generally concern ourselves with three yokes: the yoke of the Lord, the yoke of the flesh, and the yoke of the devil. As a beast can wear only one yoke at a time, so can we. We should abandon the yoke of the flesh, resist the yoke of the devil, and cherish the yoke of the Lord Jesus Christ. Only the yoke of Christ brings true freedom.

Believers Find True Freedom in Complete Surrender

True freedom is not the absence of restraint. The crack-cocaine addict who exercises his freedom to ingest cocaine is not free. The alcoholic who exercises her freedom to drink alcohol to excess is not free. The smoker who exercises his freedom to smoke cigarettes is not free. The Christian, agnostic, or atheist who exercises her freedom to ignore God is not free either.

Choices have consequences. The crack-cocaine addict can ingest cocaine, but not without consequences. The alcoholic can drink intoxicating beverages to excess, but not without consequences. The smoker can smoke cigarettes, but not without consequences. The Christian, agnostic, or atheist can ignore God, but not without consequences. Such exercises of freedom lead only to bondage. Mankind finds true freedom only in God, because mankind belongs to God.

Mankind Belongs to God

Mankind belongs to God for two reasons: God's right of creation and His right of redemption. All mankind belongs to God by His right of creation; the person who has accepted Jesus Christ as Savior also belongs to God by His right of redemption.

The person who creates an object has the right to own and control it. The individual who creates an invention owns the invention and the patent. When a married couple has a baby, the baby is their child. That particular child does not belong to anyone else. Similarly, God owns mankind by His right of creation.

Persons who pay the price of redemption for an item they gave as collateral regain their full ownership rights. God has redeemed the believer in Christ by paying the price of redemption through the sacrifice of His Son on Calvary's cross. He therefore owns every Christian by His right of redemption.

Paul identified himself as a bond servant—a voluntary slave—to the Lord Jesus Christ. He did not take the identity of being an employee of Christ. There is a vast difference between a bond servant and an employee.

Believers in Christ are not employees of God. God is always with them. They don't work for God for eight hours and then do as they please on their own time. All their time belongs to Him. They take no vacation or retirement from relying on Him or obeying Him.

Most Christians in this generation have not experienced slavery. They do not know firsthand what being a servant entails. Because of this lack of perspective, they don't fully understand what their relationship to the Lord Jesus Christ should be.

Jesus is entitled to ownership and control of all whom He has redeemed. The apostle Paul alerted the Corinthians to this fact: "Do you not know that your body is the temple of the Holy Spirit who is in you, whom you have from God, and you are not your own? For you were bought at a price; therefore glorify God in your body and in your spirit, which are God's."[17]

Believers Find True Freedom in Submission

Ironically, the believer in Christ does not find true freedom in the exercise of freedom, but in complete submission to Jesus. When Christians voluntarily become servants of Christ, they experience supernatural freedom. In this servanthood, Christians live life to its fullest. They experience supernatural revelation, peace, joy, protection, provision, and fellowship with God the Father and His Son Jesus Christ.

This is probably the most difficult part of Christianity: to refrain from exercising our freedom to guide our lives by our limited intellects rather than continually looking to God's Spirit for His guidance. God gave Adam the freedom to eat the fruit of the tree of the knowledge of good and evil, but not without consequences. Unfortunately, the way some Christians are exercising their freedom today also brings consequences, rendering them weak, insincere, uncommitted, and hypocritical.

Once again, God owns the believer in Christ by His rights of creation and redemption. The believer is free to deny God His ownership, but not without consequences. One consequence is forfeiting the fullness of the supernatural life that God is offering to all His children.

True freedom comes from choosing not to use crack cocaine, alcohol, or tobacco—not from exercising the freedom to use them. Similarly, true freedom comes from absolute submission to the Lord Jesus Christ, not from the freedom to disobey His commands or ignore the leading of the Holy Spirit.

People can walk away from God's protection and stray from His provision, but they can never escape His love. We can repent and surrender to God afresh. However, true freedom is not free.

Genuine Surrender Is Costly

The apostle Paul lived the surrendered life. He described his lifestyle to the Philippian church with these words: "Whatever was to my profit I now consider loss for the sake of Christ. What is more, I consider everything a loss compared to the surpassing greatness of knowing Christ Jesus my Lord."[18] He continued to encourage them, saying, "Practice what you have learned and received and heard and seen in me, and model your way of living on it, and the God of peace (of untroubled, undisturbed well-being) will be with you."[19]

A drowning man will not stop struggling, because he thinks he is going to die. Only when he is sufficiently exhausted will he stop struggling. The lifesaver often waits for the drowning man to become sufficiently exhausted so that he will not fight against the lifesaver but submit to his efforts to save him.

Likewise, spiritual surrender is ceasing to struggle. Instead of pursuing what Jesus has already provided in salvation, it is allowing the Holy Spirit to work the power of salvation within us and work that power through us toward other people. If we are still struggling, we are not spiritually surrendered; we are probably trying to achieve spiritual results through the work of the flesh. Like the drowning man, we must stop struggling and trust God to produce His works in and through us. He is able. He is willing. He is waiting. Let's respond with a lifestyle of surrender.

Living a Lifestyle of Surrender

It is commonly taught that God is looking for our availability more than He is looking for our ability. To be available to God, though, is not merely a matter of being mentally and physically available; it is being continually sensitive to the Spirit of God so that Christ can initiate anything at any time in and through us. It is being continually attentive to the still, small voice of God in our hearts.

The apostle Paul strongly urged the Roman believers to dedicate their bodies, including all their faculties, to God: "I appeal to you therefore, brethren, and beg of you in view of [all] the mercies of God, to make a decisive dedication of your bodies [presenting all your members and faculties] as a living sacrifice."[20] A living sacrifice is a complete and continual sacrifice.

A Living Sacrifice Is a Complete Sacrifice

A living sacrifice includes not only the physical body, but also all of its faculties—the human spirit, heart, soul, and mind. We can be continually attentive to God only if we are sensitive to our hearts. As we have seen in chapter 5, God communicates with mankind primarily in the human spirit and through the heart. Those who listen for God to speak in their minds alone miss much of what God is saying to them. When our minds are subordinated to our hearts, the thoughts of our minds and the actions of our bodies can be responsive to God's communications. When we are attentive to these communications, we can be obedient to God and become spiritually effective.

To be sensitive to our hearts, we need to live our lives in inner peace. We refuse to allow the clamor of the world to drown out the voice of God within us. God can, of course, get through to us in clamorous times, but to be sensitive to God's voice continually, we need to live a life of inner quietness.

In this present age of radios, televisions, smartphones, and other electronic devices, we are tempted to live our lives in continual audio and video stimulation. Such stimulation, even if it is wholesome entertainment, may override the inner peace we need to be attentive to the still, small voice of God.

Even so, we don't have to avoid all entertainment. We should, however, be acutely aware of when our inner peace begins to be eroded by wholesome entertainment or when our spiritual sensitivity becomes dulled, even by seemingly innocent secular tunes occupying our minds.

A Living Sacrifice Is a Continual Sacrifice

A living sacrifice is not offered periodically or occasionally, but continually. God wants us to be open to Him at all times, not just when we feel that we need His assistance. Many have fallen into the trap of being attentive to God only in their times of need. If our lives are going to be directed by God, we must be open to Him continually.

If our children listened to our advice only when they thought that they needed it, we would consider them rebellious. All children need parental advice and direction when their parents see that they need it, not just when the children think that they need it. We are God's children. If we are attentive to God only when we think we need to be, like inattentive children, we are being rebellious. We are not living a surrendered lifestyle.

Living the Surrendered Lifestyle

Many times we come to God for His advice at the time that we need it. We may ask Him a question and wait for His response, only to be frustrated by not hearing His voice. God answers prayers, not only at the time they are asked, but also at earlier or later times. If we are not continually attentive, though, we may not hear His answers.

For us to require God to answer us when and where we decide is arrogant. We should learn to make our requests to God and to know that He is faithful to answer as we continue to be attentive to His communication through our hearts. Living the surrendered lifestyle is to be continually attentive, responsive, and obedient to God's communications.

Admonition to Enter into the Surrendered Lifestyle

Allow God to form you, as the potter forms the clay. Take on the yoke of Jesus, as a beast of burden submits to the will of its master. Enter into this relationship with Christ: make a firm decision to continually know the

Father's will, to be constantly attentive to Jesus' voice, and to obey His every command. This is genuine submission. This is the surrendered lifestyle. This is ultimate freedom.

Pray for a Lifestyle of Surrender

My Father, I want to gain victory over self through surrender to the Lord Jesus Christ. I desire to be completely pliable in the potter's (God's) hands. I want to take the yoke of the master (Jesus) and become His instrument of productivity to accomplish His purpose—in His way, at His pace, and in His timing. I long to be continually attentive to Your voice. I want to be quiet in my inner being so that I am sensitive to Your communication through my heart. Please work all this within me by Your grace. All this I ask, not only for my own spiritual growth, but also that our Lord Jesus Christ, in whose name I pray, may be glorified and exalted in and through me. Amen.

Where Do We Go from Here?

Next in our maturing processes that enable us to fellowship with God the Father and the Lord Jesus Christ, we will move from surrender to Christ into intimacy with Christ. We'll see how intimacy determines our effectiveness for Christ, examine the relationship between intimacy and spiritual maturity, acknowledge the necessity of obedience, see the importance of being comfortable in the Lord's presence, and learn to relate to Christ within us.

Chapter 20

Growing into Spiritual Maturity through Intimacy with Christ

> We will in all things grow up into him who is the Head, that is, Christ.
> From him the whole body, joined and held together by every supporting
> ligament, grows and builds itself up in love, as each part does its work.
> Ephesians 4:15–16 NIV

We have defined genuine surrender as yielding our entire being to God for Him to remake us into who He created us to be and subordinating our will to God's will to do what He has for us to do. Having begun the surrendered lifestyle, we will now continue into fellowship with God the Father and the Lord Jesus Christ through spiritual maturity. Our fourth maturing process is growing into spiritual maturity through intimacy with Christ.

Next, we'll learn to increase our effectiveness in the body of Christ and see how knowing Christ intimately and spiritual maturity are directly linked. We'll enter into intimacy with Christ by (1) being obedient, (2) being comfortable in the Lord's presence, and (3) coming to know Christ as He dwells within us.

The body of Christ is composed of many members, or persons. The body as a whole is no more healthy or effective than its collective members. Unfortunately, in recent years, some Christian leaders have paid attention to teaching individual members in the body of Christ intellectually and to increasing the number of individuals in the body, but have paid little attention to spiritually maturing and unifying the individual members into one supernatural spirit-being—the body of Christ. The body of Christ is growing in size, but some of the body lacks true spiritual maturity of its members and spirit-realm unity of the body as a whole. This part of the body of Christ does not have the spiritual maturity, unity, authority, and power to be effective in its Christ-appointed mission of making disciples. Instead of making disciples, it makes mere converts.

Increasing the Effectiveness of the Body of Christ

To increase the effectiveness of the body of Christ, we first turn our attention to building His individual members spiritually. Maturing the members of the body of Christ is much more than teaching them Spiritless biblical knowledge. It is leading them into intimacy with the Lord Jesus Christ through Holy Spirit–anointed demonstration, training, and guidance. Without entering into this intimacy, the body of Christ becomes segmented, powerless, spiritually ineffective, and noninfluential in society.

Our effectiveness in life and ministry is not determined by *how much we know*, but by *how well we know* Christ. We come to intimately know the supernatural living Christ with our hearts, not with our minds.

When Jesus asked His disciples who other people were saying that He was, they answered that some thought He was John the Baptist, Elijah, Jeremiah, or one of the prophets. When Jesus asked His disciples who they said that He was, Peter replied, "You are the Christ, the Son of the living God."[1] The public saw Jesus as the Son of Man, with their minds. By the Spirit, Peter discerned Jesus as the Son of God, through his heart.

Paul informed the Corinthian church, "We once did estimate Christ from a human viewpoint and as a man, yet now [we have such knowledge of Him that] we know Him no longer [in terms of the flesh]."[2] The apostle John tells us that our relationship with the Lord Jesus Christ is with the Son of God: "What we have seen and [ourselves] heard, we are also telling you, so that you too may realize and enjoy fellowship as partners and partakers with us. And [this] fellowship that we have [which is a distinguishing mark of Christians] is with the Father and with His Son Jesus Christ (the Messiah)."[3] Knowing the Son of God personally is, accordingly, essential to our spiritual growth individually and as a whole.

Next, we increase the effectiveness of the body of Christ by developing unity. Jesus desires unity in His church. He wants believers to be one with one another, with the Father, and with Himself. Jesus prayed, "I do not pray for these alone, but also for those who will believe in Me through their word; that they all may be one, as You, Father, are in Me, and I in You; that they also may be one in Us, that the world may believe that You sent Me."[4] Notice that Jesus prayed for unity in two dimensions: that we would be one with one another and that we would be one in the Father and the Son. This two-dimensional unity is essential for the world to believe that Jesus is God's Son whom He has sent.

In order to develop individual members of the body of Christ into one supernatural, spiritually effective body of Christ, we must emphasize (1) the realm of God's presence over the natural realm, (2) inner change over outward conduct, (3) spiritual growth over numerical growth, and (4) increasing spiritual intimacy over increasing Spiritless knowledge. In order to grow spiritually into one unified body, we must let go of our mind-based concepts and opinions and enter into heart-centered, intimate fellowship with our Lord Jesus Christ. Without intimacy with Christ Jesus, there cannot be true spiritual maturity or true spirit-realm unity in the body of Christ.

Knowing Christ Determines Our Level of Spiritual Maturity

The apostle John wrote the following passage that gives us insight into the relationship between knowing Christ and spiritual maturity:

> I am writing to you, *little children*, because for His name's sake your sins are forgiven [pardoned through His name and on account of confessing His name]. I am writing to you, *fathers*, because you have come to know (recognize, be aware of, and understand) Him Who [has existed] from the beginning. I am writing to you, *young men*, because you have been victorious over the wicked [one]. I write to you, *boys* (lads), because you have come to know (recognize and be aware) of the Father. I write to you, *fathers*, because you have come to know (recognize, be conscious

of, and understand) Him Who [has existed] from the beginning. I write to you, *young men*, because you are strong and vigorous, and the Word of God is [always] abiding in you (in your hearts), and you have been victorious over the wicked one.[5]

Four stages of Christian maturity are directly linked to knowing the eternal nature of the Son of God. These stages progress into deepening intimacy and progressive revelation of the eternal nature of the Lord Jesus Christ. Although these verses are stated in the masculine gender, they apply equally to male and female. They are as follows:

(1)	Little children	1 John 2:12	for His name's sake your sins are forgiven [pardoned through His name and on account of confessing His name]
(2)	Boys (girls)	1 John 2:13	have come to know (recognize and be aware of) the Father
(3)	Young men (young women)	1 John 2:14	are strong and vigorous, and the Word of God is [always] abiding in you (in your hearts), and you have been victorious over the wicked one
(4)	Fathers (mothers)	1 John 2:13	have come to know (recognize, be aware of, and understand) Him Who [has existed] from the beginning

The distinction between young men and fathers is that young men have unsustainable faith, whereas fathers possess sustainable faith. Spiritual fatherhood is therefore essential for the body of Christ to have persevering faith. Isaiah prophesied, "Even youths shall faint and be weary, and [selected] young men shall feebly stumble and fall exhausted."[6]

Fatherhood is attained, first of all, through waiting. The prophet Isaiah exhorted the people of God: "Those who wait for the Lord [who expect, look for, and hope in Him] shall change and renew their strength and power; they shall lift their wings and mount up [close to God] as eagles [mount up to the sun]; they shall run and not be weary, they shall walk and not faint or become tired."[7] To persist in the faith over time, we must advance from the Word abiding in us and being victorious over the wicked one to knowing and understanding He who has existed from the beginning—Jesus Christ (1 John 2:13).

To know Jesus as He who has existed from the beginning, we must know Him as the Son of God, not only as the Son of Man. One way we do this is by being obedient to Him.

Obedience Produces Intimacy with Christ

To be intimate with Christ is to abide in Him. For us to abide in Him, His words must continually live within us. The apostle John admonished believers in the early church: "Let that abide in you which you heard from the beginning. If what you heard from the beginning abides in you, you also will abide in the Son and in the Father."[8] To abide is to live; His Word must live within us as we described living doctrine in chapter 13.

Becoming increasingly intimate with Christ requires our continued obedience. John advised, "By this we know that we have come to know Him, if we keep His commandments."[9] Jesus declared: "As the Father loved Me, I also have loved you; abide in My love. If you keep My commandments, you will abide in My love, just as I have kept My Father's commandments and abide in His love."[10]

Jesus disclosed the conditions we must meet for Him to reveal Himself to us: "He who has My commandments and keeps them, it is he who loves Me. And he who loves Me will be loved by My Father, and I will love him and manifest Myself to him."[11] According to this scripture, intimacy with Christ is enhanced by this progression: loving the Lord Jesus Christ, hearing His commandments, and obeying Him. Jesus reveals Himself to those who love and obey Him.

Our First Step of Obedience Is Loving God

Our obedience is to living and active persons of the Godhead—the Father, the Son, and the Holy Spirit. It should not be like that of the Pharisees in Jesus' time to a written code, but like Jesus' obedience to the Father. Obedience is our response to our Father and Savior's love—not out of duty, but out of a pure, repentant, grateful, and loving heart. Our first step of obedience is to love God; our second step is to love one another. Without these two steps, all other obedience is unfruitful (1 Cor. 13).

Obedience begins with the Great Commandment, which is to love God. When asked which commandment was the greatest, Jesus replied: "'You shall love the Lord your God with all your heart, with all your soul, and with all your mind.' This is the first and great commandment. And the second is like it: 'You shall love your neighbor as yourself.' On these two commandments hang all the Law and the Prophets."[12]

Our Second Step of Obedience Is Loving One Another

Our second step of obedience, without which all other obedience is unfruitful, is to love one another as Jesus has loved us. Jesus instructed His disciples, "This is my commandment, that you love one another as I have loved you."[13] Remember from chapter 13 that Jesus doesn't love us with a superficial love; He loves us with compassionate, unconditional, self-sacrificing love. John wrote, "This commandment we have from Him: that he who loves God must love his brother also."[14] Jesus prayed, "I do not pray for these alone, but also for those who will believe in Me through their word; that they all may be one, as You, Father, are in Me, and I in You; that they also may be one in Us, that the world may believe that You sent Me."[15]

Loving One Another Requires Openness, Genuineness, and Vulnerability

Openness, genuineness, and vulnerability are indispensable to becoming one with one another. First of all, we must openly accept other members of the Body as they really are. This is not to say that we should tolerate sin. We should not. We must, however, refuse to allow our cultural differences or personal preferences to separate us from true, spiritual fellowship with other members of the body of Christ.

Next, we must be genuine. When we try to present an image of ourselves to someone else that is different from who we really are, we cannot relate with that person in Spirit-realm fellowship. We all want to present ourselves to others as best we can, but when we misrepresent ourselves as having strengths that we do not have, or as not having weaknesses that we do have, we become deceptive. This does not mean that we should constantly display all of our faults to others. It does, however, mean that we should be genuine and not try to make others see us as something we are not.

When we are open and genuine, we become vulnerable to criticism and rejection. Not all people will love us and accept us as we are. Even Jesus was not loved and accepted by all people. Religious people in particular criticized and rejected Him. As His disciples, we too, will encounter criticism and rejection. Nevertheless, we must remain open, genuine, and vulnerable with other members of the body of Christ.

Through intimacy with Christ, we attain the courage and integrity necessary to be open, genuine, and vulnerable with our fellow believers. Through this intimacy, we grow into true spiritual maturity and true Spirit-realm unity in the body of Christ.

Loving One Another Requires Spiritual Maturity

Spiritual maturity demands that we resist the temptation to view other members of the body of Christ as our adversaries and refrain from criticizing them. This does not mean that we should not disagree with other believers. Nor does it mean that we should not correct those who are in error.

Spiritually mature believers prayerfully come together and seek God's resolution to their differences. They endeavor to keep the unity of the Spirit in the bond of peace (Eph. 4:3) because where envy and strife exist there is also confusion and every evil work (James. 3:16). Indeed, a person who sows discord among brethren is an abomination to the Lord (Prov. 6:19).

We know that we cannot love one another as Christ has loved us in our own strength. Yet John tells us that to obey God's commandments is not burdensome: "This is the love of God, that we keep His commandments. And His commandments are not burdensome."[16] God fills us with His love by the Holy Spirit. Paul disclosed to the church at Rome, "Now hope does not disappoint, because the love of God has been poured out in our hearts by the Holy Spirit who was given to us."[17] Because of God's great love for us, we can not only be obedient, but actually be comfortable in the Lord's supernatural presence.

Becoming Comfortable in the Lord's Supernatural Presence

Intimacy requires comfort. We cannot be intimate with someone without being comfortable in their presence. This is the basis of all godly relationships: we must be free of condemnation. Love gives us this freedom. The apostle John taught the early church, "There is no fear in love; but perfect love casts out fear, because fear involves punishment, and the one who fears is not perfected in love."[18] Being comfortable with Christ deepens our relationship with Him and increases our ability to freely receive, retain, and express His revelation.

Remember from chapter 6 that we know Christ as He really is with our hearts. This way, we move past only knowing the image of the man Jesus and become intimate with the Son of God, whose greatness is far beyond our human comprehension. We become more comfortable in the presence of the living Christ as we come to know Him more intimately through waiting on Him.

The apostle John referred to himself as the disciple whom Jesus loved, saying, "There was leaning on Jesus' bosom one of His disciples, whom Jesus loved."[19] When Jesus was on the cross and "saw His mother, and the disciple whom He loved standing by, He said to His mother, 'Woman, behold your son!' Then He said to the disciple, 'Behold your mother!' And from that hour that disciple took her to his own home."[20] Jesus revealed Himself to John in the book of Revelation. John probably had a more intimate relationship with Jesus as the Son of Man and with Jesus as the Son of God than did any other person.

To be comfortable in the presence of the living Christ, we release our dependence on the natural mind. This enables us to progress from our natural perception of Christ to a supernatural perception. We can then know and relate to Christ more like John did and less like Philip did, as we saw in chapter 6, and less like Thomas did, as we saw in chapter 7. We leave the deceptive, false security of the natural realm and enter into the realm of God's presence by becoming intimate with Christ within us.

Coming to Know Christ within Us

Christ will return, but until He does, His ministry is internal. He relates and ministers to us from within. Paul informed the Colossian church, "God willed to make known what are the riches of the glory of this mystery among the Gentiles: which is Christ in you, the hope of glory."[21] The apostle Paul encouraged the believers in Philippi, "It is God who works in you both to will and to do for His good pleasure."[22] Paul also labored to form Christ in the Galatian believers. He addressed them as "my little children, for whom I am again suffering birth pangs until Christ is completely and permanently formed (molded) within you."[23]

Christ resides within the heart of the believer, fills the believer with His life, and produces His fruit through the believer. In a scripture that we have quoted repeatedly, Jesus told His disciples, "I am the vine, you are the branches. He who abides in Me, and I in him, bears much fruit; for without Me you can do nothing."[24] We bear fruit when we have been filled with the life of Christ, but some Christians are looking to an external Christ.

Some Christians Are Looking to an External Christ

Some Christians are looking for an external Jesus to come and deliver them, but Christ fully formed in them is their deliverer! They look to an external Christ for guidance, healing, and deliverance. Instead of surrendering to Christ who lives in them, they persistently pursue, to no avail, a distant external Christ.

The kingdom of God is not external, but internal. When the Pharisees asked Jesus when the kingdom of God would come, He replied: "The kingdom of God does not come with observation; nor will they say, 'See here!' or 'See there!' For indeed, the kingdom of God is within you."[25]

The Pharisees were looking for a Messiah who would establish an external kingdom for the external ministry of God. Jesus rebuked them: "Woe to you, scribes and Pharisees, hypocrites! For you cleanse the outside of the cup and dish, but inside they are full of extortion and self-indulgence. Blind Pharisee, first cleanse the inside of the cup and dish, that the outside of them may be clean also."[26]

The Internal Ministry of Christ Sets the Course of Our Lives

The purity of our heart, not our outward appearance, determines our spiritual growth and effectiveness and sets the course of our lives. The crucial question is not how surrendered we are to God in outward appearance, but how surrendered we are to the rule of Christ within us. As long as we major on the external, we continue to miss the life-changing essence and power of the ministry of Christ within us. Let's stop looking to an external Messiah and look to our internal Savior and Lord in whom dwells all the fullness of the Godhead bodily.

We yield ourselves to the rule of Christ within us and become intimate with Him by regularly waiting on the Lord. Again, the prophet Isaiah proclaimed, "Those who wait for the Lord [who expect, look for, and hope in Him] shall change and renew their strength and power; they shall lift their wings and mount up [close to God] as eagles [mount up to the sun]; they shall run and not be weary, they shall walk and not faint or become tired."[27]

All the truths we discussed in this and in preceding chapters prepare us to confidently wait on the Lord and accurately discern His voice. Although there is no valid formula, I have experienced my greatest success when waiting on the Lord in a quiet place with my body relaxed; my soul quiet and restful; my mind clear and still, yet alert; and my heart peaceful and open.

Entering into this state of being requires time, patience, and perseverance. Over time, we learn to patiently wait on the Lord, steadfastly resisting the worldly pressure to get busy handling pressing matters. As we do, we become comfortable waiting in silence, even when we are hearing nothing, secure in the knowledge that the time we spend waiting on the Lord is never wasted. Somehow waiting on the Lord increases our spiritual productivity, even when we have heard nothing.

We learn by experience that the Lord responds in His time and in His way. His response is always insightful, meaningful, edifying, and productive. In this way, we come to know Christ within us and join the ranks of those who know the glorified Lord as described in chapter 6.

Admonition to Enter into Intimacy with Christ

Take time to become intimate with Christ. Attentively listen for His voice at all times. Enter into true spirit-realm unity with other believers, becoming one supernatural spirit-being with them, the body of Christ. Decide now to be obedient to His every command. Become comfortable in His presence. Look to Christ within you at all times. Surrender to Him and enjoy the life-changing essence and power of the ministry of Christ within you.

Pray to Enter into Intimacy with Christ

My Father, please forgive me for concentrating on gaining Spiritless knowledge rather than on developing intimacy with You. Please forgive me for not entering into supernatural spiritual unity with other members of the body of Christ, for not becoming one spirit-being with them, forming the body of Christ. I desire to advance into fatherhood/motherhood in Christ, into the maturity of intimately knowing Christ in increasing levels of spiritual understanding. I want to enter into intimacy with Christ through obedience with a pure heart. I long to joyfully desire Christ to live and rule within me and to become truly comfortable in the Lord's presence. Please teach me to wait on You, Lord. All this I ask, not only for my own spiritual growth, but also that our Lord Jesus Christ, in whose name I pray, may be glorified and exalted in and through me. Amen.

Where Do We Go from Here?

We have learned that we must look to Christ within us rather than looking to a distant Christ, and that we become intimate with Christ by waiting on Him. We found that true spiritual maturity is not only maturing individually, but also includes becoming one spirit-being with other believers, the body of Christ. Next, we will see that true Christianity is entering into actual personal fellowship with God the Father and the Lord Jesus Christ. This fellowship determines the quality of our relationships and the effectiveness of our ministries. We'll learn that the way we live determines our spiritual effectiveness and see that our lives and ministries are completely dependent upon our fellowship with the Lord Jesus Christ.

Chapter 21

Living Eternal Life

This is eternal life, that they may know You, the only true God, and Jesus Christ whom You have sent.
John 17:3

We have seen that intimacy with Christ advances our spiritual maturity and increases our spiritual effectiveness in the body of Christ. Being obedient to Christ and being comfortable in His supernatural presence are essential to entering into intimacy with Him. We learned to look to Christ within us rather than to a distant Christ, and to confidently wait on the Lord, accurately discerning His voice. We prayed to enter into intimacy with our Lord Jesus Christ. Now we'll continue to deepen our fellowship with God the Father and the Lord Jesus Christ by actually entering into eternal life.

The fifth and last maturing process that we'll discuss is entering into the presence of God within us through the tearing of our inner veil. We will see how God reveals His presence, describe the state of being in God's presence that is known as living in Zion, and discover how we enter into God's presence within us by the tearing of the inner veil. We will see that eternal life is knowing God the Father and the Lord Jesus Christ, and we'll become secure in knowing that we are now living eternal life. Let's start with the ways God reveals His presence.

God Reveals His Presence in Three Ways

We can identify three expressions of the presence of God: (1) His omnipresent presence, (2) His evidentiary, or manifest, presence, and (3) His communal presence. These three expressions are listed in ascending order of intimacy. Each expression requires a greater level of spiritual awareness.

God Reveals His Omnipresence

God's omnipresence is His being present everywhere. The psalmist reasoned: "Where could I go from Your Spirit? Or where could I flee from Your presence? If I ascend up into heaven, You are there; if I make my bed in Sheol (the place of the dead), behold, You are there. If I take the wings of the morning or dwell in the uttermost parts of the sea, even there shall Your hand lead me, and Your right hand shall hold me."[1] There is nowhere that God is not present.

God reveals His power and nature to all people, even to those who do not believe in Him. The apostle Paul stated this sobering fact very clearly to the church at Rome:

> The wrath of God is revealed from heaven against all ungodliness and wickedness of those who by their wickedness suppress the truth. For what can be known about God is plain to them, because God has shown it to them. Ever since the creation of the world his eternal power and divine nature, invisible though they are, have been understood and seen through the things he has made. So they are without excuse.[2]

God Reveals His Evidentiary (Manifest) Presence

God's evidentiary presence, commonly known as His manifest presence, is seen in His acts, such as answering prayers and working miracles. The children of Israel experienced God's manifest presence in many ways. They participated in God's miraculous exodus from Egypt, which included supernatural protection from the Egyptian plagues and the parting of the

Red Sea. In the wilderness, they experienced the protection and guidance of the cloud by day and the pillar of fire at night. They also ate manna that God supernaturally supplied, and they drank water that God brought forth from a rock. The children of Israel experienced God's manifest presence because Moses met personally with God and interceded for them (Ex. 32:9–14).

Today we experience God's manifest presence when He expresses His supernatural ability in naturally observable ways. Prevalent examples are answers to prayer, prophecy, tongues and interpretations, healings, and expelling demons. God's manifest presence can take place at any time and in any place, but its occurrence is usually due to someone having paid the price to enter into God's communal presence.

God Reveals His Communal Presence

Believers enter God's communal presence when He awakens their spiritual sensitivity. They experience Him firsthand, entering into Him and becoming one with Him. In the book of Exodus, Moses ascended Mount Sinai and met personally with God. He did not have God within him as believers do under the new covenant, yet he communed so closely with God that when he returned from God's presence, his face shone with such intensity that the children of Israel had him conceal his face with a veil.

Scripture tells us that God "made known His ways to Moses, His acts to the children of Israel."[3] We can say that God opened His communal presence to Moses, but He only revealed His manifested presence to the children of Israel. Because they had no personal communion with God, the children of Israel did not have enduring faith, even though they had received His supernatural benefits. Likewise, some Christians today have observed or experienced God's manifested presence but are not personally experiencing God intimately.

Living in this supernatural awareness of God's communal presence is sometimes referred to as living in Zion. Let's take a closer look.

Entering the Supernatural Realm Called Zion

There is a state of being in the presence of God where self is overthrown and obedience is most earnestly desired. Through fellowship with Christ, all believers may continually live in the presence of God, if they don't abandon that fellowship by forsaking holiness or by being inattentive because of busyness or other distractions.

Every Believer Can Live in the Presence of God

Under the old covenant, God's people worshiped Him in a building called the temple. God dwelled in a secluded part of the temple known as the Holy of Holies, which was separated from the rest of the interior by a very thick veil. Only the high priest could enter this area, and he could enter only once a year. Under the new covenant, however, every believer can enter the presence of God at any time. In fact, every believer can live in the presence of God.

This presence, called Zion, is the new covenant equivalent to the Holy of Holies. In the Old Testament, Mount Zion was a geographic location. In the New Testament, Zion is the supernatural spiritual environment of the kingdom of God in which believers who have entered fully into the new covenant spiritual dimension live. The prophet Isaiah foretold: "The Lord is exalted, for He dwells on high; He will fill Zion with justice and righteousness (moral and spiritual rectitude in every area and relation). And there shall be stability in your times, an abundance of salvation, wisdom, and knowledge; the reverent fear and worship of the Lord is your treasure and His."[4] Is this really possible?

The answer is emphatically yes! The author of the book of Hebrews exhorted believers, "You have come to Mount Zion and to the city of the living God, the heavenly Jerusalem."[5] Writing to Hebrew believers, he informed them, "You *have come* to Mount Zion." Therefore, living in Zion is not a future event in the next life, but a provision Jesus makes for every believer in this life!

Christians need not limit themselves to being in Christ positionally; all believers can enter into Christ *experientially*. Believers enter into the presence of God through time and surrender—waiting on the Lord.

Jesus Is the Connection between God and Mankind

Jesus is the connection between God and mankind. He proclaimed, "I am the Door; anyone who enters in through Me will be saved (will live)."[6] Paul enlightened the Ephesian believers with this truth: God has "blessed us with every spiritual blessing in the heavenly places in Christ."[7] He informed the church at Corinth, "All the promises of God in Him are Yes, and in Him Amen, to the glory of God through us."[8] These scriptures describe the life that God has already provided for His believers who enter into Zion.

Here is an important point to remember: any barrier between the believer and God is not outside of the person, but inside the person. It is not between the believer and God, but between the believer's soul and human spirit, because "he who is joined to the Lord is one spirit with Him."[9] (Remember our discussion of the condition of the heart and the separation of the soul and human spirit in chapter 5.) With all this in mind, we can approach Zion without fear.

We Need Not Fear Entering into Zion

Unfortunately, there are Christians who will not enter into Zion. Some are simply unaware of Zion or have not experienced this supernatural dimension of the Christian faith. Others want to maintain control of their lives rather than releasing control of them to the Holy Spirit. Some are suspicious of supernatural occurrences and refuse to have any part of them. Still others even refuse to acknowledge their existence in the world today!

We need not fear entering Zion, as the children of Israel did. They wanted Moses to be their liaison to God because they feared His presence. The writer of Hebrews admonished the Hebrew believers: "You have not come to the mountain that may be touched and that burned with fire, and to blackness and darkness and tempest, and the sound of a trumpet and the voice of words, so that those who heard it begged that the word should not be spoken to them anymore. (For they could not endure what was commanded: 'And if so much as a beast touches the mountain, it shall be stoned or shot with an arrow.' And so terrifying was the sight that Moses said, 'I am exceedingly afraid and trembling.')"[10]

Fear is probably the greatest hindrance to believers entering into Zion; it is one of Satan's most effective weapons. Satan seeks to blind us to the presence of God living within us because awareness of the life of Christ within us opens the blessings and the power of God to us. One of Satan's foremost goals is to prevent believers from entering into and living in the presence of God within them, to keep them from entering into and dwelling in Zion. Mature Christians should not be so easily intimidated.

Mature believers in Christ should regularly enter into the presence of God, live in the presence of God, and bring His presence to others as we pointed out in chapter 16. One of the most urgent needs in the body of Christ today is for leaders to enter into Zion, live in Zion, and lead believers into Zion.

How is this done? It's done by the tearing of the inner veil. Next, we'll look at how the veil of the temple was torn in the old covenant and see how it relates to the new covenant believer's communion with God.

Entering Zion by the Tearing of the Inner Veil

Remember, under the old covenant, God dwelt in the portion of the temple known as the Holy of Holies. A thick veil separated this Holy of Holies from the rest of the temple. Only the high priest could enter, and he could enter the presence of God beyond this physical veil only once a year to make atonement for the people's sins. He entered only with the blood of an animal sacrifice and only after thorough preparation, because if he did not follow God's specific instructions before entering, he would die.

This physical veil was torn when Jesus died on the cross. Luke reported: "It was now about the sixth hour (midday), and darkness enveloped the whole land and earth until the ninth hour (about three o'clock in the afternoon), while the sun's light faded or was darkened; and the curtain [of the Holy of Holies] of the temple was torn in two. And Jesus, crying out with a loud voice, said, Father, into Your hands I commit My spirit! And with these words, He expired."[11]

In the old covenant, God's presence was in the physical structure called the temple. In the new covenant, the Spirit of God lives in every believer.

Believers Are the New Covenant Temple of God

New covenant believers are the temple of God. Paul asked the believers in Corinth, "Do you not know that you are the temple of God and that the Spirit of God dwells in you?"[12] As God's presence was in the Holy of Holies in the old covenant temple, His Spirit now dwells in every

Christian. In fact, Paul told the Corinthian believers, "He who is joined to the Lord is one spirit with Him."[13]

As the physical veil in the temple separated the presence of God from the rest of the temple, an invisible barrier conceals God's presence within a believer from his or her natural consciousness. We will call this invisible barrier the inner veil.

Believers Enter into the Presence of God through the Torn Inner Veil

This inner veil separates the supernatural from the natural, the eternal from the temporal, and the human spirit from mankind's awareness. We lack full intimacy with God and with Christ while our inner veil remains intact.

A similar veil blinds the Jews from perceiving that Jesus is the Christ. Paul explained to the Corinthians: "Until this present day, when the Old Testament (the old covenant) is being read, that same veil still lies [on their hearts], not being lifted [to reveal] that in Christ it is made void and done away. Yes, down to this [very] day whenever Moses is read, a veil lies upon their minds and hearts. But whenever a person turns [in repentance] to the Lord, the veil is stripped off and taken away."[14]

As removal of this veil opens a Jew's perception to Jesus being the Christ, the tearing of the inner veil in a believer in Christ opens his or her perception to God's presence within them. The tearing of the inner veil is a deeper work than the separation of soul and spirit that we discussed in chapter 5. In the separation of soul and spirit God reveals our shortcomings to us and we allow Him to work within us. In the tearing of the inner veil we deny ourselves, take up our cross, and follow Jesus. We choose to lose our life rather than save it. We voluntarily die to self.

Through the tearing of the inner veil we enter into the presence of God within us. We enter into the supernatural environment of the kingdom of God known as Zion. We experience greater intimacy with the Lord Jesus Christ. Paul prayed for the Ephesians "that Christ may dwell in your hearts through faith."[15] He prayed this prayer for committed Christians in whom Christ was already living through salvation. There is therefore an actual dwelling of Christ in our hearts available through faith that exceeds that of salvation—experiencing Christ beyond the inner veil.

God Tears the Inner Veil As He Tore the Temple Veil

As we begin our discussion of God tearing the inner veil, let's remind ourselves of four spiritual truths. First, the kingdom of God is within the believer in Christ (Luke 17:21). Second, believers are the temple of the Holy Spirit (1 Cor. 6:19). Third, he who is joined to the Lord is one spirit with Him (1 Cor. 6:17). And fourth, Jesus said, "At that day you will know that I am in My Father, and you in Me, and I in You" (John 14:20).

As the Lord Jesus Christ entered the Holy of Holies in the heavenly tabernacle through His crucifixion, He also enters into each believer beyond the inner veil through His glorification. The writer to the Hebrews encouraged believers, saying, "This hope we have as an anchor of the soul, a hope both sure and steadfast and one which enters within the veil, where Jesus has entered as a forerunner for us, having become a high priest forever according to the order of Melchizedek."[16] When we enter into Christ beyond our inner veil we also, by being in Him, enter into the Holy of Holies in the heavenly tabernacle of God.

The writer exhorted the Hebrews, "Therefore, brethren, having boldness to enter the Holiest by the blood of Jesus, by a new and living way which He consecrated for us, through the veil, that is, His flesh, and having a High Priest over the house of God, let us draw near with a true heart in full assurance of faith, having our hearts sprinkled from an evil conscience and our bodies washed with pure water."[17] Having a true heart, being free from an evil conscience, and being washed with pure water describe holiness—without which no one will see the Lord (Heb. 12:14).

The writer encourages us to join our Lord Jesus Christ beyond our inner veil in true holiness by the blood of our resurrected Lord through the veil that is His flesh. Before the veil of Jesus' flesh was torn by crucifixion no one had the presence of God within them. After Christ's crucifixion and glorification all believers can enter the presence of God within them in their high priest—the glorified Lord Jesus Christ.

We enter the presence of God beyond our inner veil through the crucifixion of Christ and the death of our self-nature. Jesus instructed His disciples: "If anyone desires to come after Me, let him deny himself, take up his cross, and follow Me. For whoever desires to save his life will lose it, but whoever loses his life for My sake will find it."[18]

As God tore the physical veil of the old covenant temple upon the crucified death of Christ, He also tears our inner veil upon the death of our self-nature. This tearing is not a work of the flesh, but a work of the Spirit. We cannot tear our inner veil by ourselves. Only God can tear the inner veil, and He requires our self-denial. This self-denial is not a one-time event—it is a lifestyle.

No human reasoning or ability can provide entrance beyond the inner veil. The means of entry is the crucifixion of the flesh—abandonment of self. As Paul came to the end of his self-reliance in his Damascus road encounter and as Peter did when he denied Christ, our coming to the end of our self-reliance prepares us to enter through the torn inner veil.

By this tearing of the inner veil, believers in Christ become sensitive to Christ's dwelling in them, become immersed completely in His presence, and yield fully to being governed by Him from within. They enter into the communal presence of God, a much deeper experience than knowing God's omnipresence or witnessing His evidentiary (manifest) presence.

Entering into the presence of God in this way is every believer's birthright, but some Christians have sold their birthright for the price of the self-life, much as Esau sold his birthright to Jacob. This is the price for which they sold their birthright: the futility of the flesh, the arrogance of the soul, the uncleanness of the heart, and the rebellion of the mind.

Paul continued to pray for the Ephesians, "I pray that the eyes of your heart may be enlightened, so that you will know what is the hope of His calling, what are the riches of the glory of His inheritance in the saints, and what is the surpassing greatness of His power toward us who believe."[19] God is enlightening the eyes of our hearts! Therefore, we should no longer live as those who are not illuminated to the truth. We should enter God's presence through the tearing of our inner veil.

Returning in the Presence of God

The tearing of our inner veil not only gives us access into the presence of God, but it also gives the Lord Jesus Christ freedom of expression through us to others. As this invisible barrier is broken, the Lord's expression comes through us more freely and more accurately.

We enter the presence of God beyond the inner veil much as Moses ascended Mount Sinai to commune with God. Having spent time in the communal presence of God, we return in the presence of God, prepared to impart the Spirit of the message from Christ as we described in chapter 8.

To quote Paul again, "Faith comes by hearing [what is told], and what is heard comes by the preaching [of the message that came from the lips] of Christ (the Messiah Himself)."[20] The prophet Isaiah proclaimed the word of the Lord: "So shall My word be that goes forth from My mouth; it shall not return to Me void, but it shall accomplish what I please, and it shall prosper in the thing for which I sent it."[21] Notice that *the words that Christ speaks* do not return void but accomplish God's purpose. This holds true, not only for formal ministry, but also in family relationships, individual relationships, and fellowship in the body of Christ.

Entering Zion through the tearing of the inner veil is available to all believers. Not only is living in Zion available, but it's also the natural and normal Christian life. We enter by grace through faith. We enter in time spent in quietness in the Lord and through subordination of our will to God's will. This is living the eternal life that God has provided for all believers in Christ!

Living Eternal Life

Living in Zion is living eternal life on earth. Living eternal life while on this earth is the culmination of all we have discussed in progressing toward spiritual maturity. Eternal life is much more than an extension of life after physical death; it is the Lord Jesus Christ living His life in and through us now.

We can live in Christ, not only as His servants, but also as His friends. This friendship, however, is contingent upon our being obedient to Him. Jesus exhorted His disciples: "You are My friends if you do whatever I command you. No longer do I call you servants, for a servant does not know what his master is doing."[22] We can know what Jesus, our master, is doing just as Jesus knew what the Father was doing when He was on the earth. Speaking of believers, Jesus stressed: "The sheep that are My own hear and are listening to My voice; and I know them, and they follow Me. And I give them eternal life, and they shall never lose it or perish throughout the ages. [To all eternity they shall never by any means be destroyed.]"[23]

True Christianity Is Fellowship

True Christianity is entering into actual personal fellowship with God the Father and the Lord Jesus Christ. This divine intimacy is actually experienced in this life on earth! The apostle John proclaimed: "What we have seen and [ourselves] heard, we also are telling you, so that you too may realize and enjoy fellowship as partners and partakers with us. And [this] fellowship that we have [which is a distinguishing mark of Christians] is with the Father and with His Son Jesus Christ (the Messiah)."[24]

This Christian fellowship is first with God the Father and Jesus Christ His Son, and it is secondarily shared with other believers. We have seen in chapter 5 that although we can communicate with God the Father and the Lord Jesus Christ with the mind, we commune in the Spirit with them through the heart and human spirit. This communion with God enables believers to come together in the Spirit. Just as fellowship with God is supernatural, so is fellowship between believers in Christ.

Remember, we observed the spiritual influence of a believer beyond the confines of the physical body in chapters 4 and 5. Here are three examples: (1) a husband and wife are one flesh, (2) believers are members of one another in the body of Christ, and (3) believers influence other people through prayer.

Fellowship between believers is sharing their intimacy with God by the interaction of their spirit-beings through the work of the Holy Spirit. Don't forget that every believer's human spirit is one with Christ (1 Cor. 6:17). This Spirit-realm fellowship produces supernatural edification for those so engaged.

Believers who have not experienced this fellowship in the Spirit have yet to experience true Christian fellowship. Sadly, what some Christians call fellowship falls far short of fellowship in the Spirit; it is merely socializing or, at best, team building: increasing familiarity between people by bringing them together to work toward a common goal. Unfortunately, some contemporary Christians fellowship primarily with one another. Fellowship with the Father and the Son is secondary or nonexistent! Let's not settle for anything less than actual personal fellowship with God the Father and His Son Jesus Christ and genuine Spirit-realm fellowship with fellow believers.

Witnessing Is Telling Others What We Have Actually Experienced

Since Christianity is our entering into actual personal fellowship with God the Father and the Lord Jesus Christ, witnessing is telling others what we have actually experienced—not explaining a principle or a theory. The purpose of witnessing is telling other people about the actual loving fellowship we are experiencing with God the Father and the Lord Jesus Christ so that they too may enter into the same fellowship with us. This is Christianity. This is witnessing. This is a distinguishing mark of Christians.

The apostle Paul expressed how important actually experiencing fellowship with the Lord Jesus Christ was to him in his letter to the Philippians:

> [My determined purpose is] that I may know Him [that I may progressively become more deeply and intimately acquainted with Him, perceiving and recognizing and understanding the wonders of His Person more strongly and more clearly], and that I may in that same way come to know the power outflowing from His resurrection [which it exerts over believers], and that I may so share His sufferings as to be continually transformed [in spirit into His likeness even] to His death, [in the hope] that if possible I may attain to the [spiritual and moral] resurrection [that lifts me] out from among the dead [even while in the body].[25]

This Is Eternal Life

Again, eternal life is continual fellowship with God the Father and Jesus Christ His Son. In the words of the apostle John: "This is eternal life, that they may know You, the only true God, and Jesus Christ whom You have sent. You [already] have life, yes, eternal life."[26] You can live the life beyond the inner veil that costs nothing and yet costs everything. You can live in the communal presence of almighty God. You can actually live in intimate fellowship with God the Father and the Lord Jesus Christ.

Admonition to Enter into Zion and Enjoy Eternal Life

Enter into the fullness of salvation in this life—knowing God the Father and His Son Jesus Christ whom He has sent. Don't be complacent in living life outside of God's presence. Live continually in the presence of God and commune with Christ beyond the inner veil. Live in this supernatural awareness of God's communal presence known as Zion.

Enter into the presence of God where self is overthrown and obedience is most earnestly desired. Enter—not by the strength of will, self-discipline, or natural abilities—but by grace through faith.

Pray to Enter into Zion to Live and Minister Eternal Life

Father, I desire to live in and minister out of Your holy hill, out of Zion. I want to give myself to You for the crucifixion of my self-nature so that I may actually dwell with Christ beyond the inner veil. Please tear my inner veil so that I may commune with You as You intend.

Please forgive me for trying to serve You in my own strength and in my own way. Bring me into intimacy with Christ and into the fellowship of the Spirit with my fellow believers. Enable me to spend ample time with Jesus for You to express the influence, power, and authority of the ministry of Christ in and through me. By Your grace, I want to live the eternal life that You have so graciously provided for me on this earth as well as in heaven. All this I ask, not only for my own spiritual growth, but also that our Lord Jesus Christ, in whose name I pray, may be glorified and exalted in and through me. Amen.

Where Do We Go from Here?

In part 1, we opened our awareness to eight unseen spiritual realities that enable us to experience the living Christ and live in the presence of God. In part 2, we activated eight foundational truths that enable us to experience the living Christ, live in God's presence, and lead others to experience the living Christ and to live in God's presence as well.

In part 3, we yielded ourselves to five maturing processes that prepare us to live in fellowship with God the Father and the Lord Jesus Christ. We first left the realm of our intellect and entered into the realm of God's presence through our personal encounters with the Lord Jesus Christ. We then increased our spiritual strength by embracing our weaknesses. Next, we obtained ultimate freedom through genuine surrender. After that, we continued to grow into spiritual maturity through intimacy with Christ. Then we entered into the realm of God's presence called Zion through the tearing of our inner veil. We learned that eternal life is knowing God the Father and the Lord Jesus Christ, and that we already have eternal life.

God the Father intensely desires to lovingly welcome you into deep personal fellowship in Him through true personal intimacy with His Son Jesus Christ. Will you accept His invitation? The next chapter is yours to write!

My Prayer for You

My prayer for you is the same one that Paul prayed for the church at Ephesus long ago: May you "[. . . really come] to know [*practically, through experience for yourselves*] the love of Christ, which far surpasses mere knowledge [without experience]; that you may be filled [through all your being] unto all the fullness of God [may have the richest measure of the divine Presence, and become a body wholly filled and flooded with God Himself]!"[27] All this I ask, not only for your spiritual growth, but also that our Lord Jesus Christ, in whose name I pray, may be glorified and exalted in and through you. Amen.

This is experiencing the living Christ. This is living in the presence of God. This is living eternal life. This is your birthright. This is your destiny!

Endnotes

Chapter 1
Discover God's Unseen Reality

1. John 17:3 NKJV and 1 John 5:13 AMP
2. John 10:27 AMP
3. John 14:20 NASB
4. Psalm 139:7–10 AMP
5. Psalm 140:13 AMP
6. Ephesians 3:17, 19
7. John 15:4 AMP
8. John 10:27 AMP
9. Hebrews 3:7–8 AMP
10. Philippians 3:10 AMP

Chapter 2
Follow God's Pathway to Ultimate Fulfillment

1. Matthew 3:16–17
2. Luke 4:1 NIV
3. Hebrews 9: 27–28
4. John 3:16–17
5. 1 Timothy 2:3–4 NRSV
6. Romans 10:9–10
7. John 14:6
8. Colossians 2:11–12 AMP
9. Romans 6:4–6 AMP

10. 1 Peter 3:21 AMP
11. John 7:37–38
12. Acts 1:4–5
13. Acts 2:39 AMP
14. Acts 19:6 AMP
15. 2 Timothy 3:16
16. 2 Timothy 2:15 AMP
17. 1 Corinthians 2:14
18. 1 Corinthians 2:11–12
19. Matthew 4:1–11
20. Luke 4:14
21. Luke 22:41–44
22. Philippians 2:12
23. Hebrews 12:3–4

Chapter 3
Come to Know the Living Word

1. 1 Corinthians 2:14
2. 2 Timothy 3:16–17
3. John 10:10 NASB
4. 1 Corinthians 1:24 AMP
5. John 5:39–40 NIV
6. Colossians 2:20
7. Matthew 7:21–23 AMP
8. 1 Corinthians 3:6–7
9. Philippians 1:6
10. Philippians 2:13
11. John 1:1–3, 14
12. 1 Corinthians 1:24
13. Galatians 4:19 AMP
14. Hebrews 12:2
15. Mark 16:20
16. 2 Timothy 1:12
17. Colossians 1:16–17

Chapter 4
Activate Your Spirit Nature

1. Genesis 1:26–27
2. Genesis 2:7 KJV
3. 1 Thessalonians 5:23
4. Genesis 2:21–22 AMP
5. Genesis 2:24 AMP
6. Mark 10:6–8
7. Ephesians 5:31–32
8. Romans 12:5
9. 1 Corinthians 12:24–26 NIV
10. 1 Corinthians 15:46 AMP

Chapter 5
Be Released from Temporal Limitations

1. 2 Corinthians 4:16–18 NIV
2. 1 Corinthians 6:19–20
3. 1 Corinthians 6:17
4. Proverbs 20:27 NASB
5. Hebrews 4:12 AMP
6. Romans 10:9
7. Mark 16:14
8. John 7:38
9. Proverbs 4:23 NIV
10. Hebrews 4:7
11. Ephesians 3:17
12. Matthew 5:8
13. Jeremiah 17:9
14. Psalm 95:10–11 NIV
15. Hebrews 3:8–9
16. Hebrews 3:12–13
17. Romans 8:7
18. Hebrews 11:3
19. Philippians 4:8 NRSV
20. 2 Corinthians 10:5

21. Ephesians 4:23
22. Romans 12:2
23. Romans 12:2 Phillips
24. Romans 12:2
25. Romans 8:6
26. 1 Corinthians 14:14–15 NIV
27. Jeremiah 29:13
28. John 7:38 NASB
29. 1 Corinthians 2:14
30. Acts 1:8
31. 2 Corinthians 11:14 NASB

Chapter 6
Know Christ as He Really Is

1. John 7:37–39 NIV, emphasis added
2. John 1:1–3
3. John 1:14
4. Acts 10:38
5. John 3:17 AMP
6. Ephesians 1:20–23
7. John 6:26–27 NIV
8. John 6:48–49, 51
9. John 10:10
10. John 14:8–9
11. Matthew 16:15–17
12. Ephesians 1:19
13. Hebrews 1:2–4, 8–12
14. Revelation 1:14–18 AMP
15. Revelation 2:8, 12, 18; 3:1, 7, 14 AMP
16. Revelation 19:15 NIV
17. Matthew 28:18–20
18. Acts 1:4–5
19. 1 Corinthians 2:1–5

Chapter 7
Live in the New Covenant Spiritual Dimension

1. 1 Corinthians 6:17
2. Matthew 28:19–20
3. Acts 1:4–5, emphasis added
4. Acts 1:8
5. Acts 2:17–18
6. Hebrews 1:1–2 NIV
7. Romans 8:3–4 AMP
8. John 20:25
9. Romans 1:25 NIV
10. Hebrews 11:6, emphasis added

Chapter 8
Activate New Covenant Truth

1. Proverbs 3:5–6
2. Mark 10:15
3. 2 Corinthians 3:6 NIV
4. 1 John 1:3
5. Acts 3:6
6. Acts 4:10 AMP
7. Acts 4:8 AMP
8. John 1:4–5 NIV
9. Romans 10:17 AMP
10. John 15:5, 7
11. James 2:17 AMP
12. Hebrews 13:8
13. John 14:12
14. Colossians 2:10
15. Matthew 16:19 AMP, emphasis added
16. John 14:20
17. John 14:13–14 AMP
18. Acts 4:14

Chapter 9
Thirst, Come to Jesus, and Drink

1. Hebrews 2:1
2. John 15:5
3. John 10:10
4. John 1:4
5. Isaiah 55:1 AMP
6. Isaiah 55:6 AMP
7. Hebrews 11:6
8. Mark 11:24
9. James 2:17 AMP
10. Ephesians 1:18–19 AMP
11. John 14:12
12. John 14:13
13. Acts 1:4–5 AMP
14. Acts 1:8 AMP
15. John 1:33 AMP
16. Acts 2:39 AMP
17. John 14:21
18. Acts 5:31–32
19. John 14:15 AMP
20. Ephesians 4:30 AMP
21. Hebrews 12:1 AMP
22. Ephesians 3:16 AMP
23. Ephesians 1:22–23
24. Colossians 1:18
25. Hebrews 3:7–8 AMP
26. Matthew 5:6
27. John 14:23 AMP
28. Galatians 1:15–16 AMP
29. Matthew 16:16–18
30. 1 John 5:11–12
31. John 14:17 NIV
32. 1 John 2:8 AMP
33. John 1:4–5 AMP
34. Ephesians 5:8 AMP

35. Luke 11:9–10 AMP
36. John 16:12–13 NIV
37. John 4:14 AMP
38. John 6:33, 35 AMP
39. 1 Corinthians 1:9 AMP
40. John 5:6 AMP
41. John 7:40–43 NIV
42. Ephesians 4:1–6

Chapter 10
Participate in God's Supernatural Commission

1. John 18:36
2. John 18:37
3. 1 Corinthians 4:20
4. John 15:5
5. Matthew 16:18
6. Acts 2:47
7. 1 Corinthians 3:5–7
8. Matthew 26:33–35
9. Exodus 32:4
10. Exodus 32:22–24
11. Acts 7:41
12. Ephesians 4:13
13. 1 Corinthians 1:9 AMP
14. Genesis 3:6
15. 1 John 2:15–17 NRSV
16. James 4:4–6 NIV
17. Jeremiah 17:9–10 AMP
18. Psalm 139:23–24
19. Matthew 16:24
20. Philippians 2:5–8
21. Matthew 16:23
22. Acts 1:4–5
23. Acts 2:22–25, 31, 33
24. 1 Corinthians 2:1–5
25. Acts 2:38

Chapter 11
Receive Revelation through Grace in Peace

1. 2 Peter 3:16 NIV
2. John 14:27
3. Luke 10:5–7
4. James 3:18
5. Philippians 4:7 AMP
6. Proverbs 4:23 NIV
7. 1 Peter 3:11 AMP
8. Hebrews 12:14 NIV
9. Ephesians 4:2–3 NIV
10. Romans 11:6
11. 1 Corinthians 1:4–5 AMP
12. 1 Corinthians 1:7 AMP
13. Ephesians 3:7 AMP
14. Ephesians 2:8–9 AMP
15. Ephesians 4:7 AMP
16. 2 Corinthians 12:9 NIV
17. 2 Corinthians 12:8 NIV
18. Philippians 4:13 AMP
19. Hebrews 4:9–11 AMP
20. Matthew 11:28–29

Chapter 12
Give Christ Preeminence

1. Galatians 2:20
2. Romans 12:3
3. Ephesians 3:16–17
4. Hebrews 12:2
5. Romans 10:17 AMP
6. Proverbs 3:5–6
7. Romans 10:9–10
8. Colossians 2:6
9. Matthew 22:37–40
10. John 15:12

11. John 14:15
12. John 14:21
13. John 15:14
14. Galatians 5:6 KJV
15. John 12:49–50
16. John 10:27
17. Romans 10:17 AMP
18. James 2:17 AMP
19. Hebrews 11:1
20. Hebrews 11:6
21. John 14:12–14
22. John 14:3
23. John 14:12 AMP
24. John 5:19
25. John 15:5
26. 2 Timothy 1:12, emphasis added
27. Philippians 3:8, 10 AMP, emphasis added
28. 1 Corinthians 11:1
29. Matthew 8:10
30. Ephesians 3:17
31. Luke 17:20–21
32. 2 Peter 1:4
33. Colossians 2:6
34. Galatians 3:3

Chapter 13
Embrace Living Doctrine

1. 1 Corinthians 2:14
2. 2 Timothy 3:16
3. John 7:16
4. Matthew 13:9
5. John 14:26
6. Ephesians 4:14
7. 2 Timothy 3:16–17
8. 1 Corinthians 2:13 AMP
9. Romans 10:17 AMP

10. Revelation 19:10 AMP
11. Acts 1:8
12. Mark 16:17–18
13. John 14:12
14. Mark 1:22
15. Mark 1:26–27
16. Mark 7:13 AMP
17. Colossians 2:20–23
18. Galatians 1:8
19. 1 John 2:24
20. John 6:63
21. Matthew 22:37 NIV
22. Matthew 22:39 NIV
23. John 13:34 NIV
24. 2 John 9–11, emphasis added
25. Hebrews 3:4–6

Chapter 14
Come to Know the Father's Goodness

1. Deuteronomy 7:9
2. Hebrews 9:15 NIV
3. Galatians 3:16, 29
4. James 4:3
5. 2 Peter 1:4
6. Psalm 138:2 AMP
7. James 1:17
8. Hebrews 11:6
9. John 12:49–50
10. John 5:19
11. John 15:5

Chapter 15
Live a Lifestyle of Fellowship with Christ

1. Luke 10:42 NIV
2. Acts 10:44–46 NIV

Endnotes

3. Hebrews 3:5–6 NIV
4. Revelation 2:2–5
5. Revelation 2:4 AMP
6. Revelation 2:5
7. John 15:4–5
8. John 15:15
9. John 10:27
10. Philippians 3:10 AMP

Chapter 16
Allow Jesus Christ to Lead

1. Hebrews 5:12
2. John 5:19 NIV
3. John 15:5 NIV
4. Mark 1:35 NIV
5. 1 Corinthians 11:1 NIV
6. 1 Corinthians 1:9 AMP
7. Luke 10:41–42 NIV
8. Acts 6:2
9. Acts 16:6–10
10. Matthew 28:19 NIV
11. Psalm 19:13

Chapter 17
Encountering the Living Christ

1. Philippians 3:4–6
2. Acts 22:3–5
3. Matthew 23:26
4. Psalm 19:13

Chapter 18
Increasing Spiritual Strength by Embracing Weakness

1. Proverbs 3:5
2. 2 Corinthians 12:9 RSV

3. 2 Corinthians 12:10 RSV
4. 1 Corinthians 2:2–3 AMP
5. 2 Corinthians 12:9 RSV
6. Isaiah 40:29–31 AMP
7. Philippians 2:13
8. Matthew 11:28–30
9. Ephesians 2:8
10. Colossians 2:6
11. Philippians 3:3, 7–11
12. 1 Corinthians 2:4–5
13. Matthew 11:25–26 AMP

Chapter 19
Obtaining Ultimate Freedom through Genuine Surrender

1. Romans 12:1 AMP
2. Romans 12:1 AMP
3. 1 Corinthians 6:19–20
4. Galatians 2:20
5. Luke 22:42 NIV
6. Matthew 26:2
7. Psalm 24:7–10
8. Matthew 22:37
9. Revelation 3:15–16
10. Jeremiah 18:6
11. Isaiah 64:8 AMP
12. Isaiah 29:16 NIV
13. Matthew 11:28–30 AMP
14. John 5:19 NIV
15. 1 Corinthians 1:9 AMP
16. John 15:5 NIV
17. 1 Corinthians 6:19–20
18. Philippians 3:7–8 NIV
19. Philippians 4:9 AMP
20. Romans 12:1 AMP

Chapter 20
Growing into Spiritual Maturity through Intimacy with Christ

1. Matthew 16:16
2. 2 Corinthians 5:16 AMP
3. 1 John 1:3 AMP
4. John 17:20–21
5. 1 John 2:12–14 AMP, emphasis added
6. Isaiah 40:30 AMP
7. Isaiah 40:31 AMP
8. 1 John 2:24
9. 1 John 2:3 NASB
10. John 15:9–10
11. John 14:21
12. Matthew 22:37–40
13. John 15:12
14. 1 John 4:21
15. John 17:20–21
16. 1 John 5:3
17. Romans 5:5
18. 1 John 4:18 NASB
19. John 13:23
20. John 19:26–27
21. Colossians 1:27
22. Philippians 2:13
23. Galatians 4:19 AMP
24. John 15:5
25. Luke 17:20–21
26. Matthew 23:25–26
27. Isaiah 40:31 AMP

Chapter 21
Living Eternal Life

1. Psalm 139:7–10 AMP
2. Romans 1:18–20 NRSV
3. Psalm 103:7

4. Isaiah 33:5–6 AMP
5. Hebrews 12:22
6. John 10:9 AMP
7. Ephesians 1:3
8. 2 Corinthians 1:20
9. 1 Corinthians 6:17
10. Hebrews 12:18–21
11. Luke 23:44–46 AMP
12. 1 Corinthians 3:16
13. 1 Corinthians 6:17
14. 2 Corinthians 3:14–16 AMP
15. Ephesians 3:17
16. Hebrews 6:19–20 NASB
17. Hebrews 10:19–22
18. Matthew 16:24–25
19. Ephesians 1:18–19 NASB
20. Romans 10:17 AMP
21. Isaiah 55:11, emphasis added
22. John 15:14–15
23. John 10:27–28 AMP
24. 1 John 1:3 AMP
25. Philippians 3:10–11 AMP
26. John 17:3 NKJV and 1 John 5:13 AMP
27. Ephesians 3:19 AMP, emphasis added

Appendix A

Declarations with Supporting Scriptures

> Therefore, whether you eat or drink, or whatever you do,
> do all to the glory of God.
> 1 Corinthians 10:31

We have seen that to live and minister in the Spirit effectively, we must exceed the limitations of religion and move into true Christianity. We must move from a religious system of man into communion with God, from being mind-centered to being heart-centered, from knowing about God to knowing God personally, from working for God to allowing God to work through us, from our being in control to letting God be in control, and from living in bondage to our self-nature to living in the freedom of the Spirit. We have entered into Zion through the tearing of the inner veil and entered into the fullness of our salvation: knowing the only true God and His Son Jesus Christ whom He has sent.

Now let us commit to preparing ourselves to live in the presence of God. The following is a series of declarations, each followed by supporting scriptures, for personal meditation and for seeking the Lord to develop each characteristic within us. Let us commit ourselves to living each declaration continually.

Declarations

Above all, I will seek God the Father and the Lord Jesus Christ with my whole heart. I will surrender all to the Lord. I will continually prepare myself for the empowering of God's Holy Spirit in the following ways:

Surrender Completely and Unconditionally

I will give myself completely and unwaveringly to the Lord for Him to work His will and good pleasure in and through me. I will offer my body as a living sacrifice, not be conformed to this world, be transformed by the renewing of my mind, and not think more highly of myself than I should.

> I appeal to you therefore, brethren, and beg of you in view of [all] the mercies of God, to make a decisive dedication of your bodies [presenting all your members and faculties] as a living sacrifice, holy (devoted, consecrated) and well pleasing to God, which is your reasonable (rational, intelligent) service and spiritual worship. Do not be conformed to this world (this age), [fashioned after and adapted to its external, superficial customs], but be transformed (changed) by the [entire] renewal of your mind [by its new ideals and its new attitude], so that you may prove [for yourselves] what is the good and acceptable and perfect will of God, even the thing which is good and acceptable and perfect [in His sight for you].
> For by the grace (unmerited favor of God) given to me I warn everyone among you not to estimate and think of himself more highly than he ought [not to have an exaggerated opinion of his own importance], but to rate his ability with sober judgment, each according to the degree of faith apportioned by God to him.
> —Romans 12:1–3 AMP

Wait on God

I will wait quietly and attentively before the Lord on a regular, recurring, and continual basis so that I may hear His voice, know His instructions, and obey them.

> Those who wait for the Lord [who expect, look for, and hope in Him] shall change and renew their strength and power; they shall lift their wings and mount up [close to God] as eagles [mount up to the sun]; they shall run and not be weary, they shall walk and not faint or become tired.
> —Isaiah 40:31 AMP

> Wait and listen, everyone who is thirsty! Come to the waters; and he who has no money, come, buy and eat! Yes, come, buy [priceless, spiritual] wine and milk without money and without price [simply for the self-surrender that accepts the blessing].
> —Isaiah 55:1 AMP

> They will not hunger or thirst, neither will mirage [mislead] or scorching wind or sun smite them; for He Who has mercy on them will lead them, and by springs of water will He guide them.
> —Isaiah 49:10 AMP

Know Christ Intimately

I will diligently seek to know and personally experience Christ intimately, not just know about Him.

> [My determined purpose is] that I may know Him [that I may progressively become more deeply and intimately acquainted with Him, perceiving and recognizing and understanding the wonders of His Person more strongly and more clearly], and that I may in that same way come to know the power outflowing from His resurrection

[which it exerts over believers], and that I may so share His sufferings as to be continually transformed [in spirit into His likeness even] to His death, [in the hope] that if possible I may attain to the [spiritual and moral] resurrection [that lifts me] out from among the dead [even while in the body].
—Philippians 3:10–11 AMP

The person who has My commands and keeps them is the one who [really] loves Me; and whoever [really] loves Me will be loved by My Father, and I [too] will love him and will show (reveal, manifest) Myself to him. [I will let Myself be clearly seen by him and make Myself real to him.]
—John 14:21 AMP

I am the vine, you are the branches. He who abides in Me, and I in him, bears much fruit; for without Me you can do nothing.
—John 15:5

I am the Vine; you are the branches. Whoever lives in Me and I in him bears much (abundant) fruit. However, apart from Me [cut off from vital union with Me] you can do nothing.
—John 15:5 AMP

God is faithful (reliable, trustworthy and therefore ever true to His promise, and He can be depended on); by Him you were called into companionship and participation with His Son, Jesus Christ our Lord.
—1 Corinthians 1:9 AMP

[That you may really come] to know [practically, through experience for yourselves] the love of Christ, which far surpasses mere knowledge [without experience]; that you may be filled [through all your being] unto all the fullness

of God [may have the richest measure of the divine Presence, and become a body wholly filled and flooded with God Himself]!
—Ephesians 3:19 AMP

Make Love My Focus and Objective

I will love the Lord my God with all my heart, soul, and mind and love other people as myself. I will make love my focus and objective.

> Jesus said to him, "'You shall love the Lord your God with all your heart, with all your soul, and with all your mind.' This is the first and great commandment. And the second is like it: 'You shall love your neighbor as yourself.'"
> —Matthew 22:37–39

> A new command I give you: Love one another. As I have loved you, so you must love one another.
> —John 13:34 NIV

> He who has My commandments and keeps them, it is he who loves Me. And he who loves Me will be loved by My Father, and I will love him and manifest Myself to him.
> —John 14:21

> For [if we are] in Christ Jesus, neither circumcision nor uncircumcision counts for anything, but only faith activated and energized and expressed and working through love.
> —Galatians 5:6 AMP

> External religious worship [religion as it is expressed in outward acts] that is pure and unblemished in the sight of God the Father is this: to visit and help and care for the orphans and widows in their affliction and need, and to keep oneself unspotted and uncontaminated from the world.
> —James 1:27 AMP

> The object and purpose of our instruction and charge is love, which springs from a pure heart and a good (clear) conscience and sincere (unfeigned) faith. But certain individuals have missed the mark on this very matter [and] have wandered away into vain arguments and discussions and purposeless talk.
>
> —1 Timothy 1:5–6 AMP

Remain in the Spirit

I will remain in the Spirit at all times and be controlled by the Holy Spirit in everything I do.

> Are you so foolish and so senseless and so silly? Having begun [your new life spiritually] with the [Holy] Spirit, are you now reaching perfection [by dependence] on the flesh?
>
> —Galatians 3:3 AMP

> As you therefore have received Christ Jesus the Lord, so walk in Him.
>
> —Colossians 2:6

Enter into and Minister out of the Presence of God

I will live in the actual presence of God and minister out of His supernatural presence.

> Now when they saw the boldness and unfettered eloquence of Peter and John and perceived that they were unlearned and untrained in the schools [common men with no educational advantages], they marveled; and they recognized that they had been with Jesus.
>
> —Acts 4:13 AMP

Declarations with Supporting Scriptures

Demonstrate the Spirit and Power of God

I will conduct all relationships and ministry in the demonstration of the Holy Spirit and power of God.

> As for myself, brethren, when I came to you, I did not come proclaiming to you the testimony and evidence or mystery and secret of God [concerning what He has done through Christ for the salvation of men] in lofty words of eloquence or human philosophy and wisdom; for I resolved to know nothing (to be acquainted with nothing, to make a display of the knowledge of nothing, and to be conscious of nothing) among you except Jesus Christ (the Messiah) and Him crucified. And I was in (passed into a state of) weakness and fear (dread) and great trembling [after I had come] among you. And my language and my message were not set forth in persuasive (enticing and plausible) words of wisdom, but they were in demonstration of the [Holy] Spirit and power [a proof by the Spirit and power of God, operating on me and stirring in the minds of my hearers the most holy emotions and thus persuading them], so that your faith might not rest in the wisdom of men (human philosophy), but in the power of God.
> —1 Corinthians 2:1–5 AMP

> For Christ (the Messiah) sent me out not to baptize but [to evangelize by] preaching the glad tidings (the gospel), and that not with verbal eloquence, lest the cross of Christ should be deprived of force and emptied of its power and rendered vain (fruitless, void of value, and of no effect). For the story and message of the cross is sheer absurdity and folly to those who are perishing and on their way to perdition, but to us who are being saved it is the [manifestation of] the power of God.
> —1 Corinthians 1:17–18 AMP

Impart the Spirit of the Message from Christ

I will not only deliver the message of the Lord Jesus Christ to others, but I will also impart the Spirit of the message from Christ in all that I do.

> Faith comes by hearing [what is told], and what is heard comes by the preaching [of the message that came from the lips] of Christ (the Messiah Himself).
> —Romans 10:17 AMP

> It is the Spirit who gives life; the flesh profits nothing. The words that I speak to you are spirit, and they are life.
> —John 6:63

> The thief does not come except to steal, and to kill, and to destroy. I have come that they may have life, and that they may have it more abundantly.
> —John 10:10

Make My Motivation to Glorify Christ

I will make my motivation to glorify God the Father and the Lord Jesus Christ.

> So then, whether you eat or drink, or whatever you may do, do all for the honor and glory of God.
> —1 Corinthians 10:31 AMP

> Let your light so shine before men that they may see your moral excellence and your praiseworthy, noble, and good deeds and recognize and honor and praise and glorify your Father Who is in heaven.
> —Matthew 5:16 AMP

Declarations with Supporting Scriptures

Pray for God's Empowerment to Yield to Him

Father, I know I cannot achieve these declarations in my own strength or by my own abilities. I know I cannot attain spiritual results by natural means. Please empower me by Your Spirit. Please enable me to personally prepare for a life and ministry that is pleasing to You. I want to yield to You completely so that You can work Your will in me. All this I ask, not only for my own spiritual growth, but also that our Lord Jesus Christ, in whose name I pray, may be glorified and exalted in and through me. Amen.

Appendix B

Recommended Reading

Brother Lawrence, *The Practice of the Presence of God,* revised and rewritten by Harold J. Chadwick, Bridge-Logos, 1999.

Frangipane, Francis, *Holiness, Truth and the Presence of God*, Arrow Publications, Twentieth printing, 2002.

Murray, Andrew, *Andrew Murray on Prayer*, Whitaker House, 1998. This volume contains the following books:

> *Abide in Christ*
> *The Prayer Life*
> *Waiting on God*
> *With Christ in the School of Prayer*
> *The Ministry of Intercession*
> *The Secret of Intercession*

Murray, Andrew, *God's Best Secrets*, Whitaker House, 1998.

Murray, Andrew, *The Holiest of All*, Whitaker House, 1996.

Murray, Andrew, *The Practice of God's Presence*, Whitaker House, 1999. This volume contains the following books:

The Power of the Blood of Jesus
Humility
Absolute Surrender
The Secret of Spiritual Strength
Experiencing the Holy Spirit
Daily Experience with God
The Blessings of Obedience

Murray, Andrew, *The True Vine*, Whitaker House, 1982.

Nee, Watchman, *The Normal Christian Life*, Tyndale House Publishers, Inc., 1977.

Nee, Watchman, *Sit, Walk, Stand*, Tyndale House Publishers, Inc., 1977.

Nee, Watchman, *The Spiritual Man*, Christian Fellowship Publishers, Inc., 1968.

Smith, Malcolm, *Spiritual Burnout: When Doing All You Can . . . Isn't Enough*, Honor, a Division of Harrison House, Inc., 1988.

Tozer, A. W., *The Pursuit of God*, IAP—Connecting to God, 2010.

About the Author

Norman Mears, having walked with the Lord for over thirty-five years, strongly desires to help believers in Christ enter into deeper intimacy with God the Father and the Lord Jesus Christ. He has served as a deacon, an elder, and a lay-pastor—conducting home group meetings, teaching Sunday school, conducting midweek services, occasionally conducting or speaking in Sunday morning services, and ministering to individuals. Norman has also ministered in churches in eastern Europe, ministered for a season at a maximum-security prison, and occasionally taught as a nonfaculty substitute at a local Bible college. He waits regularly on the Lord and writes his impressions. He has compiled notes on a number of subjects, some of which have become these chapters.

Norman and his wife Vicki reside in North Carolina. They have five children, seven grandchildren, and three great grandchildren.

CPSIA information can be obtained at www.ICGtesting.com
Printed in the USA
BVOW03s0118140415

395968BV00003B/6/P